Foundations of Criminal and Civil Law in Canada

FOURTH EDITION

Nora Rock

Gargi Mukherji

Valerie Hoag

 emond ▪ Toronto, Canada ▪ 2017

Emond Montgomery Publications Limited
60 Shaftesbury Avenue
Toronto ON M4T 1A3
http://www.emond.ca/highered

Printed in Canada.
Reprinted July 2020.

We acknowledge the financial support of the Government of Canada.   **Canadä**

Emond Montgomery Publications has no responsibility for the persistence or accuracy of URLs for external or third-party Internet websites referred to in this publication, and does not guarantee that any content on such websites is, or will remain, accurate or appropriate.

Publisher: Anthony Rezek
Managing editor, development: Kelly Dickson
Developmental editor: Joanne Sutherland
Senior editor, production: Jim Lyons
Copy and production editor: David Handelsman
Proofreader: Michael Kelly
Permissions editor: Lisa Brant
Indexer: Michael Bunn
Cover and text designer and typesetter: Tara Agnerian
Cover image: Vlad G/Shutterstock

Library and Archives Canada Cataloguing in Publication

Rock, Nora, 1968-, author
    Foundations of criminal and civil law in Canada / Nora Rock, Gargi
    Mukherji, Valerie Hoag. — Fourth edition.

Includes index.
ISBN 978-1-77255-037-5 (paperback)

        1. Law—Canada—Textbooks.   I. Mukherji, Gargi, author   II. Hoag, Valerie, author   III. Title.

KE444.R62 2017   349.71   C2016-906324-0
KF385.ZA2R62 2017

Brief Contents

Detailed Contents

PART I

INTRODUCTION TO THE LAW: FUNCTION AND STRUCTURE

1 Introduction

2 Statute Law: Function, Jurisdiction, and Structure

3 Common Law and the Concept of Legal Precedent

8 Criminal Trial Issues and Defences

9 Criminal Offence Sentencing and Appeals

PART IV

INTRODUCTION TO CIVIL LAW DISCIPLINES

10 Contracts and Torts: The Founding Principles of Civil Law

APPENDIXES

A Abbreviations of Case and Statute Reporters

B Case Brief

Preface

It may be wildly ambitious to think that one can pull off a textbook that provides a complete overview of Canadian law, from the function and structure of the law to substantive issues within each stream. Yet we have embarked on this endeavour in order to illustrate to our students the complexity and breadth of the law in Canada—both in the private and public, criminal and civil, and legislative and common law realms. It is our hope that students from various areas of study will find this a comprehensive guide on specific areas of law.

The first edition of *Foundations of Criminal and Civil Law in Canada* was one of the very first college textbooks released by Emond Publishing. The evolution of this text has tracked the company's expansion into the college market, and reflects a deepening of understanding of the needs of students and instructors alike. With each new edition, the publisher and the authors have fine-tuned the presentation of information to stimulate interest and support practical understanding. As the book has evolved, so has our society, and the content has been adjusted to reflect major societal shifts: the recognition of same-sex marriage; changing societal attitudes about, for example, drugs, and criminal sentencing; and an evolution in the role of the police. While the fourth edition was being prepared, Canadians witnessed yet another major ideological change in the form of a new willingness on the part of our federal government to work toward a nation-to-nation relationship with our country's Indigenous peoples.

Although the audience for this textbook has shifted toward police foundations and law enforcement students, we are mindful of the intersection between criminal law and other areas of law, particularly with respect to protection and safety of the public. In Canada, there has been a shift to community policing—with greater emphasis on crime prevention and the delivery of service. Law enforcement personnel are expected to not only detect crime, but also consult and collaborate with citizens in order to maintain order and prevent bad situations from becoming worse. A working knowledge of family law, property law, and civil law is crucial in carrying out law enforcement duties.

This textbook is divided into four parts. Part I consists of the introductory chapters, which provide an overview of the sources of law, how laws are created, and the differences between common law and statute. Part II deals with rights and freedoms set out in the *Canadian Charter of Rights and Freedoms* and the role of the Constitution in Canada. Part III contains several chapters on criminal law and procedure. In Chapter 5, the structure of criminal offences and the *Criminal Code* is discussed, as well as parties to an offence. Chapter 6 provides an in-depth look at police powers of investigation, detention, arrest, and search and seizure in the context of the *Canadian Charter of Rights and Freedoms*. A new section has been added on the right to silence and how this will affect a criminal investigation. Criminal pre-trial issues are discussed in Chapter 7, from bail hearings to plea bargaining and diversion programs. Chapter 8 outlines various criminal defences that are available to an accused person at trial, with updated content on the law pertaining to self-defence. Finally, Chapter 9 highlights the sentencing and appeal process, with information on dangerous and long-term offender designations and the procedure for applying for a record suspension. Recent legislation, relating to victims of crime, is also discussed in this chapter.

Part IV is dedicated to the civil law disciplines, beginning, in Chapter 10, with an introduction to the contract and tort concepts that underpin most areas of civil law. Without burdening students with excessive detail, all of the basic principles of contract and tort are presented, and the intersection between them is explained—for example, in a case study based on *Mustapha v Culligan*, which engages issues from both fields. Also introduced is the overlap between tort law and criminal justice. New for the fourth edition is a detailed discussion of the phenomenon of tort suits seeking "public damages" from the government for rights violations. The relevant issues are illustrated through a new case study based on *Henry v British Columbia (Attorney General)*.

Chapters 11 and 12 provide a basic introduction to other key areas of law—property, residential tenancies, family law, and employment law—that are most likely to be familiar to students and to intersect with the criminal law issues that are the main focus of the book. These areas of law are categorized as either "rights to" disciplines—property, family property, and tenancies, discussed in Chapter 11—or "relationship" disciplines—divorce, custody, and support in family law, and employment law, covered in Chapter 12. In these chapters, examples focus on the intersection of civil and criminal law—for example, the impact of bail terms on outcomes within the family law system.

Acknowledgments

There are of course many other smaller changes that have been made for this edition, some of them more practical than ideological. As with all new editions, in preparation for the revision work Emond Publishing consulted with instructors teaching from the text and obtained detailed critiques. The efforts by instructor reviewers to communicate to us how they use the book, its strengths and weaknesses, and what ought to be included in a revision played a very important role in shaping the content. For those efforts we wish to acknowledge Lisa Myers, Lambton College; Cecelia Reilly, Loyalist College; and Lance Triskle, Georgian College for their contributions. We would also like to thank Emond Publishing's managing developmental editor Kelly Dickson, copy editor David Handelsman, and proofreader Michael Kelly, as well as our developmental editor, Joanne Sutherland, for their invaluable support and assistance. Emond Publishing's commitment to a consultative approach ensures that those who teach from this text can be confident that it will continue to be responsive to changes not only in the legal context but in the way the law is taught. We encourage you, as always, to let us know what you think of the latest revisions, and what you'd like to see in the *fifth* edition.

Gargi Mukherji and Nora Rock

About the Authors

Nora Rock is an Ontario JD (lawyer) working as the corporate and policy writer for LawPRO, the Lawyers' Professional Indemnity Company. Nora is author/co-author of several texts for high school, community college, and university, as well as two novels for young adults.

Professor Gargi Mukherji is a full-time faculty instructor at Sheridan College's Faculty of Applied Health and Community Studies, School of Public Safety. She currently holds the position of Public Safety Law Curriculum Coordinator for the Paralegal, Police Foundations, and Private and Public Investigations Programs at Sheridan. Professor Mukherji holds an LLB degree from the University of Manitoba, and a BEd and MEd from the University of Windsor. She has more than ten years of experience as a Crown Prosecutor in Winnipeg, Manitoba and Windsor, Ontario, and as in-house Counsel for the Windsor-Essex Children's Aid Society. Professor Mukherji has also taught at the University of Windsor, Faculty of Law, and enjoys coaching students in mock trial competitions. Her specific areas of practice and education are in criminal law and procedure, evidence and investigation, and child protection law and advocacy. She is fluent in three languages.

Valerie Hoag is a civil litigation practitioner, as a partner in a Kitchener law firm, a senior associate with a Hamilton litigation firm, and currently with her own practice in Kitchener. She has appeared before the Superior Court of Justice, Divisional Court, and the Ontario Court of Appeal, and before various tribunals in Ontario. As a full-time professor in the law and security and police foundations programs at Conestoga College Institute of Technology and Advanced Learning, Valerie designed the course curriculum for all of the law courses and taught four of those courses. She helped design the College's paralegal diploma program, Bachelor of Community and Criminal Justice degree program, and two post-diploma programs. She was a member of the College's Research Ethics Board and currently she is a member of the University of Waterloo Clinical Research Ethics Committee.

PART I

Introduction to the Law: Function and Structure

Introduction

1

LEARNING OUTCOMES

After completing this chapter, you should be able to:

- Describe the various functions of law in society.

- List the stages in the life cycle of a law.

- Describe the origins of and differences between common law and statute law.

- Describe the relationship between common law and statute law.

- Distinguish between criminal law and civil law.

- Understand the distinction between substantive law and procedural law.

This book is designed to provide an introductory overview of Canadian law. Although it will not make readers experts in any of the many specific areas of the law, it will provide an understanding of how the Canadian legal system is structured and how the law changes as society changes.

Why Make Laws?

All societies in all parts of the world govern themselves according to what can be described as codes of law. As societies develop, members develop, communicate, and observe certain norms of organized and predictable behaviour so that they can live together peaceably and govern their affairs efficiently. As a group of members living together grows larger, the potential for conflict and the need for organization increase. In response to these changes, the group's code of behavioural norms—or laws—increases in complexity and in formality.

Religious and Secular Laws

Not all codes of behavioural norms resemble "laws" as we typically recognize them. Some groups identify their rules as being part of their religion, given to them by a god or gods. Some groups live by rules that are never explicitly spoken. Consider, for example, a high school clique, membership in which depends on "being cool"—either students are cool (understand the unspoken rules and govern themselves accordingly) or are not (haven't cracked the admission code).

secular
non-religious

In some societies, codes of religious rules actually evolve into laws for governing society (sometimes called "civil laws"); in other societies, a separate civil code emerges and evolves parallel to the religious code—hence the distinction between religious laws and **secular** laws. For many Canadians, secular laws have come to assume much greater importance than religious laws for governing behaviour, but aspects of the parallel systems remain. For example, a modern Jewish (or Christian, or Muslim, and so on) wedding ceremony incorporates the solemnization of both religious and secular contracts, each with different provisions and implications.

Leading up to the passage of Bill 27, the *Family Statute Law Amendment Act, 2006*,[1] the Ontario government considered, then rejected, a proposal to apply religious law, such as sharia (Islamic law), under the *Arbitration Act, 1991*.[2] As well, most nations have deliberately separated religious and secular laws.

In Canada, this separation doesn't preclude government efforts to foster individual citizens' religious freedom, and doesn't mean the end of debate of religious issues in our society. The right (or not) of citizenship candidates to wear the niqab when taking the oath of Canadian citizenship was a polarizing issue in the 2015 federal election. In the same year, law societies across the country considered whether or not they would admit into legal practice the graduates of a proposed Christian law school that would require students to sign a covenant prohibiting sex outside of marriage between a man and a woman.

Of course, many codes of social rules coexist with religious and secular laws—that is, every school, every family, and even every friendship has its own code.

The Life Cycle of Laws

Because of the many codes that everyone uses to govern their lives, most people are already familiar with, whether they realize it or not, the "life cycle" of rules. For example, they know that rules are born when they are proposed by a member and adopted by the group, and that rules often evolve to accommodate changes in the group's composition or circumstances. Rules also become increasingly complex. As a group's membership expands, rules that were once either unspoken or communicated orally may become **codified** or formalized—that is, written down in an organized way for easier dissemination. As social circumstances change, rules go through the processes of amendment and reform whereby some rules are revised and others are replaced because they no longer meet the needs of the society.

Civil or secular laws (simply "laws" from here on) follow a similar life cycle, which may include some or all of the following stages:

1. introduction,
2. debate and discussion,
3. adoption,
4. codification,
5. **amendment**, and
6. reform/**repeal**.

Laws are valuable to a society only insofar as they meet that society's existing needs and deal adequately with the variety of circumstances that its members may experience. When a law stops meeting the needs of or taking into account the circumstances of the society, it must evolve or be amended.

This need to respond to change and to be flexible is the reason that all of our laws cannot simply be written down in one comprehensive (albeit lengthy!) and final code for everyone's reference. It is also the reason that we need lawyers to keep track of the myriad intricacies of the law, we need courts to settle disputes that arise over interpreting those intricacies, and we need a legislature to create new laws to handle emerging issues. Basically, the judicial and legislative systems are the mechanisms by which laws are formulated, designed, and interpreted in a consistent and orderly way.

> **codify**
> formalize a law or rule by incorporating it (usually in print form) into an existing or new code

> **amend**
> change a law or rule

> **repeal**
> terminate the application of a statute or statutory provision

Sources of Law: Common Law and Statute Law

Our legal system in Canada has two sources of law: common law and statute law. Statutes are made by the federal and provincial levels of government. Laws passed by the third level of government—the municipal level—are called bylaws. Each of these levels passes laws through the life cycle described in the preceding section. The other source of law in Canada (in all provinces and territories except Quebec[3]) is common law, or case law, where the courts make law by judicial decisions.

Common Law

The role of the **common law** in our legal system is a direct result of our history as a British colony; we have inherited the common law as part of our law-making system. The common law is the body of judicial decisions made by courts in England and in Canada that establishes legal rules and principles dealing with specific issues. The common law has evolved over many years and reflects changes in society. Other legal systems—for example, code-based systems—exist in other parts of the world. See Figure 1.1 for a map of world legal systems.

> **common law**
> a legal rule or a body of legal principles, established through judicial decisions, that deals with particular legal issues or subject areas

FIGURE 1.1   Map of Legal Systems Around the World

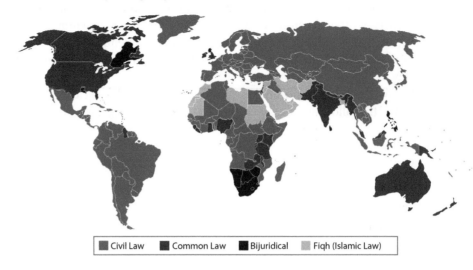

Source: Public domain.

precedent
a court decision that
influences or binds future
decisions on the same
issue or similar facts

The use of common law to guide judicial decision-making is based on the concept of **precedent**. A precedent is a judicial decision on a particular legal issue that sets the law for the same or similar cases that follow. The courts in these later cases will apply the precedent and make the same or a similar decision, thereby reinforcing the legal principle of the precedent. The body of law—these cases—makes up part of the common law.

The advantage of the common law system is that it provides consistency across decisions and predictability. Parties to a case will consider the decisions made in previous, similar decisions, and the parties should be able to predict what the result in their particular court case may be, barring any unforeseen developments. For example, a person charged with driving while impaired may want to challenge the manner in which the breath test was conducted. This person, with the assistance of a lawyer, can review the large body of cases that have already considered this issue to determine whether there is a valid argument to be made to the court. In the context of the civil (non-criminal) court system, the same predictability promotes out-of-court settlements in many cases, which saves money for the parties and time and resources for the legal system.

One advantage that the common law system has over statute law is its ability to respond to changes in society and to particular fact situations. The change, in 2003, to the common law definition of marriage is a good example of the flexibility of precedent. Previously, the common law definition of marriage prohibited people of the same sex from marrying each other. Various court decisions had supported that prohibition. However, societal views changed in the 10 to 15 years leading up to 2003. That summer, the Ontario Court of Appeal, in *Halpern*,[4] considered decisions made by other courts (cases) to help it decide whether the definition of marriage should be changed to include same-sex couples. The Ontario Court of Appeal decided that it would be discriminatory not to change the definition of marriage to include same-sex couples. This decision became the law in Ontario and applies to any other cases in lower courts involving this issue. The decision was **binding** in Ontario.

binding
in common law, the
determinative quality of
a legal decision on future
decisions (assuming
similar facts) if it was
decided in a court of
superior jurisdiction

persuasive
the quality of a legal
decision or precedent
that influences later
decisions on the same
or similar legal issues

Courts of appeal in other provinces heard cases regarding whether the common law definition of marriage should be changed. The Ontario Court of Appeal decision acted as a precedent and it was **persuasive** to the other provincial courts of appeal. They came to the same decision although they were not required to because the Ontario decision was not binding on them. The combined force of these decisions across Canada (and a decision from the Supreme Court of Canada, the highest court in the land) helped persuade the federal government to proceed with legislation in Parliament to change the definition officially. The *Civil Marriage Act*[5] came into effect in July 2005, allowing people of the same sex to marry each other. Prior to its enactment, the statute was hotly debated both within and outside Parliament, demonstrating that the courts and the legislature may not always agree on what the law should be.

In fact, during his time in office (2006-2015), Prime Minister Stephen Harper made no secret of his displeasure about a number of high-profile rulings of the Supreme Court of Canada. These included a ruling that the country's prostitution offences were unconstitutional,[6] a rejection of mandatory minimum sentences for gun crimes,[7] a declaration of Tsilhqot'in First Nations title to a large area of land in British Columbia,[8] a ruling striking down laws prohibiting physician-assisted suicide,[9] and a ruling that the prime minister's appointment of Marc Nadon to the Supreme Court was invalid.[10]

Statute Law

Governments make **statute law**, whether federal, provincial, or municipal (bylaws). Typically, the governing party in Parliament or the provincial legislature will introduce a bill—a proposed piece of legislation—designed to address an issue or a procedure. A new bill, if proclaimed, can become a new statute, can add new provisions to an existing statute, or can create or amend a regulation made under a statute. For example, the Ontario government introduced a bill in 2013—Bill 77, the *Hawkins Gignac Act (Carbon Monoxide Safety), 2013*[11]—that sought to make carbon monoxide detectors mandatory in all Ontario homes. The Bill was introduced after a family of four from Woodstock, Ontario died as a result of a carbon monoxide leak in their home, which had no carbon monoxide detector installed. This Bill was proclaimed as an amendment to an existing regulation—the *Fire Code*[12]—and came into force on October 15, 2014.

This method of changing the law may be more time-consuming than having a court create a new precedent because of the democratic process of debate and review that is an important part of our parliamentary process. However, once the statute has been passed and becomes law, there is stability and consistency in that "the letter of the law" has been published and is available for all to read. For example, drivers of automobiles should know that there is legislation that prohibits speeding, careless driving, "running a stop sign," and using hand-held devices while behind the wheel. The requirements for safe driving are not up to an individual's whim, but are codified by statute, and are enforced accordingly.

Statutes may also reflect government policy objectives. For example, all provinces and territories in Canada have human rights statutes that mandate the fair treatment of all employees and prohibit discrimination on specified grounds. In Ontario, for example, employees have a right to equal treatment in the workplace regardless of race, ancestry, place of origin, colour, ethnic origin, citizenship, creed, sex, sexual orientation, gender identity, gender expression, age, record of offences, marital status, family status, or disability.[13] Having a statute that prohibits discrimination in the workplace on the basis of a prohibited ground sends a message to all employers about the government's expectations and places them at risk of being investigated and penalized for violations. A statute is a more effective and efficient way of regulating behaviour than leaving the issue to a judge to determine and monitor on a case-by-case basis.

Similarly, if a statute becomes outdated, no longer reflects the government's policy objectives (if the government changes after an election), or is no longer in step with societal values, then the government may decide to repeal the statute and the statute is no longer in force.

statute law
legal provisions, in codified form, that are developed and adopted by the parliamentary and legislative process

Box 1.1   Statute "Gathering"

One reason statutes may be repealed is to allow the gathering of related areas of regulation under a single umbrella statute, so that those related or similar topics are regulated in a consistent manner.

This "gathering" makes it easier for people to manage their legal obligations by bringing predictability and familiarity into the law. The following are two examples of initiatives that resulted in the repeal of a number of individual statutes in favour of a harmonized umbrella scheme.

The Ontario Technical Standards and Safety Act

This long and detailed statute creates a harmonized system of safety standards for a wide range of equipment used in Ontario (elevators, boilers, amusement park rides, etc.). When it was proclaimed in 2001, it repealed and replaced the *Boilers and Pressure Vessels Act*, the *Amusement Devices Act*, the *Elevating Devices Act*, the *Energy Act*, the *Gasoline Handling Act*, the *Operating Engineers Act*, and the *Upholstered and Stuffed Articles Act*.

The Manitoba Regulated Health Professions Act

This Act, which was passed in 2009, was designed to repeal more than 20 individual pieces of legislation regulating a wide range of professions in Manitoba (nurses, chiropractors, speech therapists, midwives, naturopaths, opticians, etc.). Transition provisions were designed to manage the replacement of the various administrative schemes with one consistent scheme. Many discipline-related details under the new statute are managed through regulations. (Regulations are discussed in Chapter 2.) This transition, for Manitoba, happened very slowly, with some health professions having not made the transition by the end of 2016, a problem that reflects the reality of bringing such a wide range of self-regulating systems under a central regime.

Sources: *Technical Standards and Safety Act, 2000*, SO 2000, c 16; *The Regulated Health Professions Act*, CCSM c R117.

The Relationship Between Common Law and Statute Law

As we have just discussed, common law and statute law come from different sources and each has advantages and disadvantages in terms of advancing the state of the law. The two systems do not operate independently of each other, however; the nature of the relationship could be likened to a "chicken and egg" dilemma—which comes first? Both influence each other and both have the capacity to change each other. In using the same-sex marriage example, the courts redefined the common law definition of marriage, and Parliament followed suit. Yet in a future case, the courts may well look to the *Civil Marriage Act* to further refine this area of the law.

The tension between common law and statute law comes from two competing concepts: rule of law and parliamentary supremacy. Rule of law means that no one is above the law, including governments, so that if a government passes an "illegal" law or a statute that was contrary to its authority, the courts can strike down that law, effectively cancelling or revoking it. On the other hand, parliamentary supremacy means that Parliament makes the laws, not the courts. The tension between these two concepts is often covered by the media after controversial court decisions. However, both concepts are fundamental to our legal system and are directly inherited from the British legal system.

A great deal of statute law has resulted from the government's decision to codify the case law on a particular legal issue. The government may make this decision because it believes that the common law rules are appropriate and worthy of entrenchment in statute, or because it disagrees with the common law rules that have developed on a certain legal issue and wants to ensure that changes are made. Once the legislation is passed, the common law will evolve because the courts will be called upon to interpret and apply the new statute. For example, the first time a property owner who has been charged for not having carbon monoxide detectors installed decides to fight the charge, the court will be required to interpret and to apply the new law. The decision by the court will have an impact on both the common law and the statute.

The *Criminal Code*,[14] for example, provides a statutory framework of rules that are **considered** by case law. Therefore, law enforcement students cannot simply carry around a pocket *Criminal Code* and be confident that all the law they need to know is contained in its pages. Much of the detail they will need to know to do their job properly can be found only in the common law—in the rules (and police practices) that develop out of the *Criminal Code* sections through daily judicial interpretation and reinterpretation of the words used in the Code. For example, a number of *Criminal Code* offences are based on possession—possession of a weapon, of proceeds of crime, of child pornography, etc. To understand whether a person is guilty of an offence based on possession, law enforcement officers must be familiar with how the law defines "possession." As it turns out, the definition of "possession" varies depending on what is possessed, and is quite complicated. For example, the 2014 Ontario Court of Appeal decision in *R v Tyrell*[15] considered the relationship between **wilful blindness** and **constructive possession**, with respect to the issue of whether an accused whose ex-girlfriend had a loaded gun in a closet was or was not in possession of the gun despite being "wilfully blind" to the presence of the gun.

While criminal law has the *Criminal Code* as its statutory framework, many other areas of law, such as contracts and torts, are based almost completely in common law, with some specific subtopics the subject of statutes. Contract and tort law are covered in Chapter 10. For example, family law statutes and landlord and tenant statutes, discussed in Chapters 11 and 12, demonstrate the implementation of government policy objectives and the influence of societal values in changing the common law.

Criminal Law Versus Civil Law

When considering distinctions within the law, it's worthwhile to examine the difference between criminal law and non-criminal law, which is sometimes called "civil law."

The term "civil law" is a confusing one, because it has at least three recognized usages. First, as mentioned earlier in this chapter, it can be used to describe "laws for governing society" in general (all of those laws). Second, it can be used to distinguish the civil law system (a code-based system used in many countries around the world and also in the province of Quebec) from the common law system (a precedent-based system) used in the other Canadian provinces.

But there is a third usage of the term "civil law," and that is to distinguish non-criminal laws and the procedures used to enforce them from criminal laws and their procedures. This third usage is the one that is discussed in this text.

One of the most important differences between criminal and non-criminal (civil) cases is that while the parties to civil cases can be anyone (private individuals, corporations, government agencies, etc.), one of the parties in every criminal case is the state (the government). Although there is such a thing as a "private prosecution," the overwhelming majority of criminal prosecutions are brought by the government against a private party.

considered
applied or interpreted in a court case; refers to statutory provisions

wilful blindness
a person is wilfully blind to something when he deliberately fails to turn his mind to that thing despite the fact that he could be expected to know about it

constructive possession
a person can be found to be in possession of something, under the criminal law, when she acquiesces to another person's (unlawful) actual possession of the thing while they are together

first instance
the first time a dispute appears before the court (at the original trial level, not the appeal level)

Also, because criminal charges can have a serious impact on a person's freedom and/or reputation, there are special procedures incorporated into criminal proceedings that are not used for civil proceedings. To support these separate procedures, criminal trials and civil trials are heard (decided) in separate courts, at least at **first instance** (at the trial level).

At many places in this book, the differences between criminal laws and procedures and non-criminal (civil) laws and procedures are highlighted. For law enforcement officers and others who work with the law on a regular basis, understanding these distinctions poses many practical problems. For example, when a commercial transaction goes wrong because one party intentionally substitutes the wrong product for the product ordered, is this a breach of contract (non-criminal law), is it the crime of fraud (criminal law), or is it both? And is sorting out the problem the job of the police, or must one party sue the other in the civil court system? We will revisit the boundaries between criminal and civil law whenever they are pertinent to the topic being covered.

Substantive Law Versus Procedural Law

substantive law
law that addresses the substance or factual content of a legal issue

procedural law
law that establishes the process by which substantive issues will be addressed

Another distinction that law enforcement students should be aware of is the difference between **substantive law** and **procedural law**. Substantive law describes the type of conduct that is acceptable and unacceptable. Procedural law describes the process to be followed when there is a violation of substantive law.

For example, colleges have codes of student conduct that cover cheating. Cheating, as described in its various forms in a college's code of conduct, is the substantive law. If a student violates the prohibition against cheating, there is also a prescribed process whereby members of faculty and/or administration conduct an investigation and render a decision, in which a penalty may be assessed. This process is the procedural law and includes such matters as what forms are used, what the student is expected to do, and whether the student can appeal.

In criminal law, the *Criminal Code* contains both substantive law ("Every one commits robbery who …") and procedural law ("A judge … may … release an appellant …"). The *Criminal Code* tells us what the offences are and what happens if an offence is committed. Both aspects of the *Criminal Code* are explored further in later chapters.

In civil law, there are statutes and cases that describe the substantive aspects of civil claims, such as liability for injuries suffered in a motor vehicle accident or in a slip-and-fall accident on an icy sidewalk. The procedures that govern requirements such as the documents to be served and filed and the time limits that must be met are contained in a separate instrument; the Ontario version is called the *Rules of Civil Procedure*.[16] Some of these requirements will be discussed later.

For law enforcement personnel, it is as important to respect procedural law as it is substantive law. Procedural law provides the "same rules" for all participants in the process to follow. Failure to follow the procedural law can be very serious for law enforcement officers, law clerks, paralegals, and other participants, as will be discussed in more detail later.

CHAPTER SUMMARY

Laws permit groups (societies) to live together harmoniously by defining, communicating, and enforcing accepted behavioural norms. These norms can be religious or secular; both kinds of norms can evolve into laws as we know them.

As societies grow and become more complex, laws follow suit. To permit flexibility and adaptability, laws follow a typical pattern and have a life cycle. In general, laws are proposed or introduced; they are debated; they evolve (before and/or after being adopted); they may be codified; they are sometimes amended; and, when no longer needed, they are repealed or replaced.

Canada has two systems of law that exist side by side: the common law evolves through judges' precedent-based decisions in court cases, and statute law is passed by governments. Each system has advantages and disadvantages, and the systems inform and complement each other. An important advantage of the common law is its ability to respond to changes in society and to particular fact situations. Statute law, on the other hand, provides stability and consistency because it is codified and available for all to read.

Within the law, there are various subdivisions and classifications. A well-known distinction is between criminal and non-criminal (civil) law, but laws can also be distinguished on the basis of whether they are substantive (they provide a description of regulated conduct or conditions) or procedural (they provide a description of how to deal with breaches of substantive law).

KEY TERMS

amend, 5
binding, 6
codify, 5
common law, 5
considered, 9

constructive possession, 9
first instance, 10
persuasive, 6
precedent, 6
procedural law, 10

repeal, 5
secular, 4
statute law, 7
substantive law, 10
wilful blindness, 9

NOTES

1   Bill 27, *Family Statute Law Amendment Act, 2006*, SO 2006, c 1.

2   *Arbitration Act, 1991*, SO 1991, c 17.

3   Quebec's legal system is somewhat different. Quebec has a *Civil Code*—a general code of provincial law that addresses a wide range of legal issues that, in other provinces, are covered primarily by case law.

4   *Halpern v Canada (Attorney general)*, 2003 CanLII 26403 (Ont CA).

5   *Civil Marriage Act*, SC 2005, c 33.

6   *Canada (Attorney General) v Bedford*, 2013 SCC 72, [2013] 3 SCR 1101.

7   *R v Nur*, 2015 SCC 15.

8   *Tsilhqot'in Nation v British Columbia*, 2014 SCC 44, [2014] 2 SCR 257.

9   *Carter v Canada (Attorney General)*, 2015 SCC 5, [2015] 1 SCR 331.

10   *Reference re Supreme Court Act, ss 5 and 6*, 2014 SCC 21, [2014] 1 SCR 433.

11   *Hawkins Gignac Act (Carbon Monoxide Safety), 2013*, SO 2013, c 14.

12   *Fire Code*, O Reg 213/07, a regulation made under part IV of the *Fire Protection and Prevention Act, 1997*, SO 1997, c 4.

13   *Human Rights Code*, RSO 1990, c H.19, s 5(1).

14   *Criminal Code*, RSC 1985, c C-46, as amended.

15   *R v Tyrell*, 2014 ONCA 617.

16   *Rules of Civil Procedure*, RRO 1990, Reg 194.

EXERCISES

Multiple Choice

1. Statute law offers the following advantage(s) over case law:
   a. it allows easier public access to the state of the law
   b. it can provide policy directions for specific groups to follow
   c. it addresses all possible fact situations
   d. a and b
   e. all of the above

2. Some laws are described as procedural because they
   a. regulate the performance of complex scientific procedures
   b. are less important than substantive laws
   c. prescribe the process by which justice is to be achieved
   d. can be applied only by courts of superior jurisdiction
   e. none of the above

3. The life cycle of a law includes the following stages:
   a. introduction, amendment, citation, repeal
   b. introduction, debate, codification, citation, statute, substantiation
   c. adoption, termination, repeal, substantiation
   d. introduction, debate and discussion, adoption, codification, amendment, reform/repeal
   e. introduction, debate and discussion, adoption, repeal, codification, amendment

4. Common law is
   a. the set of laws that are common, everyday occurrences
   b. a body of legal principles established through court decisions
   c. a set of statutes passed by Parliament
   d. a body of cases established through court decisions and codified as statutes
   e. the set of bylaws passed by a municipal government

5. Substantive law
   a. describes an expectation of behaviour or responses
   b. is designed to govern the way the law is brought to bear on a dispute
   c. is a body of legal principles established through the judicial process
   d. is a body of statutes passed by Parliament
   e. is also called civil or secular law

True or False?

_____ 1. Converting a common law rule into statutory form ensures that it will no longer evolve in response to court decisions.

_____ 2. All criminal law is statute law because it is contained in the *Criminal Code*.

_____ 3. Religious laws no longer apply in the common law world.

_____ 4. Religious laws are not interpreted or applied by Canadian legal courts.

_____ 5. Procedural law governs the way substantive law is brought to bear on a dispute.

_____ 6. When it comes to non-criminal statute law, the substantive provisions and the procedures for applying those provisions are often contained in separate statutes.

____ **7.** A statute can be repealed by a parliament only if it is first declared unconstitutional by the Supreme Court of Canada.

____ **8.** There are three distinct meanings of the term "civil law" in Canada.

____ **9.** A particular behaviour is illegal only if it is specifically referenced by a statute; for example, you can be charged with distracted driving for texting on a cellphone, but not for tying a fishhook onto fishing line.

____**10.** Because religious law is not recognized by Canadian courts, religious leaders cannot enforce customary religious laws within a religious community; for example, a religion can no longer enforce a rule that its leaders cannot marry, or be female.

Short Answer

1. Based on your understanding of this chapter, draft a definition of the word "law."

2. This chapter describes many of the practical advantages of statute law. What are the advantages of case law?

3. The *Charter of Rights and Freedoms*, part of Canada's Constitution, was drafted broadly, with the expectation that its provisions would be interpreted by case law. Why do you think the drafters chose to be vague about such important legal issues?

4. This chapter mentioned that the Conservative government and Prime Minister Harper, in power for nine years leading up to October 19, 2015, were frustrated with the outcome of a series of Supreme Court of Canada decisions made in the years 2013-2015. If the government can pass new laws to achieve its preferred social policy objectives, why would it care about "unfavourable" Supreme Court decisions?

5. Why are statutes more effective than common law precedents as a way for governments to shape behaviour (for example, corporate behaviour)?

Research Question

1. Under the heading "Common Law," we mentioned that the Supreme Court, in a 2013 decision (*Canada (Attorney General) v Bedford*), declared Canada's anti-prostitution regime (some of the *Criminal Code* provisions prohibiting aspects of prostitution) to be unconstitutional. After a ruling like this, what happens, practically speaking?

   a. Were new laws regulating prostitution passed, and if so, how was this achieved?

   b. What did police forces do in the meantime, when they encountered suspects engaging in behaviours that would have been illegal under the former legislation (that has now been declared unconstitutional)? Did it still apply until it was replaced, or not? Was prostitution "legal" until it was replaced?

   c. What about individuals who were charged under the previous legislation before it was struck down, but who had not yet gone to trial for these offences? Were they released if they were in custody? Did they still go to trial? Would they simply be re-charged under the new regime even though their "crime" happened under the old regime?

Statute Law: Function, Jurisdiction, and Structure

2

LEARNING OUTCOMES

After completing this chapter, you should be able to:

- Explain the concept of jurisdiction with respect to law-making.

- List the principal levels of law-making jurisdiction in Canada.

- Describe the function of the Constitution in establishing law-making jurisdiction.

- Describe, in general terms, the division between, and scope of, provincial and federal jurisdiction.

- Explain how to locate a statute.

- Describe the typical structure of a statute.

- Describe the function of regulations.

The Concept of Law-Making Jurisdiction

jurisdiction
authority to make law,
either by governments
or by courts

As explained in Chapter 1, statute law (legislation) is the formal, written law enacted by governments. Canada has three principal levels of government—federal, provincial, and municipal—and each level has a specific law-making **jurisdiction**, or sphere of appropriate legislative action, reserved to it.

In countries with a federal system of government (a system that contains a number of semi-autonomous units), these levels are a common way of organizing legislative responsibility. However, the degree of control given to the smaller government units varies widely from federation to federation. As a general rule, the central government in a federation tends to reserve to itself jurisdiction over very important issues or issues of national importance, including serious crime, national security, immigration, and trade. Issues of daily life, such as employment and family law, are assigned to the smaller government units. In Canada, a comparatively large degree of legislative responsibility is delegated to the provinces and territories—that is, there are many more provincial statutes, and accompanying regulations, than there are federal ones.

A coherent organizational scheme for assigning jurisdiction is important because it prevents legislative overlap while ensuring that all of the issues that need to be addressed are covered. An organizational scheme also allows for shared governmental responsibility, including financial responsibility, for administering the legal system.

Decisions about which level of government has jurisdiction over a particular issue often create political tension in a federation. While the smaller government units often prefer to have the power to decide a particular issue, having that power usually means being responsible for the cost of its administration. See the Case in Point feature below for an example of how courts decide questions about constitutional jurisdiction.

How Is Legislative Jurisdiction Assigned?

cite
describe or refer to, orally
or in writing, a legislative
provision or legal decision

In Canada, as in many federations, legislative jurisdiction has been established by a constitution. A constitution is considered to be the law that creates, or "constitutes," a nation. It is a basic plan for the government of a major political unit, in our case, Canada. Canada was created in 1867 by an act passed by the British Parliament **cited** now as the *Constitution Act, 1867*,[1] previously known as the *British North America Act 1867*. In 1982, the British Parliament passed the *Canada Act 1982*,[2] which contained the *Constitution Act, 1982*.[3] The *Constitution Act, 1982* was passed by our Parliament and includes the *Canadian Charter of Rights and Freedoms*.[4] The passage of these pieces of legislation by both the British and Canadian parliaments meant that Canada officially had a constitution and that this constitution was completely Canadian. The *Constitution Act, 1982* states that it, and therefore the Charter, is the supreme law in Canada. No single government, federal or provincial, can change the Constitution. The Charter will be discussed in greater detail in Chapters 4 and 6.

One of the most important tasks performed by any constitution is the assignment of legislative jurisdiction. In the case of the *Constitution Act, 1867*, this assignment is made by sections 91 and 92, which read, in part, as follows:

> 91. It shall be lawful for the Queen, by and with the Advice and Consent of the Senate and House of Commons, to make Laws for the Peace, Order, and good Government of Canada, in relation to all Matters not coming within the Classes of Subjects by this Act assigned exclusively to the Legislatures of the Provinces; and for greater Certainty, but not so as to restrict the Generality of the foregoing Terms

of this Section, it is hereby declared that (notwithstanding anything in this Act) the exclusive Legislative Authority of the Parliament of Canada extends to all Matters coming within the Classes of Subjects next hereinafter enumerated; that is to say,

   1. Repealed.
1A. The Public Debt and Property.
   2. The Regulation of Trade and Commerce.
2A. Unemployment insurance.
   3. The raising of Money by any Mode or System of Taxation.
   4. The borrowing of Money on the Public Credit.
   5. Postal Service.
   6. The Census and Statistics.
   7. Militia, Military and Naval Service, and Defence.
   8. The fixing of and providing for the Salaries and Allowances of Civil and other Officers of the Government of Canada.
   9. Beacons, Buoys, Lighthouses, and Sable Island.
10. Navigation and Shipping.
11. Quarantine and the Establishment and Maintenance of Marine Hospitals.
12. Sea Coast and Inland Fisheries.
13. Ferries between a Province and any British or Foreign Country or between Two Provinces.
14. Currency and Coinage.
15. Banking, Incorporation of Banks, and the Issue of Paper Money.
16. Savings Banks.
17. Weights and Measures.
18. Bills of Exchange and Promissory Notes.
19. Interest.
20. Legal Tender.
21. Bankruptcy and Insolvency.
22. Patents of Invention and Discovery.
23. Copyrights.
24. Indians, and Lands reserved for the Indians.
25. Naturalization and Aliens.
26. Marriage and Divorce.
27. The Criminal Law, except the Constitution of Courts of Criminal Jurisdiction, but including the Procedure in Criminal Matters.
28. The Establishment, Maintenance, and Management of Penitentiaries.
29. Such Classes of Subjects as are expressly excepted in the Enumeration of the Classes of Subjects by this Act assigned exclusively to the Legislatures of the Provinces.

And any Matter coming within any of the Classes of Subjects enumerated in this Section shall not be deemed to come within the Class of Matters of a local or private Nature comprised in the Enumeration of the Classes of Subjects by this Act assigned exclusively to the Legislatures of the Provinces.

   92. In each Province, the Legislature may exclusively make Laws in relation to Matters coming within the Classes of Subjects next hereinafter enumerated; that is to say,

   1. Repealed.
   2. Direct Taxation within the Province in order to the raising of a Revenue for Provincial Purposes.
   3. The borrowing of Money on the sole Credit of the Province.

4. The Establishment and Tenure of Provincial Offices and the Appointment and Payment of Provincial Officers.

5. The Management and Sale of the Public Lands belonging to the Province and of the Timber and Wood thereon.

6. The Establishment, Maintenance, and Management of Public and Reformatory Prisons in and for the Province.

7. The Establishment, Maintenance, and Management of Hospitals, Asylums, Charities, and Eleemosynary Institutions in and for the Province, other than Marine Hospitals.

8. Municipal Institutions in the Province.

9. Shop, Saloon, Tavern, Auctioneer, and other Licences in order to the raising of a Revenue for Provincial, Local, or Municipal Purposes.

10. Local Works and Undertakings other than such as are of the following Classes:

    (a) Lines of Steam or other Ships, Railways, Canals, Telegraphs, and other Works and Undertakings connecting the Province with any other or others of the Provinces, or extending beyond the Limits of the Province:

    (b) Lines of Steam Ships between the Province and any British or Foreign Country:

    (c) Such Works as, although wholly situate within the Province, are before or after their Execution declared by the Parliament of Canada to be for the general Advantage of Canada or for the Advantage of Two or more of the Provinces.

11. The Incorporation of Companies with Provincial Objects.

12. The Solemnization of Marriage in the Province.

13. Property and Civil Rights in the Province.

14. The Administration of Justice in the Province, including the Constitution, Maintenance, and Organization of Provincial Courts, both of Civil and of Criminal Jurisdiction, and including Procedure in Civil Matters in those Courts.

15. The Imposition of Punishment by Fine, Penalty, or Imprisonment for enforcing any Law of the Province made in relation to any Matter coming within any of the Classes of Subjects enumerated in this Section.

16. Generally all Matters of a merely local or private Nature in the Province.

tribunal
a formal body established, often under a statute, for the purpose of adjudicating disputes within the ambit of the statute

CASE IN POINT

Constitutional Jurisdiction and Services in Indigenous Communities

The question of whether a government activity falls under federal or provincial jurisdiction is especially complicated where the activity takes place on First Nation reserve territory. First Nations and other indigenous communities in Canada often have their own systems of government, and there is an increasing willingness, on the part of non-indigenous governments in Canada, to interact with these governments on a quasi nation-to-nation basis (the way one country interacts with another country under international law).

However, as provided by treaties and other agreements, indigenous communities often receive funding from other Canadian governments, both at the federal and the provincial/territorial level. Typically, funds from a province are given to support on-reserve activities that are analogous to services under provincial jurisdiction, while federal funding often has a more general purpose (to support self-governance efforts and efforts to achieve an acceptable standard of living in reserve communities).

In the case in question, a **tribunal** formed in 2012, the British Columbia Human Rights Tribunal (BCHRT), heard arguments in *Prichard v Tla'Amin Community Health Board Society and others*. In this case, an individual named Hugh Prichard was fired as the executive director of the Tla'Amin Community Health Board Society ("the Society"), an agency that operated on a First Nations reserve and offered services similar to those provided by a provincial or territorial child and family services society. Prichard alleged discrimination in relation to the termination, and filed complaints with both the (federal) Canadian Human Rights Commission and the (provincial) British Columbia Human Rights Commission, because he was unsure which commission had jurisdiction over the case.

The BCHRT was required to decide which human rights commission had jurisdiction over the case. Previous decisions (jurisprudence) about these kinds of cases make it clear that the answer in these cases is highly fact-specific: the tribunal must consider all of the relevant evidence and cannot just rely on one deciding factor in making its determination. The jurisprudence also made it clear that facts related to funding ("Where does the money to run the service come from?") and also facts related to the nature of the service ("Is it more like a provincial, or more like a federal service?") are relevant to the analysis that the tribunal must undertake.

The BCHRT noted that the Sliammon First Nation (where the Society operated) receives funding from the federal government "for the provision of health programs and services." However, the First Nation argued that the Society operated independently of the First Nation. The Society itself received funding from the province of British Columbia, to permit it to offer child welfare services (as an alternative to having the First Nation come within the operational jurisdiction of the province's own child protection department). (This arrangement exists on several reserves, because many First Nations consider the right to provide their own child welfare services to be an important aspect of self-government.) Child and family welfare services have long since been recognized as falling within the jurisdiction of the provinces and territories.

In essence, then, the question before the tribunal was whether the operations of the Society were

a. more like provincial child and family services, which would mean the matter would fall under the jurisdiction of the provincial human rights commission; or

b. more like a matter involving "Indians, and Lands reserved for the Indians" (s 91, item 24, of the *Constitution Act, 1867*),[5] which could theoretically make the Society a federal agency, which would be governed, for the purpose of labour relations disputes, by the federal human rights commission.

The tribunal decided that, based on the facts it had to consider, the Society fell under the jurisdiction of the province, and therefore the British Columbia Human Rights Commission would be charged with handling Prichard's complaint.

In finding that the operations of the Society were not primarily about "Indians, and Lands reserved for the Indians," the BCHRT reflected the modern-day tendency to, where possible, move away from the older historic pattern of federal influence and control over indigenous peoples, and instead to support reserves' progress toward autonomy over the provision of services on their lands.

Questions for Discussion

1. Do you believe that treating services provided on reserve as analogous to provincial services is consistent with a nation-to-nation approach to relations with indigenous peoples in Canada? Why or why not?

2. Notice that although he was employed by an agency operated by a First Nation, Prichard needed to bring his complaint before an agency operated by the province of British Columbia (the British Columbia Human Rights Commission). From the perspective of the First Nation, does this requirement support or undermine its goal of greater autonomy? Should First Nations create their own human rights commissions? What would the benefits, drawbacks, and/or obstacles likely be?

Source: *Prichard v Tla'Amin Community Health Board Society and others*, 2012 BCHRT 152.

Considering the hundreds of statutes currently in force in Canada, it is surprising that this jurisdiction plan is relatively simple. Because the plan was created in 1867, many of the issues that are currently the subject of legislation had not even been contemplated by the constitutional drafters (consider, for example, legislation designed to regulate telecommunications). How, then, do the provinces and the federal government determine which has jurisdiction over new or unique issues? The answer: by analogy. When an issue that requires legislation comes up, it is compared with the matters specifically addressed in the jurisdiction sections of the Constitution (ss 91 and 92), and it is then assigned to either the provinces or the federal government based on where the issue seems to fit according to the intentions behind the original division of powers.

In many cases, this is an easy decision and is a matter of agreement between the levels of government. When the decision is more contentious, the courts are called on to interpret the application of the Constitution to the new issue. For example, credit cards, such as Visa or MasterCard, are regulated by federal law, even though credit cards did not exist in 1867. Banks handle the business of credit cards; therefore, by analogy, it makes sense to have credit cards fall under federal jurisdiction.

To help clarify how the division of powers works in practice, here are two lists of statute names. The statutes in the first list are federal statutes, and the statutes in the second list are provincial statutes:

Federal statutes (passed by the Parliament of Canada):

- the *Criminal Code*[6]
- the *Immigration and Refugee Protection Act*[7]
- the *Aeronautics Act*[8]
- the *Oceans Act*[9]

Provincial statutes (passed by provincial legislatures):

- the *Family Law Act*[10] (Ontario)
- the *Workers' Compensation Act*[11] (Alberta)
- the *Human Tissue Gift Act*[12] (British Columbia)
- the *Municipal Act, 2001*[13] (Ontario)

Municipal Jurisdiction

bylaws
laws made by a municipality that govern such issues as parking, noise control, licensing, and property standards; can include offences and penalties

Sections 91 and 92 of the Constitution, reproduced above, include scant mention of municipal jurisdiction. However, certain legal issues in Canada are addressed by municipalities (cities and towns). You will notice that specific items in section 92 of the Constitution refer to municipal or local matters (see items 8, 9, and 10) and thus the provinces have jurisdiction over municipalities. Laws passed by municipalities are called **bylaws**, and usually deal with issues of a very local nature, such as parking, waste collection, and community services. Municipalities hold the authority to regulate these issues by delegation (passing down of responsibility) from the provinces and territories. Although many issues that are considered part of municipal jurisdiction may seem minor in comparison with national concerns, the smooth management of a large municipality is an incredibly complicated task and can give rise to an enormous number of bylaws. Municipal law is a very complicated discipline and, apart from this brief mention, is beyond the scope of this text.

Criminal Law, Civil Law, and the Administration of Justice

Criminal law and civil law are the primary themes of this text. As was discussed in Chapter 1, it is important for all students of the Canadian justice system, whether in police foundations, law and security administration, or law clerk programs, to be aware of the distinction between these two areas of law. The distinction plays out in a variety of ways. For example, as noted in Chapter 1, the procedures used to enforce the criminal law are very different from those used to enforce the civil law. Another example is the source of authority for a police officer or a security officer: does the authority to act (for example, to arrest or to charge) come from a federal statute, a provincial or territorial statute, or a municipal bylaw? A third example lies in the administration of justice.

You may have noticed in the lists of legislative jurisdiction above that there appears to be an overlap in the area of criminal law. Criminal law is discussed under section 91, item 27, as a federal matter but it is also discussed under section 92, item 14, as a provincial matter under the topic of the administration of justice. A closer examination of these items shows that federal jurisdiction and provincial jurisdiction are divided: "Procedure in Criminal Matters" comes under federal authority, but the "Constitution of Courts of Criminal Jurisdiction" does not; that function comes under provincial authority.

As you progress through the courses in your program, the practical effects of these two areas of legislative jurisdiction will become more apparent. For now, it is sufficient for you to know that the federal government has the authority to set out the criminal law (for example, through the *Criminal Code*) and to prescribe the procedure for processing criminal charges, while the provincial and territorial governments have the authority to run the courts and to set the procedure for civil matters (when a person or company sues another person or company).

Researching Statute Law

The Criminal Code

The statute that police consult most often is the *Criminal Code*. The most current version of this statute is cited as RSC 1985, c C-46 (the significance of the elements of this citation will be discussed below). Because it is one of the most frequently consulted Canadian statutes, the *Criminal Code* is often published by commercial publishers in pocket and annotated (with commentary) editions, many of which contain the text of other related statutes, such as the *Youth Criminal Justice Act*,[14] the *Canada Evidence Act*,[15] and others creating criminal or quasi-criminal offences. These editions will typically include, as well, the text of the *Charter of Rights and Freedoms*. A current, commercially published edition of the *Criminal Code* will serve most research needs, but because such Codes are usually published only once a year, new provisions or amendments may not be included in the edition. To be absolutely sure that the information is up to date (to prepare for a court appearance, for example), one needs to update, or "note up," research results by consulting an **official source**—a version of a statute or regulation that meets the courts' standards for legitimacy, accuracy, and currency—for the legislation, as described below.

official source
a version of a statute or regulation that meets the courts' standards for legitimacy, accuracy, and currency

Other Statutes

Although the *Criminal Code* figures prominently in legal research, there will be occasions to apply or be familiar with other statutes that have a quasi-criminal component—for example, the *Smoke-Free Ontario Act*.[16] (Many of these statutes will be discussed in a course on provincial offences.)

Because these other statutes are not as commonly applied by police officers, usually no convenient pocket edition is available. Finding these statutes requires performing basic legal research in the same way that a lawyer or paralegal does—either in a traditional law library or on a computer. There are a number of computerized databases, including government websites (which contain cases, statutes, and regulations), the Canadian Legal Information Institute website (called CanLII, which is managed by the Federation of Law Societies of Canada), and commercial online resources such as LexisNexis Quicklaw and WestlawNext Canada.

Is the Legal Problem Covered by a Statute?

In some cases, it may be necessary to research a legal problem without even knowing whether the problem is covered by a statute (remember, a great deal of Canadian law is case law, as explained in Chapter 1). In such a case, the first step might simply be to describe the problem to a more experienced colleague or to a law librarian, who may be able to identify the relevant statute. Figure 2.1 may help you visualize the typical steps used when researching a legal issue.

A statute may also be identified by performing a keyword search. For example, if the problem deals with a tenant who claims to have been locked out of his or her apartment by the landlord, the search for the relevant statute might be based on the words "landlord" or "locked out."

Resources are often available in both electronic and paper form. Which form is used may depend on availability, cost, and ease of use. Common examples of each form are discussed below.

FIGURE 2.1   Researching a Legal Issue

> **Researching a Legal Issue**
>
> Is it legal in Ontario to refuse to rent an apartment to a dog owner?
>
> **Step 1: Is renting apartments a provincially or federally regulated matter?**
>
> Try
> - Check list of topics in ss 91, 92 of the Constitution
> - Do an Internet keyword search—restricting results to Canada—to see which statutes come up
>
> Answer
> - s 92(13) mentions "Property and Civil Rights in the Province"
> - Web search brings up province-specific hits
>
> **Step 2: Search Ontario provincial laws**
>
> Try
> - Go to www.ontario.ca/laws
> - Browse statute names or search using logical keywords
>
> Answer
> - a search for the word "Landlord" brings up the *Residential Tenancies Act, 2006*[17]
>
> **Step 3: Read the Table of Contents of the statute**
>
> Try
> - s 14: "No pet" provisions void
>
> Answer
> - s 14 reads, "A provision in a tenancy agreement forbidding the presence of animals in or about the residential complex is void"
>
> That's great news! But as you have learned, Canadian law is more complex than just the content of the provisions in statutes.

Electronic Sources

An electronic source for legal research, such as a database or website, will likely have a search function that allows searches by keyword. The kinds of documents generated by such a source will depend on the type of source, but if there is a statute governing the problem, there is a good chance that it will be found in this way. As with any website, the user should make sure that the site contains accurate and current information.

The federal government and most provincial governments maintain websites that include the full text of statutes. Current versions and consolidated (updated) versions of the statutes and regulations found on Ontario's e-Laws website now have official status. Similarly, all consolidated statutes and regulations found on the federal government's Department of Justice website (<http://www.justice.gc.ca>) are official versions.

Paper Sources

Legal research can also be done in a law library using paper sources. The librarian can identify any encyclopedic sources that may be available. The most common ones are the *Canadian Abridgment* (Carswell), a huge, multivolume legal encyclopedia that is searchable in many different ways (it is a good idea to ask a librarian how best to use it), and the *Canadian Encyclopedic Digest* (Carswell), another large encyclopedia that is organized primarily by subject matter. The Digest has regional editions, so the appropriate one for the region can be used.

Although these encyclopedias may look daunting, a keyword search will often very quickly reveal the name of a statute (or a case) dealing with the particular legal problem. In the case of the above lockout example, a search under "landlord" will almost certainly lead to a provincial or territorial landlord and tenant statute. All of the provinces have one of these.

Using the Citation to Find the Statute

A reference to a statute will also likely provide the statute's **citation**—a list of letters and numbers following the statute name that represent that statute's "address" for the purpose of research.

A federal statute's citation looks like this:

- *Criminal Code*, RSC 1985, c C-46; or
- *Immigration and Refugee Protection Act*, SC 2001, c 27.

A provincial statute's citation looks like this:

- *Provincial Offences Act*, RSO 1990, c P.33; or
- *Employment Standards Act, 2000*, SO 2000, c 41.

A statute citation is designed to direct the reader to the most current official print source of the legislation. Each Canadian legislature, federal or provincial, publishes a print collection of its statutes. This collection includes new volumes, printed in each year, containing all new legislation passed by the legislature. In the past, people consulted these print sources as their primary means of accessing the content of statutes. Previously, the practice had been to publish a collection of statutes, with any changes or revisions, periodically. For example, Ontario published its revised statutes every ten years. Now that most people access statutes online, the creation of print "revisions" (consolidations) has stopped.

citation
an expression, in standard form, of the bibliographical information for locating a case or legislative document

The two or three letters that immediately follow the statute name in the citation identify whether it is in the revised statutes or in the annual statutes: "RSC 1985" means *Revised Statutes of Canada*, 1985 revision, while "SC 1994" means *Statutes of Canada*, 1994. The same is true for provincial legislation: "RSO 1990" means *Revised Statutes of Ontario*, 1990 revision, and "SO 1995" means *Statutes of Ontario*, 1995. (The abbreviations differ for other provinces. For example, "RSA" means *Revised Statutes of Alberta*. See Appendix A for a list of abbreviations.) This part of the citation, then, identifies which volume contains that statute.

The rest of the citation is a chapter reference (indicated by lowercase "c")—it tells where in the volume to look for the statute. Revised statutes are usually catalogued or cited by a combination of the first letter of the statute and the numerical position under that letter. For example, the *Criminal Code* is "c C-46." Statutes that have been passed since the last revision of statutes for that government are numbered consecutively for the year that the statutes were passed.

In the past, if a researcher needed to review a statute (or amendment) so recent that it wasn't in the last annual volume, he or she would need to consult a print publication called a bills service. Now, bills and their status are widely available online. Also, when amendments have been passed but are not yet in force (sometimes there is a delay, for example, where an administrative system needs to be created to support the changes), the "pending" provisions appear in grey-scale in the text of the online statute so that the researcher can see what changes are contemplated.

Updating a Statute

While the citation directs researchers to the statute, this is never the end of the process. Most statutes, not only "busy" ones like the *Criminal Code*, are updated occasionally by Parliament through the process of amendment, which involves passing new substatutes that make changes to the main statute. These amending statutes may be found in the statute volumes following the most recent revised statute volumes. The revisions are incorporated into the statutes on the government websites.

Reading a Statute: Basic Principles of Statutory Organization

Having found a statute, a researcher needs a plan of attack for reading it, especially if it is long. A few statutes—especially longer ones—are published with tables of contents and even indexes, but most are not. Fortunately, most are organized according to a standard pattern, which may include the following features:

1. *Long title* Usually, "An Act respecting … (the subject matter of the statute)." The long title is rarely used to refer to the statute.

2. *Short title* The name by which the statute is commonly known, which may be provided at the beginning or at the end of the statute. If a short title is provided, it is the only way the statute may be properly cited.

preamble
an introduction, made up of one or more provisions, that sets out the objectives and guiding philosophy of a statute

3. ***Preamble*** An introduction, made up of one or more provisions, that sets out the objectives and guiding philosophy of the statute. The preamble can often provide some interesting insights into the socio-political context of the statute. It is also an official component of the statute for interpreting and enforcing the statute.

4. *Introductory provisions* These often include a list of defined terms, a description of the scope of application of the statute, and details about how the statute will be administered.

5. *Body of the statute* The sections in this part deal with the substantive issues covered by the legislation. In a long statute, the body may be divided into a number of parts, each of which deals with an aspect of the statute. Provisions dealing with the same aspect are grouped together in the same part of the statute. Where a statute imposes penalties for breach of its terms, these provisions are often found near the end of the body or near the end of individual parts.

6. ***"Housekeeping" provisions*** These provisions, found at the end of some statutes, deal with administrative issues, such as the timing of coming into force of individual provisions.

Briefly skimming a statute before beginning to actually read it may help to identify sections that are most likely to contain the information sought, especially if the statute contains shoulder notes—brief references in the margins that describe the content of the provisions. Shoulder notes are not officially part of the statute, but are meant to help readers access the different provisions. Headings are helpful for the same purpose.

"housekeeping" provisions
provisions found at the end of some statutes that deal with such administrative issues as the timing of coming into force of individual provisions

Regulations

Many statutes are accompanied by a type of subordinate legislation known as regulations, particularly where the subject matter being covered is of a technical nature. Unlike statutes, regulations are not passed by Parliament or provincial legislatures. They are prepared and published by administrative officials (department or ministry staff), under the authority of the relevant statute, to deal with the technical issues. Regulations tend to be very practical and can include lists, schedules, diagrams, forms, and charts. The rules of various levels of courts are generally published in the form of regulations.

The information contained in regulations is just as important as that found in the primary legislation. It is often even more current because regulations do not require the formalities of the legislative process to be created—they can and do change frequently. This flexibility is one of the reasons they are used. For example, Ontario's *Employment Standards Act, 2000*[18] has numerous regulations, including one describing minimum wages to be paid. If a statute has regulations made under it, the regulations will be published in their own volumes, separate from the statute, and will be revised according to the same schedule as the statute itself. However, regulations cannot exist on their own without a parent statute. For a regulation to lawfully exist, the statute must include a provision that designates regulation-making authority. If no such provision exists, no regulations can be drafted. Regulations are available online on government websites. For example, in Ontario, statutes and regulations are available on e-Laws at <https://www.ontario.ca/laws>.

CHAPTER SUMMARY

Jurisdiction for making laws is divided between the federal government and the provincial governments; the division of jurisdiction is found in the *Constitution Act, 1867*. When new demands and challenges in society create the need for new legislation, jurisdiction must be determined. This is done through a process of analogy, in which the new issue is compared with issues enumerated in the Constitution and assigned to either the federal government or a provincial government based on where it best fits. In this way, the specific areas of powers of these two levels of government are expanded.

It is important to keep the distinction between criminal law and civil law clear. Criminal law is an area of law under federal jurisdiction, while civil law is largely a matter of provincial jurisdiction. However, the administration of justice in a province—that is, the constitution of the courts and the operation of the courthouses, both civil and criminal—is under provincial jurisdiction.

Statute law is one source of law. One of the most frequently consulted Canadian statutes is the *Criminal Code*, which is often published by commercial publishers in pocket and annotated editions. Many of these contain the text of related statutes such as the *Youth Criminal Justice Act*. Other statutes can be found either by visiting a law library and consulting a print source such as the *Canadian Abridgment* or by accessing a computerized database or website such as CanLII.

A statute's citation is designed to direct readers to the most current version of the statute. However, researchers must check for amendments to a statute on government websites. The structure of a statute follows a set pattern, which aids a researcher in finding the desired information within the statute. Many statutes are accompanied by subordinate laws called regulations that provide important practical information about the statute.

KEY TERMS

bylaws, 20	"housekeeping" provisions, 25	preamble, 24
citation, 23	jurisdiction, 16	tribunal, 18
cite, 16	official source, 21	

NOTES

1 *Constitution Act, 1867* (UK), 30 & 31 Vict, c 3, reprinted in RSC 1985, Appendix II, No 5.

2 *Canada Act 1982* (UK), 1982, c 11.

3 *Constitution Act, 1982*, being Schedule B to the *Canada Act 1982* (UK), 1982, c 11.

4 *Canadian Charter of Rights and Freedoms*, Part I of the *Constitution Act, 1982*, being Schedule B to the *Canada Act 1982* (UK), 1982, c 11.

5 This section, which refers to "Indians," has been interpreted by courts to include all indigenous peoples in Canada, including not only Anishnaabe or First Nations peoples (who were once called Indians) but also Inuit and Metis peoples.

6 *Criminal Code*, RSC 1985, c C-46, as amended.

7 *Immigration and Refugee Protection Act*, SC 2001, c 27.

8 *Aeronautics Act*, RSC 1985, c A-2.

9 *Oceans Act*, SC 1996, c 31.

10 *Family Law Act*, RSO 1990, c F.3.

11 *Workers' Compensation Act*, RSA 2000, c W-15, as amended.

12 *Human Tissue Gift Act*, RSBC 1996, c 211.

13 *Municipal Act, 2001*, SO 2001, c 25.

14 *Youth Criminal Justice Act*, SC 2002, c 1.

15 *Canada Evidence Act*, RSC 1985, c C-5.

16 *Smoke-Free Ontario Act*, SO 1994, c 10.

17 *Residential Tenancies Act, 2006*, SO 2006, c 17.

18 *Employment Standards Act, 2000*, SO 2000, c 41.

EXERCISES

Multiple Choice

1. Legislative jurisdiction over a particular subject matter is determined
   a. by the courts
   b. by the Constitution
   c. by analogy
   d. on a first-come, first-served basis
   e. a, b, or c

2. If you suspect that the statute you are seeking was passed within the last 12 months, you could look for it
   a. in the most recent statute volumes
   b. in the newspaper
   c. in the *Canada Gazette* or a provincial bills service
   d. any or all of the above
   e. b or c

3. The preamble of a statute
   a. deals with substantive issues covered by the legislation
   b. deals with administrative issues
   c. sets out the objectives and guiding philosophy of the statute
   d. lists housekeeping provisions
   e. gives the long title of the statute

4. The abbreviation "RSC 1985" stands for
   a. *Revised Substantive Code*, 1985 revision
   b. *Revised Statute Constitution*, 1985 revision
   c. *Revised Statute Citations*, 1985 revision
   d. *Revised Statutes of Constitution*, 1985 revision
   e. *Revised Statutes of Canada*, 1985 revision

5. A bill
   a. is a draft statute that is being considered by Parliament
   b. is a statute that has just been passed by Parliament
   c. is a provision of a new statute
   d. is a statute that is in the process of being amended
   e. is a substatute of an existing statute

True or False?

_____ **1.** If a provincial statute is currently in force, you will always be able to find it in the revised statutes of the relevant province.

_____ **2.** All statutes have accompanying regulations.

_____ **3.** Marriage licences are issued by provincial agencies, but divorce is governed by a federal statute.

_____ **4.** Canada's Constitution was actually passed as a statute of the British government.

_____ **5.** Diagrams, schedules, and charts are common features of regulations.

_____ **6.** A commercially published edition of the *Criminal Code* is an official statutory source.

_____ **7.** All services delivered on First Nations reserves fall within the jurisdiction of the federal government.

_____ **8.** The building and management of railways falls under federal jurisdiction.

_____ **9.** Municipalities have the authority to provide services because those services are delegated to them by provincial, territorial, or federal governments.

_____**10.** The procedures that apply in criminal courts are prescribed by the *Criminal Code* itself, not by the *Rules of Civil Procedure*.

Short Answer

1. Consider the names of the statutes below and the division of powers set out in sections 91 and 92 of the Constitution. Which level of government do you think passed each of these statutes? For each statute, cite an item number from section 91 or section 92 to support your answer.

   a. *Workplace Safety and Insurance Act*

   b. *Bank Act*

   c. *Meat Inspection Act*

   d. *Highway Traffic Act*

   e. *Broadcasting Act*

   f. *Business Corporations Act*

2. You are a police officer who receives a telephone complaint from a citizen who is irritated by the loud flapping of his neighbour's Confederate flag. The large flag is mounted prominently above the neighbour's front door. The complainant also believes that the flag is a racist symbol because of its connection to the historical practice of black slavery in the American South. As a black Canadian, the complainant feels that as well as being a source of noise pollution, flying this flag in a suburban Ontario neighbourhood is a form of racial harassment.

   Identify and locate legislation that deals with the issues (noise, flag-flying, racist symbols) raised by this complaint. Is the flag-flying neighbour guilty of any offence in your jurisdiction?

3. One of the campaign promises made by Prime Minister Justin Trudeau was to "decriminalize marijuana." At the time of writing, no changes have been made to the management of marijuana in Canada. Review the constitutional division of powers described in this chapter, consider what you now know about statutes, and answer the following questions:

   a. Where (in what statute) is marijuana currently "criminalized"? Is that the *only* statute? Are the statutes that govern marijuana use, possession, and distribution federal or provincial/territorial?

   b. Marijuana is a crop. Which level of government regulates agriculture?

   c. There was speculation, when this question was written, that in Ontario, marijuana might be sold through the Liquor Control Board of Ontario (LCBO). What statute governs the operation of the LCBO?

    d. If it were to become legal to import marijuana into Canada, rules that govern the operation of border crossings would have to be changed. What legislation governs border security in Canada?

    e. Considering the answers to the above questions, and that the answers to question c relate only to Ontario and that different distribution arrangements would need to be made in each province or territory, how simple is it to "decriminalize marijuana"?

4. You learned, in this chapter, that the municipal level of government regulates issues such as waste collection, parking, and community centres through delegation of regulatory authority from a province or territory. Research the following issues with respect to municipal jurisdiction.

    a. Are all Canadian communities within organized municipalities?

    b. Does this mean that there is no government waste collection in some communities?

5. Identify a statute (for example, using an Internet keyword search about an issue, such as "water quality testing" or "student loans"). See if you can answer the following questions about the statute:

    a. Is it federal or provincial/territorial?

    b. In what year was it introduced?

    c. Who proposed it (for example, was it a government-sponsored statute, or was it a private member's bill)?

    d. What prompted the passage of the statute—was it a court decision, an event such as an accident or natural disaster, the emergence of a new social problem, or some other circumstance?

Common Law and the Concept of Legal Precedent

3

LEARNING OUTCOMES

After completing this chapter, you should be able to:

- Explain the process by which a body of common law develops to resolve a legal issue.

- Explain the concept of legal precedent.

- Describe the application of precedent to a novel legal issue.

- Describe the various levels of court in Canada and how they determine the value of cases as precedents.

- Explain how to locate a body of case law.

- Explain how to locate an individual case.

- Prepare a case brief.

How Common Law Works

Chapter 1 introduced the common law system and explained that the judgments—usually judges' written **reasons for decision**—produced by individual court cases act as links in a chain of legal principles that make up various areas of law. But how does this work in practice? How does everyone keep track of the current state of the law and the direction in which it is growing?

How a Link Is Added to the Legal Chain

It may help to explain that every new court judgment is only a *potential* link in the common law chain. In reality, many judgments are left out of the chain because

- they don't really add anything new to the state of the law;
- they serve only to apply existing law to a novel set of facts without changing the existing law;
- in retrospect, the decision that was reached is considered by future decision-makers to be wrong and is explicitly **overruled** (rejected);
- the decision is for some reason unpopular, and while not actually overruled, it is ignored by future decision-makers; or
- the decision is superseded by a decision of a higher court within the system of precedent.

The decision about whether a court decision will earn a place in the chain of the law is made through the process of citation. In presenting their arguments to the court, the parties in a case—usually plaintiff and defendant, or Crown and defence in criminal cases—support their conclusions by relying on prior decisions in the legal chain. A party (usually through a lawyer) typically makes a point and then *supports* that point by citing an **authority**—that is, by mentioning a previous case in which the same point was accepted by a judge. If the judge in the new case accepts the cited authority and mentions it in his or her judgment, the case has been "cited with approval" and lives on as part of the law.

Often, only a few words of a case, often described as the ***ratio decidendi*** (reasons for decision) or simply *ratio*, live on in this way. In many instances, a frequently cited *ratio* will take the form of a rule or test that can be successfully applied to fact situations that differ from the facts in the original case. Very strong *ratios* can live on for hundreds of years in this way and become as familiar as proverbs to the lawyers and judges specializing in a particular area of law.

Sometimes a party can't find an authority that fits his or her situation precisely. If this is the case, the lawyer must suggest an entirely new principle, or propose an extension or modification of a principle set out in a pre-existing case that comes closest to his or her situation. If this new principle or extension of an existing principle is accepted by the judge and forms the basis for a judgment in that party's favour, a new link in the chain of common law has been made. If the new judgment, in turn, is cited by a future judge, the place of this newborn link in the chain of law is established.

reasons for decision
the written expression of a legal decision; some decisions include reasons from more than one judge or justice

overruled
rejected or contradicted in a decision of a court of higher jurisdiction

authority
a previously decided case that supports a particular position or conclusion about a question of law

ratio decidendi
Latin for "reasons for decision," but often used to describe the few words or phrases that form the most essential part of a legal decision for precedent purposes

How a Link Is Tested

A new link in the legal chain is a fragile thing. After all, the link earned its place through the actions of only a few people—the lawyer who suggested it, the judge who accepted it, and possibly another one or two lawyers or judges who cited it. Whether the new link will be popular in the wider legal community has yet to be tested.

The test comes when a new case arises in which it would make sense for the new link to be applied. The lawyers in this new case, if they have done their research thoroughly, will come across the new link in the online or printed reports of case law (these will be discussed later in this chapter). If a party likes the link and it supports their position, they will cite it. If they don't like it, either they will argue that their own situation is so different from the situation in issue when the link case was decided that the link case should not be applied to their case (this is called "distinguishing" the link case), or they will argue that the link case was decided incorrectly and should not be followed by the judge in the present case. It will be up to the judge to decide whether the link is binding on the new case. In theory, if a link in the legal chain has addressed the same issue as that before the present court, it is a binding precedent and a judge cannot ignore it. He or she *must* acknowledge it as law and apply it to the new situation.

There are two important points to remember when considering whether a link is binding or not. First, the link must be from within the same territorial jurisdiction as the case in question. For example, a decision from a court in British Columbia is not binding on a court in Ontario, and vice versa. Second, a link forged in a court of inferior (lower) jurisdiction need not be followed by a higher court, either on appeal of the same case or in a totally new case. The court of higher jurisdiction has the power to reject the decision of a lower court, knocking it right out of the chain of precedent. A case that is "knocked out" in this manner is said to be overruled and should not thereafter be applied by any other court. Both points will be expanded upon in the remainder of this chapter.

The Role of Jurisdiction in the System of Legal Precedent

As explained above, judges are not free to decide cases in any way that they want. They are bound by the system of legal precedent, which forbids them to ignore principles that have been added to the chain of the common law. However, the binding nature of legal precedents (existing links) is limited by the level of jurisdiction in which those links were formed.

If we think of the levels of court as the rungs of a ladder, starting with small claims courts at the bottom, rising through the trial courts and provincial courts of appeal, and ending with the Supreme Court of Canada at the top, the binding power of an individual decision becomes clear: the judge of a court is bound by the decisions of all courts within the province that are at a higher level and by the decisions of the Supreme Court of Canada. So, for example, all courts in the country except the Supreme Court of Canada are bound by the decisions of the Supreme Court of Canada; all courts in a specific province, except the province's court of appeal and the Supreme Court of Canada, are bound by the decisions of the province's court of appeal, and so on.

Administrative tribunals, which adjudicate a large proportion of disputes in Canada, exist somewhat apart from this system; however, some tribunal decisions can be reviewed by traditional courts. See Box 3.1 for an overview of the role of tribunals.

Box 3.1   Administrative Tribunals

Not all decisions that affect the rights of Canadians are made within the court system. Many disputes are resolved instead by administrative tribunals.

These tribunals are court-like bodies that are created by statutes or regulations to administer a particular legislative scheme. For example, the Landlord and Tenant Board is an Ontario tribunal that administers the rules created by the Ontario *Residential Tenancies Act*.[1]

Tribunals create a mechanism by which expert decision-makers can bring their specialized expertise to bear within a specific context. They also often provide efficiency and reduced cost for the parties involved. The way in which administrative tribunals make decisions varies widely—some tribunals are as formal as courts, while others have a more relaxed process. A set of rules generally exists to help participants understand how to bring their dispute before the tribunal.

The decisions of tribunals are meant to be final and binding on parties. Some sophisticated tribunals—for example, provincial labour relations boards—have multiple levels and an appeal system to deal with situations in which parties are not satisfied with an initial decision. In some cases, where a party has exhausted his or her rights of appeal within a tribunal, he or she can seek what is called a judicial review, which means that the decision of the tribunal (or other administrative body) can be brought before a "traditional" justice system court—for example, the Court of Appeal of New Brunswick—for review. Because tribunal decision-makers are generally technical experts, judges in mainstream courts typically defer to tribunal decisions with respect to facts, and only overturn cases in which there has been unfairness (for example, bias), or an error in applying the law.

Some examples of tribunals:

- the Workers Compensation Board of Manitoba
- the Nova Scotia Assessment Appeal Tribunal
- the Parole Board of Canada
- the British Columbia Securities Commission

Levels of Court in Canada

The concept of jurisdiction was introduced in the context of statute-making authority in the legislative system in Chapter 2. Jurisdiction also has a role to play in the judicial system, but here jurisdiction is quite different. While legislative jurisdiction is designed to facilitate the ordinary administration of government business and to reduce overlap in the subject matter of what is being legislated, judicial jurisdiction serves different functions. In the system of judicial jurisdiction, with the exception of certain special courts and tribunals designed to deal with specific types of cases (such as the federal Tax Court of Canada, the Family Court branch of Ontario's Superior Court of Justice, or the Ontario Human Rights Tribunal), subject matter is not important. Instead, the system is designed to sort cases based on how far along they are on the road to resolution and whether the parties deserve the opportunity to make use of the system and its resources to appeal decisions that they feel are not satisfactory.

To understand the role of jurisdiction in the judicial system, it is important to know something about the judicial structure.

Trial Courts

Each province has at least two levels of court: trial courts and appeal courts. Trial courts are divided into various divisions based on the subject matter of the disputes brought before the courts or the money value of the disputes. For example, the Ontario court system has separate courts for small claims (where the amount of damages claimed by the plaintiff falls below a certain maximum), for criminal law matters, for youth justice matters, and for family matters. In some counties, courts are further subdivided, with specialized courts reserved for, for example, specialized commercial transactions. In Ontario, not all of these trial courts are at the same level. In some limited situations, a plaintiff can appeal a decision of a low-level trial court to a higher-level trial court. For example, the decisions of a judge in a Small Claims Court may be appealed to a judge of the Ontario Superior Court of Justice.

Appeal Courts

Each province has a court of appeal that represents the highest level of court in the province. Decisions made in trial courts can be **appealed** (challenged) by either party to the court of appeal, where the decision will be reconsidered. (The rules regarding the right to appeal are more complicated in the criminal law context and will be discussed in Chapter 9.) If the appeal is allowed, the lower-court decision will be reversed. If the appeal is denied, the lower-court decision will be preserved. In terms of precedent, courts must give greater persuasive weight to an appeal court decision than to a trial court decision.

appeal
a review or challenge of a legal decision in a court of higher jurisdiction

The Supreme Court of Canada

The Supreme Court of Canada is the highest-level court in the country. It decides only a limited number of cases every year, and there is no automatic right to appeal a civil (non-criminal) case to this court. There is an automatic right of appeal in certain criminal matters. Otherwise, only parties with cases of national importance and general public interest are granted **leave to appeal** to the Supreme Court of Canada, and a decision rendered here creates a precedent that supersedes all lower-level judgments in all jurisdictions—it is the final word.

Because of the role of jurisdiction in creating precedents, a party or lawyer trying to argue a point of law in any level of court will strive to support his or her argument with authorities from the highest possible level of court. This is an important consideration to keep in mind when doing legal research.

leave to appeal
permission to file an appeal

How to Find a Body of Case Law

Throughout this chapter we have been using the analogy of a "chain" of law, but most legal writers describe the bundle of judicial decisions on a particular legal issue or in a subject area as a "body of law." This section explains how to find the particular body of law, or **case law**, that addresses a particular legal issue.

First, if the issue has a statutory connection and the relevant statute is already known (from using the instructions in Chapter 2), the first place to look for cases is "under" the statute. Cases that elaborate on a statutory provision can be found in online legal databases (more on these later) by conducting a keyword search for the statutory provision—for example, by searching for the text of the provision and/or the section number. Cases decided under a statute can also be found in legal encyclopedic sources, such as the *Canadian Abridgment* (Carswell). Encyclopedic sources include a section that lists statutes considered—that is, references to statutory material found within cases. Some frequently applied statutes, such as the *Criminal Code*, are published in **annotated** form, which means they are available in an edition that contains references to relevant cases, and even summaries of the cases, directly below the statute provisions themselves.

case law
reported decisions of judges from trials or appeals that are used to interpret the law

annotate
supplement published statutes by giving references to cases that have considered the application of statutory provisions

With no statute to start from, the researcher must perform a subject-matter or keyword search, either in an online database of cases or in an encyclopedic paper source such as the *Canadian Encyclopedic Digest* (Carswell) in a library.

How to Locate a Specific Case

Once a reference to a body of law dealing with a particular issue is found, the researcher will come across references to individual cases (usually the most important ones) within that body of law. These cases are referred to by the names of the two parties. In criminal law cases, one of the parties is always the Crown. The Crown is identified by the initial "R." The "R" stands for either "*Regina*," which is Latin for "the Queen," or "*Rex*," which is Latin for "the King." The latter is used if there was a king in power in the Commonwealth at the time the case was decided. Therefore, the case name in a criminal law case is typically "*R v* [Name of accused]" and is indexed under the name "[Name of accused]."

The case name is immediately followed by the case citation, a letter and number code that serves as an "address" for the case online or in print. This address is used to locate a copy of the case.

Online Legal Research: The New Starting Point

While legal research has been conducted using print sources for many centuries, it is now more common to search for cases online. Online versions of cases offer many useful innovations. For example, many online databases provide

- information about whether a case has been appealed (with a link to the appeal decision(s));
- links to related decisions—for example, motion decisions (technical hearings within the main case) and sentencing decisions;
- information about whether the case has been cited in other decisions, which can help a researcher determine whether it has been overruled, or whether it has been relied upon in higher courts; and
- internal links to cases, statutes, and even academic articles or textbooks relied upon by the judge in crafting the reasons for decision.

Case citations either are "neutral" (more on this below) or direct the reader to a case reporting service—either an online database or a set of volumes published by a commercial publisher. Not every case is reported. What gets added to an online database or published in print commercially depends on the decisions of the editorial board and what it views as its reporting mandate.

Neutral Citations

neutral citation
a form of citation for a case that is not tied to a particular report series or database, but includes the year of the decision, the court or tribunal that made the decision, and a number indicating the place in sequence of the decision

A **neutral citation** consists of the following basic elements:

- the case name—for example, *R v Fearon*;
- the year in which the case was decided—for example, 2014;
- a court or tribunal identifier—for example, SCC (an abbreviation of "Supreme Court of Canada"); and
- a sequential number—for example, 77.

The above examples become the following neutral citation:

- *R v Fearon*, 2014 SCC 77

In this example, the parties to the case are the Crown ("R") and Fearon; the court that made the decision is the Supreme Court of Canada; and the sequential number that helps make this citation unique is 77.

Case Reporter Citations

Case reporters choose the cases they report based on particular criteria:

- Jurisdictional reporters, like the *Ontario Reports*, report significant or major cases decided in a certain geographical jurisdiction.
- Court-specific reporters, like the *Supreme Court Reports*, report cases decided in a particular court.
- Subject-specific reporters, like *Canadian Criminal Cases*, report cases that deal with a particular area of law.

Most case citations assigned by a case reporter contain the following elements:

- the case name—for example, *R v Ford*;
- a year in round or square brackets—for example, (1982) or [1982]—which is either the year in which the case was decided (round brackets), or the year of the reporter volume in which it is reported (square brackets);
- a number that represents the volume number of the series of case reports in which the case is reported—for example, 65;
- letters that represent the initials of the case reports in which the case is reported— for example, CCC for *Canadian Criminal Cases* (see Appendix A); these initials may be followed by a series number if the case reporter has been published in more than one series—for example, "(2d)" means "second series";
- the page number in the case reporter where the case can be found—for example, 392; and
- in parentheses, a short form of the name of the court from which the decision comes—for example, SCC for Supreme Court of Canada—if the court is not obvious from the name of the reporter.

The above examples become the following case citation:

- *R v Ford* (1982), 65 CCC (2d) 392 (SCC)

This means that the case of *R v Ford*, which was decided by the Supreme Court of Canada in 1982, can be found in volume 65 of the second series of *Canadian Criminal Cases* at page 392.

Two or more different citations may be given for the same case, which means that it is reported in more than one place. For example, *R v Ford* can also be found at

- [1982] 1 SCR 231 (in the *Supreme Court Reports*), and
- (1982), 133 DLR (3d) 567 (in the *Dominion Law Reports*, third series).

Online Case Law Databases

Online databases may use both the citations provided by case reporters and their own citation system. By looking at the structure of the citation, the reader can often figure out which online system the case came from. For example, CanLII uses the following types of citations:

- the citation provided by a case reporter;
- a neutral citation (where one is issued by a court) that is the same as the court's citation except that "(CanLII)" is added to the end of the citation; and
- an original CanLII citation that consists of the case name, the year of the decision, "CanLII," a sequential number, and an abbreviation of the court or tribunal in parentheses.

Here are examples of each:

- *R v Ford* (1982), 65 CCC (2d) 392 (SCC)
- *R v Fearon*, 2014 SCC 77 (CanLII)
- *R v Stone*, 1999 CanLII 688 (SCC)

It is clear from the structure of the last two citations that their online source is CanLII.

Figuring out what the initials for the name of the court or case reporter stand for can be a challenge. See Appendix A for a list of abbreviations. Most encyclopedic sources provide a list of case and statute reporter abbreviations. A law librarian can help find a name that isn't listed. Practising with a few different cases helps make the process clear.

How to Read and Summarize a Case

Although some terms and phrases are unique to legal writing, legal judgments are usually quite readable and interesting. Most judges strive to present their judgments according to a logical organization, often providing a general statement of the facts, followed by an expression (sometimes even a list) of the issues to be decided, and finally, the decision itself, with an explanation of the legal principle or doctrine on which it is based.

Being able to grasp the meaning of a particular case often depends on how heavily the decision is influenced by earlier decisions (precedents) that the researcher may not have read. Where a case deals with issues that have a long common law history, the researcher may need to seek out and read earlier cases in the chain of reasoning to put that particular case into context. On the other hand, where a case is, for example, the first case decided under a particular statutory provision that the researcher has already looked up and read, it may make perfect sense. Remember that cases build on each other, so grasping them may require more searching.

The length of legal judgments varies enormously. Some are a page or two long; others can be over 100 pages, with decisions (sometimes conflicting) by more than one judge. Figuring out how to distill what's important—the *ratio decidendi*—from several pages of text is an essential research skill that is developed through practice. While a written judgment may provide a detailed history of the facts of the particular case—the legal precedents, tests, and rules influencing the decision—the most important part of the judgment is the part that describes the reason for the judge's final decision. This section may be only a sentence or two long; it may be as simple as "Applying the common law test to the facts,

I find that …" in cases where the common law rules are simply applied, or it may be much more complex when the existing common law rule is changed, expanded, or amended in some way. This statement will live on as part of the development of the common law, and it will have a binding effect on subsequent cases.

To get a feel for how to isolate the *ratio* of a case, try this exercise:

1. Choose a case to read by locating a citation under an interesting *Criminal Code*[2] provision in an annotated *Criminal Code*. Do not read the description of the case in the annotated Code.

2. Find the case on the library shelf and flip past the **headnote**—the summary that precedes the full text of the case. (This is not an official part of the judgment but is prepared by the editors of the case reporter.)

3. Read the case from beginning to end.

4. Read the headnote and consider how the case has been summarized. Which points did the editor seem to feel were most important? Do you agree?

5. Finally, read the even shorter summary of the case in an annotated *Criminal Code*.

The above process can help a person gain a basic understanding of how to reduce a legal decision to its most concise form. But remember: shorter is not always better. To understand a complicated legal issue *fully*, it often helps to review the full decision so that the result can be put into its factual context.

headnote
an unofficial summary of reasons for decision that may precede the full text of a published case in a commercial case reporter or an online legal database

Preparing a Simple Case Brief

Someone who will be reading multiple cases in the course of researching an issue may find that reading notes are needed to help him or her remember what is learned along the way. A particularly effective way to prepare reading notes is to write a **case brief** for each case. A simple plan for a case brief follows, but for personal use, any model that best suits the researcher's needs is fine.

A basic case brief may contain the following:

case brief
a summary of a legal judgment prepared for research purposes

1. the full name and citation for the case, including the court in which it was decided;

2. the names of all the parties to the decision;

3. the names of all the judges who wrote the judgment(s);

4. a short summary of the key facts and issues of the case;

5. the decision and concise reasons for it;

6. the verbatim, or word-for-word, wording of any new legal rule or test that was formulated by the decision;

7. any facts or details that make the case of particular interest to the researcher—for example, any facts that are particularly similar to or different from those of the fact situation that is being researched; and

8. any other information that the researcher wants to remember later.

For an example of a simple case brief, see Appendix B.

CHAPTER SUMMARY

Under Canada's common law system, judges' written decisions act as links in a chain of legal principles that make up various areas of law. Each new decision is only a potential link in the chain and must earn a place in the chain of the law through the system of legal precedent. However, a new link is fragile and may be broken if, in a subsequent case, a judge finds that the case is not binding, and the case is then overruled or ignored. For a link to be binding, it must address the same issue as that before the present court, be from within the same territorial jurisdiction as the case in question, and be from a court of superior jurisdiction.

Each province has two basic levels of court. The trial level is broken down by subject matter (for example, small claims, family, or criminal). The other level is the appeal level; the court of appeal hears appeals of cases from the trial level. A case from a provincial court of appeal may be appealed to the Supreme Court of Canada, if the case satisfies the criteria for being heard at the highest court in Canada.

There are two main strategies for researching a body of case law. If the issue being researched has a statutory connection and the relevant statute is known, the researcher can find cases that discuss the statute using an online search, or by consulting an encyclopedic source. If there is no statute to start from, the researcher can perform a subject-matter or keyword search in an online database of cases or in an encyclopedic paper source. Specific cases within a body of law are published by case reporters in report series, which are available online or in print. Report series are categorized by jurisdiction, court, or subject matter. Citations assist the researcher in locating the case. Researchers who must read multiple cases often prepare reading notes in the form of a case brief to help them remember the important points in each case.

KEY TERMS

annotate, 35

appeal, 35

authority, 32

case brief, 39

case law, 35

headnote, 39

leave to appeal, 35

neutral citation, 36

overruled, 32

ratio decidendi, 32

reasons for decision, 32

NOTES

1 *Residential Tenancies Act, 2006*, SO 2006, c 17.

2 *Criminal Code*, RSC 1985, c C-46, as amended.

EXERCISES

Multiple Choice

1. Despite the principle of legal precedent, case law continues to evolve because
   a. no two fact situations are exactly the same
   b. legislative provisions can intervene to change the course of the common law
   c. the reasons for and effect of a particular decision may be interpreted and applied differently in different courts
   d. a and c
   e. all of the above

2. When considering the application of a current *Criminal Code* provision, it is important to review any court cases decided under the provision because

   a. the provision may have been overruled by a court

   b. the provision may have been held not to apply to the current fact situation

   c. other *Criminal Code* provisions may also apply to the fact situation

   d. doing so may give the researcher insights into the meaning of ambiguous words in the provision

   e. all of the above

3. A full case citation *does not* provide information about

   a. the year in which the case was decided or the year of the reporter volume

   b. the judge who wrote the reasons for the decision

   c. the case reporter in which the case is reported

   d. the level of court in which the case was decided

   e. the names of the parties to the case

4. The judge of a court is bound by the decisions of

   a. all courts within his or her province

   b. only the court of appeal of his or her province

   c. all courts within his or her province that are at a higher level

   d. all courts within his or her province that are at a higher level and the Supreme Court of Canada

   e. only the Supreme Court of Canada

5. A case name

   a. gives the names of the parties to the case

   b. cites the case reporter in which the case can be found

   c. gives the date of the case

   d. indicates the court in which the case was tried

   e. indicates the province in which the case was tried

True or False?

_____ **1.** A statutory rule is the product of the cooperation of many different people (including politicians, lobby groups, and legal drafters), but a common law rule can be created by a single judge.

_____ **2.** A precedent created by the Supreme Court of Canada can never be changed.

_____ **3.** When a party cannot find an authority that fits his or her situation precisely, the party's lawyer may propose a new principle.

_____ **4.** The cases described in the annotations to a *Criminal Code* provision typically demonstrate the application of that statutory provision to particular fact situations.

_____ **5.** Given an identical fact situation, a judge of the Ontario Superior Court of Justice must decide a legal issue in the same way that the issue was previously decided in the Ontario Court of Appeal.

_____ **6.** The fact that a case can be found in a print reporter or online database means that the case has not been overruled by a court.

_____ **7.** The newer a statute, the less likely it is that there will be cases decided under its provisions.

___ **8.** When a judge finds that a statutory provision does not apply to the case he or she is deciding, his or her reasons for decision overrule the provision and it is no longer in effect.

___ **9.** The decision of a dissenting judge, if any, should be included in the *ratio* of a case for the purpose of a case brief.

___ **10.** The headnote of a case is written not by the judge, but by an editor who works for an online legal database or commercial publisher.

Short Answer

1. Imagine that the Ontario Superior Court of Justice is hearing a case about an issue that has never been addressed before in the Ontario court system. The same issue *has*, however, been litigated up to the Court of Appeal level in British Columbia and New Brunswick, and at the trial level in Alberta. All of these three decisions are consistent with each other, and none of them has been further appealed.

   a. Are the Court of Appeal decisions in the other provinces binding on the Ontario Superior Court of Justice?

   b. Is the Alberta trial-level decision binding on the Ontario Superior Court of Justice?

   c. If you answered "no" to questions a and b, do you believe that the Ontario judge will or should completely ignore the decisions from the other jurisdictions? Why or why not?

2. For clarity reasons, this chapter did not discuss dissenting judgments. Do your own research to answer these questions:

   a. What is a dissenting judgment?

   b. Why do you think justices bother writing dissents?

3. What is it about subject-matter-specific administrative tribunals that makes them more efficient than generalist courts?

4. Why is it important for judges to write detailed reasons for decision, especially when deciding novel issues?

Activity

Choose a case mentioned in your annotated *Criminal Code*. Locate the full text of the decision in the library, read the case, and prepare a short case brief. How does your case affect or illustrate the application of the provision under which it was decided?

PART II

Introduction to Constitutional Law

The Canadian Charter of Rights and Freedoms: Introduction and Selected Provisions

4

LEARNING OUTCOMES

After completing this chapter, you should be able to:

- Describe the origin of the *Canadian Charter of Rights and Freedoms* and the role of the Constitution in Canadian law.

- Explain the function of the Charter and its application to government law and action.

- Describe how Charter rights are enforced.

- Describe the application of the fundamental freedoms described in section 2 of the Charter.

- Understand the nature of the democratic rights guaranteed by section 3 of the Charter.

- Understand the nature of the mobility rights guaranteed by section 6 of the Charter.

- Explain the scope and application of the equality rights guaranteed by section 15 of the Charter.

Introduction

The **Canadian Charter of Rights and Freedoms**[1] plays a very important role in enforcing the quasi-criminal law and criminal law, and law enforcement officers cannot properly carry out their responsibilities without a solid understanding of how the Charter works and the rights that it protects.

The Charter is not a statute: it is part I of the Constitution of Canada, the *Constitution Act, 1982*.[2] The Constitution is the supreme law of Canada, a fact that is emphasized in section 52 of the Constitution:

> 52. The Constitution of Canada is the supreme law of Canada, and any law that is inconsistent with the provisions of the Constitution is, to the extent of the inconsistency, of no force or effect.

Any law that is inconsistent with the Constitution is, *to the extent of the inconsistency*, invalid or of no force or effect. The phrase "to the extent of the inconsistency" is important in that it preserves those parts of a statute that do not violate the Constitution but nullifies any part that does violate the Constitution. The Constitution is unlike other statutes, whether federal or provincial, in that it cannot be changed or amended except by one of the amending formulas that are described in the Constitution.

The Charter's 34 provisions form the first part of the *Constitution Act, 1982*. The Charter is, therefore, part of the law that is above all other laws in the country. If any law passed in Canada or in any of the provinces or territories contravenes the terms of the Charter, that law may be declared unconstitutional and of no force and effect by a court of competent jurisdiction. Also, any action of an agent or representative of any level of government that contravenes any right or freedom protected in the Charter may attract a remedy under section 24 of the Charter.

The proclamation of the Charter in 1982 marked the culmination of a complicated initiative to entrench, under constitutional legislation, certain rights and freedoms that the government felt should be guaranteed to *all* people in Canada. The Charter was designed to help accomplish one of the most important constitutional functions—to express the fundamental values and principles of our society.

The provisions of the Charter were the subject of spirited consultation between the federal government and the provinces because, unlike other human rights legislation, the provisions have the force of constitutional law. This means that if other laws—even pre-existing laws—are proven to be inconsistent with a provision, the Charter takes precedence and the offending legislation is rendered invalid, sometimes called **struck down**.

Application of the Charter

Section 32 provides for the Charter's application to all matters under the authority of the Parliament of Canada and provincial parliaments. This means, for practical purposes, that

- no level of government (federal, provincial, or municipal) can pass legislation or enforce existing law that is contrary to the provisions of the Charter, and
- neither the government nor its agents, which include a very wide range of officials (including police officers and correctional officers), can take any administrative, judicial, or other kind of action, whether legislatively based or not, that is contrary to the provisions of the Charter.

The precise scope of the Charter's application has been a matter of debate and litigation. Although it is clear that the Charter applies to the content and effects of government law and to the nature and effects of government action, it has sometimes been difficult to define what is meant by "government" action. Many organizations, undertakings, and regulated industries in Canada have some connection to government; there have been many cases argued that turn on whether the actions of a quasi-governmental organization is government action. Unregulated private activity within a province is not intended to be subject to the Charter. For example, the courts have found that a hospital regulation requiring physicians to retire at age 65 was not government law or administration subject to review under the Charter. Even though the hospital's regulations needed to be approved by the minister of health before they could be passed, they were still considered to be part of the hospital's internal management regime—and thus private activity.[3]

Limits on Charter Rights

The rights guaranteed by the Charter are important but are not without limits. Some rights-granting provisions contain an internal limitation. For example, section 7 guarantees the right to "life, liberty and security of the person and the right not to be deprived thereof *except in accordance with the principles of fundamental justice*" (emphasis added). The content of "the principles of fundamental justice" has been a matter of judicial consideration (it has been interpreted by case law), and legal tests have evolved to determine whether a particular violation of a section 7 right will be deemed to be in accordance with the principles of fundamental justice.

There is also a more general limitation on the guarantee of Charter rights, expressed in section 1:

> 1. The *Canadian Charter of Rights and Freedoms* guarantees the rights and freedoms set out in it subject only to such reasonable limits prescribed by law as can be demonstrably justified in a free and democratic society.

Because of section 1, even if a piece of government law or a government action is proven to violate a right or freedom guaranteed under the Charter, the law or action may still be upheld (it will not be invalidated or give rise to a remedy) if the government can show that the apparent Charter violation constitutes "a reasonable limit prescribed by law as can be demonstrably justified in a free and democratic society." The reasonableness of such a limit is currently determined by the application of a two-part legal test called the *Oakes* test (because it originated in the decision in *R v Oakes*).[4] The *Oakes* test is a common law rule and has been expressed in many ways in different cases. In general, it requires that the Crown prove

1. a "pressing and substantial objective" underlying the law or government action that imposes the limitation; and

2. that the law and its effect on rights are proportionate to the interest or objective being protected, which means that the law does not infringe on people's rights to a degree not warranted by the importance of the goal that the law is supposed to accomplish. This second arm of the test has, through common law, developed into the following three-part test:

   a. there must be a rational connection between the objective and the means by which it is sought to be achieved,

   b. the law must result in a minimal impairment of the right(s) sought to be limited, and

c. there must be a proportionality between the effects of the limitation on rights and the importance of the government objective.

Finally, although not truly a limit, not all of the Charter rights are available to every person in Canada. The legal or "criminal law" rights are available to everyone, but the democratic and mobility rights apply only to citizens of Canada. Thus, it is important to look at the language of each section to determine who is entitled to the protection of the different rights in the Charter. For example, section 3 states:

> 3. Every citizen of Canada has the right to vote in an election of members of the House of Commons or of a legislative assembly and to be qualified for membership therein.

The words "Every citizen of Canada" make clear that this right is not available to non-citizens.

How Charter Rights Are Enforced: Charter Challenges

Charter challenges are simply legal arguments, made by a party in the course of litigation, that assert the violation of a Charter right. Charter challenges require a multistep process.

First, a person who is claiming that one or more of his or her Charter rights have been violated must prove the violation, and must prove that it happened by the operation of law or by government action.

Once proof of a violation has been established, the burden falls to the government to prove that the right in question can be limited in accordance with the law (and why).

As explained above, some limits on Charter rights are expressed within the Charter's rights-granting sections themselves (see, for example, s 7). In a case dealing with one of these limited rights, the Crown will first try to prove that circumstances exist to support the limitation of the right in the particular case. If the Crown fails in this, or if the right is not subject to an internal limitation, the Crown must try to prove that the limitation sought is "demonstrably justified in a free and democratic society," according to the wording of section 1. This part of section 1 is sometimes called the "saving provision" because it can be relied upon to "save" a law that would otherwise be found to impose an unacceptable limit on a Charter right.

Remedies for Breach of a Charter Right

When alleging a breach of a Charter right, a person can choose one of two routes to a remedy. For breaches involving unconstitutional action (for example, when police conduct an illegal search to find evidence of a crime), the person who was subject to the search will usually make a claim for a remedy that "the court considers appropriate and just in the circumstances" under section 24 of the Charter.

The court can choose from a broad range of remedies available under this section. One remedy provides for excluding from use at trial evidence obtained in a manner that infringed a person's Charter rights (see s 24(2)). In other words, because the evidence was obtained in a manner that is in breach of the Charter, the judge may rule it inadmissible at trial, meaning the Crown cannot use it to attempt to secure a conviction of the person.

When a person has alleged that a law (including common law) is unconstitutional, the court may order that the offending section be amended or repealed, or make a declaration that the legislation is of no force or effect. These remedies can be requested under section 52(1) of the *Constitution Act, 1982*.

Overview of Selected Sections

Part III of this text, and in particular Chapter 6, discusses some of the individual Charter rights that have particular application to the criminal law. The full scope of "criminal law" rights include:

- section 7—the right to life, liberty, and security of the person;
- section 8—the right to be free from unreasonable search or seizure;
- section 9—the right not to be arbitrarily detained or imprisoned;
- section 10—procedural rights upon arrest or detention;
- section 11—procedural rights in the course of a criminal prosecution;
- section 12—the right not to be subjected to cruel and unusual treatment or punishment;
- section 13—certain rights against self-incrimination; and
- section 14—the right to an interpreter in a trial.

This chapter will focus instead on the rights that arise outside the context of a criminal prosecution.

analogous
sharing similar qualities or characteristics in some aspects, yet being different in other aspects

read into
process of interpretation that allows the reader to insert or to include a meaning in a passage that is not specifically there

CASE IN POINT

Charter Challenge Leads to Redefinition of Marriage

The *Halpern* case, referred to in Chapter 1, involved a challenge to the common law definition of marriage. At issue were sections 2(a) (freedom of conscience and religion) and 15(1) (equal benefit of the law without discrimination). The primary issue was whether the common law definition of marriage resulted in different treatment of opposite-sex couples and same-sex couples, on the basis of one of the grounds set out in section 15(1). Section 15(1) includes sex as an enumerated ground but not sexual orientation.

However, previous decisions of the Supreme Court of Canada had stated that sexual orientation was an **analogous** or similar ground, such that it could be **read into** or be treated as part of the section. In Chapter 2, we discussed how the division of powers between the federal government and the provincial governments has been expanded by the use of analogous grounds. Charter provisions can likewise be expanded by the application of analogous grounds.

The Ontario Court of Appeal made its decision by expanding section 15(1) to include sexual orientation. Finally, the court looked at whether there was a discriminatory effect of the definition of common law marriage. In a challenge involving section 15(1), it is not necessary that there be a discriminatory purpose to the law, only that there is a discriminatory effect. The court concluded that the definition of marriage had to be rewritten because the common law definition discriminated on the basis of sexual orientation.

Questions for Discussion

1. Does the use of analogy to expand the application of a statutory provision make understanding the law more complicated for the ordinary reader? Was there any other solution (other than making an analogy) open to the court, once it had decided that the gender restriction within the definition of common law marriage was unwarranted?

2. Is sexual orientation really analogous to sex? Explain your opinion.

Source: *Halpern v Canada (Attorney General)* (2003), 65 OR (3d) 161 (CA).

Does the Charter Protect Canadians from the Actions of Other Countries?

While the Constitution provides a clear path to a remedy for rights abuses by Canadian government actors, the situation becomes murkier with respect to the abuse of Canadian nationals' Charter rights by other governments. In 2010, the Supreme Court of Canada found that Canadian national Omar Khadr was subject to numerous violations of his Charter rights while detained in the US prison in Guantanamo Bay for several years; however, the court declined to order a remedy, citing an unwillingness to engage in foreign policy-making.

In a commentary on the Khadr case and the influence of government prerogative (prerogative is a concept based on government's autonomy and power to take unfettered action in certain situations) on constitutional law generally, David Schneiderman of the Faculty of Law, University of Toronto, explained:

> As the prerogative over foreign affairs has not been displaced by statute, the Court preferred to defer to "the executive to make decisions on matters of foreign affairs in the context of complex and ever-changing circumstances, taking into account broader national interests." The Court opted to "leave it to the government to decide how best to respond to this judgment in light of current information, its responsibility for foreign affairs, and in conformity with the Charter" (para. 39).[5]

In the summer of 2010, Omar Khadr asked the Federal Court to rule on whether, in responding to the Supreme Court's findings, the Canadian government was required to apply principles of procedural fairness. The Federal Court found that the executive branch of government was required to follow those principles, and that it had failed to do so. Justice Russell Zinn ordered that the government of Canada put forward, within seven days, a proposed remedy for the failure to provide Khadr with procedural fairness. However, the order was stayed (put on hold) because the government of Canada filed its intention to appeal the Federal Court decision.

In October of 2010, Omar Khadr made it clear that he was considering a plea bargain in the US criminal case against him. He was proposing to plead guilty to all five charges against him in exchange for a sentence no longer than ten years, and a transfer to custody in Canada after the first year as provided by the *Treaty between Canada and the United States of America on the Execution of Penal Sentences*.[6] The Canadian government advised the US government that it was willing to accept Khadr, and so on October 31 Khadr entered his guilty pleas and was sentenced to eight years' imprisonment.[7] Because of certain administrative delays, Khadr was not transferred to Canada until September 29, 2012. Once in Canada, he was placed in a series of federal penitentiaries—first Millhaven in Ontario, then the Edmonton Institution, and finally Alberta's Bowden Institution.

While at the Edmonton Institution, Khadr filed an application for *habeas corpus* (an administrative remedy that essentially means "free the prisoner") on the basis that, based on the terms of his sentence, under Canadian law, he belonged in a provincial prison, not a federal penitentiary.

His application failed at trial, but succeeded on appeal. The Alberta Court of Appeal found that "the eight-year sentence imposed on Khadr in the United States could only have been available as a youth sentence under Canadian law, and not an adult one, had the offences been committed in Canada," and for that reason, under the rules created by the *International Transfer of Offenders Act*,[8] Khadr could be placed only in a provincial prison. He was transferred to a medium-security facility, and then a minimum-security facility. On May 7, 2015, he was paroled on strict conditions, many of which were lifted by late 2015.

Questions for Discussion

1. Do you agree with the Supreme Court's reasoning in declining to order a remedy for the violation of Khadr's Charter rights?

2. Do you believe that Supreme Court decisions are very influential, somewhat influential, or have no influence at all on the actions of the executive branch of government? How can the public support the influence of decisions like the *Khadr* decision?

Sources: See the Supreme Court decision about rights violations: *Canada (Prime Minister) v Khadr*, 2010 SCC 3; the Federal Court decision about procedural fairness: *Khadr v Canada (Prime Minister)*, 2010 FC 715; the Alberta Court of Appeal decision about place of detention: *Khadr v Edmonton Institution*, 2014 ABCA 225; and Professor Schneiderman's commentary at <http://www.law.utoronto.ca/blog/faculty/khadr-and-prerogative-power>.

Section 2: Fundamental Freedoms

Section 2 is designed to guarantee rights often associated with democratic values and self-expression. It provides that

> 2. Everyone has the following fundamental freedoms:
>   (a) freedom of conscience and religion;
>   (b) freedom of thought, belief, opinion and expression, including freedom
> of the press and other media of communication;
>   (c) freedom of peaceful assembly; and
>   (d) freedom of association.

Charter challenges that have arisen under this section have been based on such issues as

- the right of businesses to operate on Sundays (and to require employees to work on that day);
- the reciting of prayers of particular religions in public schools;
- controversial historical teachings (such as in the case of teachers who teach an account of the Holocaust that contradicts the factual events that occurred);
- restrictions on advertising (such as advertising tobacco products or advertising that is directed at young children);
- hate speech, racist propaganda, and the assembly and association rights of racist groups;
- "obscenity" and the regulation of sexually explicit art, literature, and film (including expressions of homosexuality); and
- whether or not to admit to the bar of a province the graduates of a proposed law school that requires students to sign a covenant promising to avoid sexual relations outside the context of marriage between a man and a woman (that is, to promise not to have premarital sex or gay sex).

As you might imagine, litigation under this section is often politically and morally charged, and involves the court in a difficult struggle to balance majority and minority opinions. Canada prides itself on being a free and democratic country in which individual opinions, however controversial, can flourish, but our government must balance this value against the need to protect society's more vulnerable members.

Section 3: Democratic Rights

Section 3 of the Charter establishes the right to vote or to be elected:

> 3. Every citizen of Canada has the right to vote in an election of members of the House of Commons or of a legislative assembly and to be qualified for membership therein.

As discussed in Chapter 12, this guarantee of the right to vote is supported by provincial employment standards legislation, which allows for short-term leave from work for the purpose of voting.

Charter challenges have been brought by prison inmates who were denied the right to vote because of their incarceration. The decisions have made it clear that inmates are entitled to vote in federal and provincial elections.[9] Restrictions on their voting have been held not to be "reasonable limits" on the inmates' rights for the purpose of section 1 of the Charter, and policies preventing inmates from voting are unconstitutional.

Note that although many Charter rights are guaranteed to people who live in Canada regardless of citizenship, the wording of section 3 makes it clear that the right to vote is guaranteed to every *citizen* of Canada—that is, citizenship is a prerequisite to the eligibility to vote in most elections.

Section 6: Mobility Rights

Section 6 of the Charter is designed to address some of the special challenges of a federal system of government by guaranteeing mobility rights.

> 6(1) Every citizen of Canada has the right to enter, remain in and leave Canada.
>
> (2) Every citizen of Canada and every person who has the status of a permanent resident of Canada has the right
>> (a) to move to and take up residence in any province; and
>> (b) to pursue the gaining of a livelihood in any province.
>
> (3) The rights specified in subsection (2) are subject to
>> (a) any laws or practices of general application in force in a province other than those that discriminate among persons primarily on the basis of province of present or previous residence; and
>> (b) any laws providing for reasonable residency requirements as a qualification for the receipt of publicly provided social services.
>
> (4) Subsections (2) and (3) do not preclude any law, program or activity that has as its object the amelioration in a province of conditions of individuals in that province who are socially or economically disadvantaged if the rate of employment in that province is below the rate of employment in Canada.

The rights guaranteed by this section are qualified by several internal limitations of the kind described above. These limitations reflect the practical use, for many purposes, of residency requirements to control access to certain government programs. Population patterns in Canada, which tend to be characterized by heavy population in southern urban areas and lighter population in northern regions, pose many challenges for provinces, and issues relating to restrictions on place of practice for certain professionals (such as doctors) have been the subject of Charter challenges.[10]

Section 15: Equality Rights

Section 15 protects the rights of people to equal treatment under the law regardless of their own intrinsic differences. It provides that

> 15(1) Every individual is equal before and under the law and has the right to the equal protection and equal benefit of the law without discrimination and, in particular, without discrimination based on race, national or ethnic origin, colour, religion, sex, age or mental or physical disability.
>
> (2) Subsection (1) does not preclude any law, program or activity that has as its object the amelioration of conditions of disadvantaged individuals or groups including those that are disadvantaged because of race, national or ethnic origin, colour, religion, sex, age or mental or physical disability.

Despite the general wording of this section, Canadian courts have taken a relatively narrow approach to interpreting equality rights, allowing only those discrimination claims based on the grounds specifically listed in section 15 or on grounds that can be shown to be *analogous* to those grounds.

CASE IN POINT

Are Decisions About Events Included in the Olympics Subject to Charter Challenge?

Canada hosted the 2010 Winter Olympics at several venues in British Columbia. A number of new sporting events were introduced for this Olympics, including men's and women's ski cross and snowboard cross. Not included, despite requests from potential competitors, was women's ski jumping.

After learning that there were no plans to include a women's ski jumping event at the 2010 Winter Olympics, 14 women described as "highly-ranked women ski jumpers" launched a Charter challenge based on the equality rights provision of the Charter (s 15). The women argued before the British Columbia Supreme Court that

> a failure to plan, organize, finance and stage a ski jumping event for women violates their equality rights, as guaranteed in section 15(1) of the *Canadian Charter of Rights and Freedoms*, and is not saved under section 1.

The judge at the trial level (BC Supreme Court) agreed with the women's suggestion that the actions of the Vancouver Organizing Committee (VANOC), the organization responsible for hosting the Games, were government actions subject to the Charter. That court, however, declined to grant the women a remedy, holding that only VANOC's activities and decisions in *delivering* the Games could be challenged on Charter grounds, and that the choice of events could not.

The women appealed. On appeal, the BC Court of Appeal also declined to provide a remedy, but on different grounds, holding that

- the case law makes it clear that the Charter applies only to government legislation and activity, and not to transactions between private parties; and
- VANOC was not a government agency, nor was it substantially controlled by any Canadian government.

However, the court acknowledged that the Olympic Games would not have come to Vancouver had it not been for a bid process and financial backing from both the federal and BC provincial governments, and so there was some element of government involvement in hosting the Games. But the court ultimately concluded that

- although a local organizing committee based in the host country handles the delivery of the Games, the decision about which events will be staged rests with the International Olympic Committee (IOC); and
- the Vancouver Organizing Committee did not make the decision not to stage women's ski jumping, and did not have the power to alter the decision, and so the decision not to host women's ski jumping did not violate the Charter because the decision was made by a body (the IOC) outside the jurisdiction of the Charter.

Perhaps more importantly, the BC Court of Appeal held that even if hosting the Olympics were a government activity, and even if the decision about which events to include had been made by a Canadian party, the appellants could still not have succeeded under section 15. The reason: the chance to participate in an Olympic sport is not a *benefit provided by law*. The court explained:

> Section 15(1) sets out constitutional guarantees of equality that are broad in scope, but it does not constitute a general guarantee of equality. Rather, the section guarantees equality only in the way that the law affects individuals. Where the law is not implicated in discrimination or inequality, s. 15(1) is not engaged.

The appellants sought leave to appeal this decision to the Supreme Court of Canada, but leave to appeal was denied.

Questions for Discussion

1. Besides the courts' stated grounds for denying a constitutional remedy for the applications, might there have been more practical reasons for declining to rule on VANOC's choice of included events?

2. The BC Court of Appeal noted that "where *the law* is not implicated in discrimination or inequality, s. 15(1) is not engaged" (emphasis added). Do you know of any other Canadian legal provisions—outside the Charter—that may be "engaged" when discrimination results because of something other than the application of a law?

Source: *Sagen v Vancouver Organizing Committee for the 2010 Olympic and Paralympic Winter Games*, 2009 BCCA 522, 2009 BCSC 942.

Many legal tests for establishing discrimination have been developed by the courts and are applied when new cases arise.

Courts applying the **formal equality** test have defined discrimination by reference to equality (and inequality) of opportunity. For example, a government program might violate section 15, according to this test, if it extends small-business assistance only to urban, and not rural, small-business owners.

The **substantive equality** test has been used to prescribe a finding of discrimination wherever there is an inequality of outcome. This test, which involves the examination of adverse effect discrimination, allows the courts to look more closely at laws or government actions that appear, on their face, to be objective but that cause unfair results. For example, one plaintiff successfully argued that the British Columbia health care system, while on its face providing equal benefits to hearing people and deaf people, actually discriminated against deaf people because a lack of funding for sign language interpreters within the system reduced access to health services for deaf people.[11]

Approaches to equality issues will no doubt continue to evolve along with changing social values.

formal equality
a measure of equality based on equality or inequality of opportunity

substantive equality
a measure of equality based on equality or inequality of outcomes, regardless of opportunity

CHAPTER SUMMARY

The Canadian Constitution is the supreme law in Canada, and the *Canadian Charter of Rights and Freedoms* forms part I of the Constitution. Any statute or part of a statute that is inconsistent with the Constitution is invalid, to the extent of that inconsistency.

The Charter applies to all levels of government in Canada. This means that no level of government may pass legislation or enforce laws that are contrary to the Charter and that the actions of governments and their agents must not be inconsistent with or contrary to the Charter.

However, there are two important limits on Charter rights and freedoms: internal limitations contained in specific provisions (such as s 7), and a general limitation in section 1 stating that the rights and freedoms in the Charter are subject to "such reasonable limits prescribed by law as can be demonstrably justified in a free and democratic society." As well, not all Charter rights are available to all persons in Canada. The language of each section must be considered to determine who is entitled to the right or freedom described in that section.

Charter rights are enforced through Charter challenges in the courts. Once proof of a violation is established, the government must prove that a limitation applies. If it cannot, the court provides a remedy, such as an order to exclude improperly obtained evidence, or a declaration that an unconstitutional law is invalid or must be amended.

Some Charter rights, such as the right to be free from unreasonable search or seizure, have particular application to the criminal law (these are discussed in Chapter 6); others arise outside the context of criminal prosecutions.

Section 2 sets out fundamental freedoms, which include freedom of conscience and religion, freedom of belief and expression (written, spoken, or artistic), freedom of the press, freedom of association, and freedom of assembly. There are some limits on these freedoms. For example, the right to freedom of speech does not include the right to engage in hate speech.

Section 3 protects citizens' democratic rights, notably the right to vote and to run for office. Challenges under this part of the Charter have been mounted by, for example, inmates in prison who successfully sought the opportunity to participate in the democratic process.

Section 6 sets out mobility rights, which include the right to move freely across provincial and territorial borders, and to work in the jurisdiction of one's choice. There are some limits on mobility rights. For example, there are in some cases residency requirements as a prerequisite to access to social services.

Finally, section 15 of the Charter guarantees individuals' rights to the equal protection and benefit of the law without discrimination, regardless of intrinsic differences.

KEY TERMS

analogous, 49
Canadian Charter of Rights and Freedoms, 46

formal equality, 54
read into, 49
struck down, 46

substantive equality, 54

NOTES

1   *Canadian Charter of Rights and Freedoms*, Part I of the *Constitution Act, 1982*, being Schedule B to the *Canada Act 1982* (UK), 1982, c 11.

2   *Constitution Act, 1982*, being Schedule B to the *Canada Act 1982* (UK), 1982, c 11.

3   *Stoffman v Vancouver General Hospital*, [1990] 3 SCR 483.

4   *R v Oakes*, [1986] 1 SCR 103.

5   David Schneiderman, "Khadr and Prerogative Power" (1 April 2010), online: <http://www.law.utoronto.ca/blog/faculty/khadr-and-prerogative-power>, citing *Canada (Prime Minister) v Khadr*, 2010 SCC 3.

6 *Treaty between Canada and the United States of America on the Execution of Penal Sentences*, 2 March 1977, Can TS 1978 No 12 (entered into 19 July 1978).

7 Khadr was actually sentenced to 40 years' imprisonment, because the military commission that accepted his plea was not aware of the plea bargain; however, the convening authority that creates military commissions "approved" only 8 years of the 40-year sentence.

8 *International Transfer of Offenders Act*, SC 2004, c 21.

9 See e.g. *Sauvé v Canada (Chief Electoral Officer)*, 2002 SCC 68, [2002] 3 SCR 519.

10 See e.g. *Wilson v British Columbia (Medical Services Commission)* (1987), 9 BCLR (2d) 350, 1987 CanLII 2558.

11 *Eldridge v British Columbia (Attorney General)*, [1997] 3 SCR 624.

EXERCISES

Multiple Choice

1. To be a "reasonable limit prescribed by law as can be demonstrably justified in a free and democratic society," a limit on a Charter right must
   a. further a pressing and substantial government objective
   b. be rationally connected to the government objective
   c. minimally impair the right that would otherwise be guaranteed
   d. be in proportion to the objective that is sought to be achieved
   e. all of the above

2. A person alleging the violation of a Charter right must always prove that
   a. he or she is a member of a disadvantaged group in society
   b. he or she is a Canadian citizen
   c. there is no internal limitation on the right asserted
   d. the violation was the result of government action or government law
   e. all of the above

3. A person who has succeeded in proving a Charter violation may be entitled to a remedy
   a. under section 34
   b. under section 52
   c. under section 15
   d. in the form of the exclusion of illegally obtained evidence
   e. b or d

4. The Charter is
   a. part of Canada's Constitution
   b. a statute
   c. part of the law that is above all other laws in Canada
   d. designed to entrench certain fundamental rights and freedoms
   e. a, c, and d

5. Once a violation of a Charter right is established, the burden of proving that this right can be legally limited falls on

  a. the victim of the violation

  b. the government

  c. the Supreme Court of Canada

  d. the judge

  e. the jury

True or False?

_____ **1.** To argue discrimination under the Charter, a complainant must base his or her claim on one of the types of discrimination specifically listed in section 15.

_____ **2.** As constitutional legislation, the provisions of the Charter take precedence over all other legislation, whether federal or provincial.

_____ **3.** Section 6 of the Charter guarantees Canadians the right to work and earn a living.

_____ **4.** All of the rights prescribed by the Charter are subject to the "reasonable limits" described in section 1.

_____ **5.** Only legislation—not common law—can be challenged under the Charter.

_____ **6.** Business transactions between private individuals are governed by the Charter.

_____ **7.** Sexual orientation is an enumerated ground of discrimination under section 15 of the Charter.

_____ **8.** Prison inmates are entitled to vote in federal elections.

_____ **9.** A formal equality analysis under section 15 of the Charter involves considering whether a law or government action that appears to be objective leads to discriminatory results when it is applied.

_____**10.** Most sections of the Charter apply to all people residing in Canada regardless of immigration status, but section 3 applies only to citizens.

Short Answer

1. The results of certain challenges under the Charter have made it clear that the right to self-expression guaranteed in section 2 does not include the right to engage in hate speech.

  a. What do you think would have been the greatest challenges for the parties arguing for this limitation and for the courts in coming to this conclusion?

  b. Are there any pitfalls for a society that decides to limit hate speech? If so, what would these be?

2. A busy, expensive restaurant in a fashionable neighbourhood is decorated with several stylized sculptures of what appear to be female genitalia. The sculptures are the work of the restaurant's owner, an amateur sculptor. After receiving two complaints from patrons, one in February 2010 and another in May of that same year, police charge the restaurateur with the offence of corrupting morals under section 163 of the *Criminal Code* and order that the artwork be removed. Section 163 reads in part as follows:

> 163(2) Every one commits an offence who knowingly, without lawful justification or excuse,
>> (a) sells, exposes to public view or has in his possession for such a purpose any obscene written matter, picture, model, phonograph record or other thing whatever;
>> (b) publicly exhibits a disgusting object or an indecent show; …

(3) No person shall be convicted of an offence under this section if the public good was served by the acts that are alleged to constitute the offence and if the acts alleged did not extend beyond what served the public good.

The police allege that the sculptures are either "obscene matter" or "disgusting objects." The restaurant's owner argues that they are tasteful *objets d'art*, and that the charge constitutes an infringement of his Charter-guaranteed freedom of self-expression.

a. Who is right? Why?

b. What will the restaurant's owner have to prove to establish a violation of his rights? What kind of evidence do you imagine he would need to gather?

c. If the owner is successful, what remedy or remedies will he likely seek? Under which section(s) of the Charter?

PART III

Basic Principles of Criminal Law and Procedure

The Criminal Code and the Structure of Criminal Offences

5

LEARNING OUTCOMES

After completing this chapter, you should be able to:

- Identify the different types of statutes that create offences.

- Describe the basic structure of the *Criminal Code*.

- Understand the differences between federal criminal offences and provincial quasi-criminal offences.

- Explain the difference between *actus reus* and *mens rea*.

- Describe the different levels of intent.

- Understand how absolute and strict liability offences differ from specific and general liability offences.

- Explain the various ways in which people not directly involved in committing an offence can still be convicted for their role in the offence.

Creating Offences

As discussed in Chapters 2 and 4, our Constitution divides the power to make laws between the federal and provincial governments. This means that the legislatures of both levels of government can create statutes that make it illegal to commit certain acts, as long as the subject matter of these acts falls into the particular legislature's jurisdiction. For example, the *Constitution Act, 1867*[1] gives the provinces jurisdiction over the establishment and management of hospitals in the province (s 92, item 7). This has been extended, through interpretation, to mean that provinces have legislative jurisdiction over the public health care system in each province. Because of this, a law restricting the use of restraints on a mentally ill patient would be found in a provincial statute—for example, the Ontario *Mental Health Act*.[2]

While the *Criminal Code*[3] (a federal statute) is by far the best known of the offence-creating statutes, there are many laws at both levels of government that prohibit certain acts and create penalties for those who commit them. At the provincial level, quasi-criminal statutes such as the Ontario *Highway Traffic Act*[4] are designed to support the enforcement of activities that fall within provincial responsibility under the Constitution. At the federal level, offence-creating statutes other than the *Criminal Code* are typically created to govern subject areas for which the government has a discrete enforcement mission, strategy, scheme, or philosophy. Examples of such subject-specific statutes include the *Controlled Drugs and Substances Act*,[5] and the *Crimes Against Humanity and War Crimes Act*.[6]

Offence-creating statutes not only prohibit certain acts; many also make certain acts mandatory. For example, Ontario's *Compulsory Automobile Insurance Act*[7] requires persons who own and operate motor vehicles on public highways to have liability insurance on their vehicles and to carry evidence of such insurance in the vehicles at all times.

As you learned in Chapter 1, in the Canadian legal system there are important differences between criminal law and non-criminal law. When thinking about offence-creating statutes, it is useful to remember that a person can suffer legal consequences from his or her actions under *both* the criminal and the non-criminal (civil) law. The fact that a person has been charged with a criminal offence based on an act or omission does not protect him or her from also being sued in civil court over the same incident. For example, if a person committed the criminal act of "uttering" (trying to use) counterfeit money as defined in the *Criminal Code*, he could be charged with an offence under section 452 of the Code; but he could probably also be sued in contract, under the civil law system, by the person who accepted the counterfeit money in exchange for goods or services.

This chapter introduces the concept of offence-creating statutes and sets out a useful guide to the most important offence-creating statute: the *Criminal Code*. The chapter then discusses the topic of **offences** in greater detail.

offence
an act or omission that breaches a law and leads to a penalty; a crime codified in a statute such as the *Criminal Code*

The Criminal Code

Criminal law is a subject matter that is federal in some aspects and provincial in others. Under our Constitution, the federal government has jurisdiction over the creation of criminal law, while the provinces have jurisdiction over the administration and enforcement of criminal law. All criminal laws are enacted by the Parliament of Canada and are codified in the Canadian *Criminal Code*, which creates the offences, sets the rules of procedure for criminal matters, and establishes guidelines for sentencing. The provincial court system then administers the criminal procedure according to the *Criminal Code*.

Criminal law is detailed and complex. The *Criminal Code* is constantly being revised by the federal Parliament. At the same time, dozens of court cases that affect the common law (non-codified) aspects of the criminal law are decided every year. To assist readers in managing these constant changes, commercial editions of the *Criminal Code* include a comprehensive index that helps people become familiar with the legislation and the offences it creates. Some annotated versions of the Code also include an **offence grid** that gives a helpful summary of the offences and their penalties, as well as a table of cases.

The annotated versions of the Code (for example, *Martin's Annual Criminal Code*, published by Canada Law Book) often also include the text of the *Canadian Charter of Rights and Freedoms*,[8] as well as other major federal criminal law or offence-creating statutes: the *Canada Evidence Act*,[9] the *Controlled Drugs and Substances Act*, the *Crimes Against Humanity and War Crimes Act*, and the *Youth Criminal Justice Act*.[10]

offence grid
a feature of some annotated versions of the *Criminal Code* that provides, in chart form, a summary of the elements, punishment, and other aspects of different offences

Basic Structure of the Code

It is easy to become lost in the maze that is the *Criminal Code*. Even without annotations, it is a long statute with more than 849 numbered sections, many of which have numerous subsections. To make navigation easier, publications of the Code generally include a detailed table of contents and index.

The Code is divided into 28 parts, each numbered with a Roman numeral, and seven additional subparts, each numbered with a Roman numeral followed by a digit. A quick scan of the table of contents provides a clear idea of how these divisions work.

Parts II through XIII either create offences or deal with subtypes of offences (such as attempts and conspiracies to commit offences). The name of each section helps the reader determine under which part an offence falls; for example, Firearms and Other Weapons (part III) deals with how the use of a gun affects an offence or an offender, and Offences Against Rights of Property (part IX) deals with issues such as theft and robbery.

Parts XIV through XXVII are procedural in nature. They set out the rules for how offences are to be investigated, prosecuted, tried, and, if necessary, appealed. Parts XIX, XX, and XXVII establish the different types of offences (indictable, hybrid, and summary conviction offences, respectively, which will be discussed in more detail later in this chapter and in Chapter 8) and the procedures that go with them. Part XXIII deals with sentencing, while part XXI covers appeals of indictable offences (see Chapter 9).

Parts XX.1 and XXI.1 are newer parts of the Code. Part XX.1 sets out rules for accused persons suffering from mental disorders. Part XXI.1 creates a procedure by which an accused whose normal rights of appeal have been exhausted can apply to the minister of justice to consider his or her conviction, or his or her designation as a dangerous or long-term offender, on the ground that the court decision being complained of constitutes a "miscarriage of justice." Part XXIV deals with dangerous offenders.

The final part, XXVIII, contains the various forms used in investigating and trying criminal offences.

How to Read the Code—An Example

The Code contains cross-references that, to be properly understood, require the reader to move back and forth through the text. The simplest way to use the Code is to begin with the offence being considered, and then to work outward. For example, if the facts suggest that the appropriate charge may be attempted murder, the first place to look is in the index under "murder," which gives a number of subcategories, including attempted murder.

Not surprisingly, attempted murder falls under part VIII, Offences Against the Person and Reputation. Section 239(1) defines the offence itself, along with the potential sentence for the offence:

> 239(1) Every person who attempts by any means to commit murder is guilty of an indictable offence and liable
>
>> (a) if a restricted firearm or prohibited firearm is used in the commission of the offence or if any firearm is used in the commission of the offence and the offence is committed for the benefit of, at the direction of, or in association with, a criminal organization, to imprisonment for life and to a minimum punishment of imprisonment for a term of
>>
>>> (i) in the case of a first offence, five years, and
>>> (ii) in the case of a second or subsequent offence, seven years;
>>
>> (a.1) in any other case where a firearm is used in the commission of the offence, to imprisonment for life and to a minimum punishment of imprisonment for a term of four years; and
>>
>> (b) in any other case, to imprisonment for life.

A reader who is familiar with the Code will realize that several terms included in the definition of attempted murder are dealt with in more detail elsewhere in the Code: "attempts," "murder," "indictable offence," "restricted firearm," "prohibited firearm," "firearm," and "criminal organization." To understand the offence of attempted murder, the reader must also consider the precise terms used to describe it. These included terms may be defined either in other parts of the Code, or in common law decisions that have interpreted the Code's provisions.

The next step is to review the meaning of "attempts." The Code deals with attempts, conspiracies, and accessories in part XIII. This turns out to be something of a dead end, however, because part XIII indicates that attempted murder is one of the few "attempt" offences that is covered in a separate section of the Code. Since the Code doesn't define the word "attempt," a definition must be found in the common law—in the cases about attempted murder that have been decided under section 239. The 1986 case of *R v Marshall*[11] established that an attempt means "to do anything, by any means, to carry out the intent of causing the death of a human being."

If the offence is the attempt to commit a murder, it is also necessary to understand exactly what murder is. The Code deals with the offence of murder in a number of sections, beginning at section 229. This section defines murder as "culpable homicide." Further research must now be done to discover the meaning of "homicide."

The next term in the definition of attempted murder is "indictable offence." The Code discusses the procedure for trying indictable offences in parts XIX and XX.

The final terms that require further investigation are those relating to firearms and to criminal organizations, since attempting murder with a firearm or at the behest of a criminal organization carries a potentially more serious punishment than does attempting murder in the absence of those aggravating factors. Part III of the Code, Firearms and Other Weapons, explains the scheme for the classification of firearms, as well as what constitutes use of a firearm in committing an offence. The definition of "criminal organization" appears in part XIII, in section 467.1(1).

Once a researcher has a good understanding of the offence, he or she may want to move on to review the procedures for trying an indictable offence such as attempted murder, the principles and procedures for **sentencing** for such an offence, and maybe even the process for appealing a conviction. All of these matters are discussed in the Code. The researcher will also need to take into account the principles of the Charter (discussed in Chapter 4),

sentence
the punishment imposed on a person convicted of an offence

because the protection of an accused's Charter rights permeates every aspect of Canadian criminal procedure.

A later section of this chapter discusses the structure and elements of offences in more detail.

Quasi-Criminal and Regulatory Offences

The *Criminal Code* and its related federal statutes are not the only laws that create offences. The Constitution gives the provinces (and, by delegation, the municipal governments that are created by the provinces) the power to make laws in a number of areas, and many of these laws include offences of their own. Such provincial or municipal offences are often called **quasi-criminal** offences.

These offences are usually punished by a penalty (such as a fine or term of imprisonment) or a forfeiture (the loss of a driver's licence, for example). Provincial offences often require a lower level of **intent** than do *Criminal Code* offences, and provincial offences usually attract less serious penalties.

For example, to obtain a conviction, the Crown prosecutor must prove that a person charged with the *Criminal Code* offence of attempted murder intended to cause the death of his or her victim, and if a conviction is obtained, the punishment could be imprisonment for life. The Crown prosecutor dealing with a driver who is charged with the provincial offence of failure to stop at a red light, contrary to the Ontario *Highway Traffic Act*[12] (provincial legislation), does not have to prove that the person *intended* to disobey the light, simply that he disobeyed it. If convicted of the provincial offence, the driver will not have a criminal record but will receive a fine and demerit points on his or her driver's licence.

What Is an Offence?

Defining the word "offence" is not easy. In simple terms, an offence is an **act** or **omission** that violates a law and from which some form of penalty follows.

Police officers are responsible for enforcing laws of all kinds, not just those created under the criminal law. Enforcing the law involves not only preventing the commission of offences, but also investigating offences that have already been committed. The investigation of offences requires law enforcement officers to collect **evidence** that will support a **conviction**. The collection of appropriate evidence, in turn, requires an understanding of the elements of the offence in question, as defined by the offence-creating statute and the common law.

Chapter 6 discusses the investigation of offences in more detail. This section introduces the elements of an offence, so that you can better determine what evidence is required and which facts must be proven to support a conviction in court. While this chapter focuses primarily on *Criminal Code* offences, the discussion that follows also applies, for the most part, to offences created by other legislation.

Classification of Offences

Our criminal justice system classifies *Criminal Code* offences into three categories according to their seriousness and the procedure used to deal with the accused—the person charged with the offence—in court: summary conviction, indictable, and hybrid offences.

---

quasi-criminal
similar in nature to offences listed in the *Criminal Code*, but under provincial or municipal jurisdiction

intent
the mental element of an offence; see also *mens rea*

act
something done or committed

omission
a failure to do something that is required by statute or by common law

evidence
oral or physical proof of the truth of an allegation

conviction
a guilty verdict, where an accused is found, beyond a reasonable doubt, to have committed an offence

In general, **summary conviction offences** are less serious offences that carry light penalties. Any charge tried by summary conviction is tried in the provincial court before a judge alone. (In Ontario, the provincial court is called the Ontario Court of Justice. The names of the courts vary across provinces, but the general structure and appeal route are the same.) No preliminary hearing is held.

Indictable offences are more serious crimes that usually carry stiffer penalties. Any charge tried as an indictable offence is tried, according to the election (choice) of the accused, either

1. in the provincial court before a judge alone,
2. in the superior court of the province (in Ontario, the Superior Court of Justice) before a judge alone, or
3. in the superior court of the province before a judge and a jury.

In most cases, the accused has the right to a preliminary hearing as well.

Hybrid offences are a combination of the summary conviction and indictable offences. The section of the Code that creates a hybrid offence gives the prosecution the option of electing to treat the offence as a summary conviction offence (and thus subject to lesser penalties) or as an indictable offence (and thus subject to stiffer penalties).

Chapter 7 discusses elections and preliminary hearings in more detail.

Parts of a Criminal Code Section

In general, each offence is dealt with in an independent section of the *Criminal Code*. Each section is made up of three parts:

- the **substantive part**, which describes the offence itself;
- the **procedural part**, indicating whether the offence is a summary conviction, indictable, or hybrid offence, which identifies the way in which the offence will be dealt with in court; and
- the **penalty part**, which sets out the maximum or minimum (or both) punishment that may be imposed on anyone convicted of committing the offence.

The offence of attempted murder under section 239(1) of the Code provides a good example of the three parts of an offence section:

239(1) Every person who attempts by any means to commit murder is guilty of an indictable offence and liable

    (a) if a restricted firearm or prohibited firearm is used in the commission of the offence or if any firearm is used in the commission of the offence and the offence is committed for the benefit of, at the direction of, or in association with, a criminal organization, to imprisonment for life and to a minimum punishment of imprisonment for a term of

        (i) in the case of a first offence, five years, and

        (ii) in the case of a second or subsequent offence, seven years;

    (a.1) in any other case where a firearm is used in the commission of the offence, to imprisonment for life and to a minimum punishment of imprisonment for a term of four years; and

    (b) in any other case, to imprisonment for life.

The substantive part of the section is "Every person who attempts by any means to commit murder." (Paragraphs (a) and (a.1), through the addition of wording about firearms and criminal organizations, create additional, related offences.)

The words "is guilty of an indictable offence" make up the procedural part of the section, setting out the procedure by which the offence will be dealt with in court.

The penalty part of the section is actually divided into four parts, according to the presence or absence of aggravating factors. If there are no aggravating factors, paragraph (b) applies, imposing no minimum penalty and a maximum penalty of imprisonment for life. If a firearm was used, but the offence was not committed with the involvement of or for the benefit of a criminal organization, paragraph (a.1) applies and there is a minimum penalty of four years, and a maximum of life. If the offence was committed with a firearm and for a criminal organization, and has resulted in the offender's first conviction for this kind of offence, subparagraph (a)(i) applies and the minimum penalty is five years, and the maximum is life. However, if this is a second or subsequent offence (as defined in s 239(2)) for this offender, subparagraph (a)(ii) applies and the minimum penalty is seven years, and the maximum is life.

The following discussion relates almost exclusively to the substantive part of offences. Chapter 8 covers the procedural part in detail, while Chapter 9 focuses on the penalty aspect.

Substantive Part of an Offence

The substantive part of the offence section is the part that describes the actions or omissions that constitute the offence. In some cases, a particular mental state—for example, intent, recklessness, or negligence—is also described here. These actions, omissions, and/or mental states are called the **elements** of the offence. These elements must be proven in court through **oral testimony**, **physical evidence**, or both. For most offences, a finding of guilt depends on proving two separate kinds of elements:

- the objective component—the ***actus reus***—which is the physical act, an omission, or a state of being involved in committing the offence; and
- the subjective component—called the ***mens rea***—which is the state of mind, or level of intention, attributed to the accused, that establishes his or her fault in committing the physical act or omission.

For example, in the case of assault and battery (s 265 of the *Criminal Code*), physically striking the victim is the *actus reus* and intending to strike is the *mens rea*.

Perhaps the easiest way to understand the substantive part of an offence is to think of it as a math equation: *actus reus* + *mens rea* = offence. Both the *actus reus* and the *mens rea* may involve more than one element as well, making the equation more complex.

Using the example of attempted murder, the *actus reus* of the offence involves an effort to end another person's life that fails: effort + failure = *actus reus*. If a firearm is added to the equation (effort + failure + firearm), the offender is subject to the more severe punishment set out in penalty part (a) of the offence. The *mens rea* of the offence of attempted murder is the intention to end another person's life. If the offender simply wants to injure the victim, he or she does not have the required mental state to be guilty of attempted murder. (However, he or she may be guilty of a lesser, included offence, such as assault. Included offences are discussed below.) The offender must intend to kill the victim for attempted murder to be proven.

element
a part of an offence that must be proven

oral testimony
evidence provided verbally by witnesses

physical evidence
proof of the truth of an allegation in the form of actual objects (for example, a gun, bloody clothes, photographs)

actus reus
Latin for "criminal act"; the objective element of an offence, which may be an act, an omission, or a state of being

mens rea
Latin for "guilty mind"; the subjective element of an offence that describes the state of mind or required intention necessary of the accused

Therefore, to support a conviction of a person accused of attempted murder with a firearm under section 239 of the *Criminal Code*, the police must provide convincing proof (evidence) supporting each element of the offence equation: effort + failure + firearm + intention to end the life of the victim = conviction.

Actus Reus

The objective element, or *actus reus*, of an offence can be a state of being, an omission, or an act. To establish the *actus reus* of a *Criminal Code* offence, the relevant Code section must be considered in its entirety. If the prosecution fails to prove any required element of the *actus reus*, it fails to prove the specific offence and the accused may be acquitted (not convicted). If, for example, the police cannot provide convincing evidence that the accused made some sort of effort to kill the victim (even if the accused carried a firearm and intended to kill the victim), the accused will be acquitted of the offence of attempted murder.

The accused's mental state is not considered when looking at whether the *actus reus* is made out. For example, Person A holds a gun to Person B and tells Person B to steal lottery tickets from a convenience store; Person B then steals lottery tickets from the store out of fear for his personal safety. The *actus reus* of theft is made out even though Person B felt compelled to steal the lottery tickets.

New Offences and Included Offences

As you can see from the structure of section 239(1) of the *Criminal Code*, new offences can be created or greater penalties can be imposed within a single section through the addition of a new element to the *actus reus*. Consider effort + failure + intent to kill = attempted murder, which has no minimum penalty (so a judge could find a person guilty of the offence but sentence him or her to only one day in jail). Adding a firearm to the equation (effort + failure + firearm + intent to kill) makes the penalty potentially more severe: a minimum of four years' imprisonment.

In much the same way, separate *Criminal Code* offences can build on each other to create more serious crimes. For example, assault with a weapon (s 267(a)) and assault causing bodily harm (s 267(b)) build on the offence of simple assault (s 266) by adding either a circumstance (the use of a weapon) or a consequence (bodily harm). This scheme also makes it possible for less serious offences to be **included** in more serious ones.

included offence
a less serious offence that might be proven even when the more serious offence charged is not

This has important practical implications for law enforcement officers. If a person is charged with assault causing bodily harm (striking another + injuries caused + intention to strike), but there is insufficient evidence to prove that the actions of the accused caused injuries to the victim, the accused may still be convicted of simple assault (striking another + intention to strike). The police are not required to charge the accused with both offences, because simple assault is considered to be included in assault causing bodily harm. Note, however, that if the prosecution fails to prove that the accused struck the victim, the accused cannot be convicted of either offence.

The table in Box 5.1 shows how aggravating factors build on the crime of assault to create more serious offences. Included crimes are discussed below it.

Box 5.1   Aggravating Factors for Assault

Action	Crime
accused touches victim accidentally	no crime
accused touches victim intentionally	(simple) assault (s 266)
+ bodily harm or with a weapon	assault with a weapon or causing bodily harm (s 267)
+ wounding, maiming, disfiguring, or endangering life (with or without a weapon)	aggravated assault (s 268)
+ by an official, to punish, intimidate, or obtain a statement, but not necessarily wounding or with a weapon	torture (s 269.1)
+ victim is peace officer	assaulting a peace officer (s 270)
+ sexual nature of assault	sexual assault (s 271)
+ sexual nature of assault and use of a weapon	sexual assault with a weapon (s 272)
+ sexual nature of assault and wounding, maiming, etc.	aggravated sexual assault (s 273)

Because these crimes build upon each other, the less serious versions are included in the more serious ones. This means that where an accused is charged with a crime that includes aggravating factors, but the prosecution fails to prove one or more aggravating factors, the accused may be convicted of an included crime. For example:

1. An accused is charged with aggravated assault, but the jury finds that the victim's injuries do not meet the definition of "wounding, maiming, disfiguring, or endangering life." In this case, the accused may be convicted of assault causing bodily harm.

2. An accused is charged with assaulting a peace officer, but the prosecution cannot prove that the officer was on duty, or that the accused knew that the officer was an officer. In this case, the accused may be convicted of (simple) assault.

3. An accused is charged with sexual assault, but the prosecution cannot prove that the sexual integrity of the victim was violated, or that the offence occurred in a sexual context, but can prove non-consensual touching. In this case, the accused may be charged with (simple) assault.

State-of-Being Offences

Most state-of-being offences are offences of **possession**: of weapons, of controlled drugs, of break-in tools, and so on. The *actus reus* for such an offence is simply the fact of being in possession and control of the particular item. This is where the *mens rea* becomes especially important: legal "possession" generally requires knowledge on the part of the accused as to what he or she possessed, or **consent** on the part of the accused to possess it.

possession
ownership based on rights acquired or conferred through physical occupancy or control

consent
the informed, voluntary approval by one party of the actions of another

A person cannot be guilty of possession of a weapon, for example, if he or she has no knowledge of having it on his or her person (someone dropped it into the person's backpack without the person knowing it, for example).

Some state-of-being offences involve being present at a place that is deemed unlawful. For example, the offence of being found at a common bawdy house without lawful excuse is an offence under the *Criminal Code*. The prosecution need only prove that a person is present at the location in order to satisfy the *actus reus* component.

Offences of Omission

In some cases, the law requires a person to take a particular action in a particular circumstance, so it is an offence *not* to take the required action. These rules are sometimes called Good Samaritan laws, and many of them have been created by the common law. For example, a parent is required to care for his or her child, and a doctor or teacher is required to report child abuse. In addition to creating offences based on these common law duties, statutes have imposed circumstance-specific statutory duties in response to dangerous behaviour. These include a driver's duty to give a breath sample when requested to do so by the police.

In determining whether a duty has been breached, the courts have traditionally compared the behaviour of the accused with the standard of behaviour of a **reasonable person** in the same circumstances, and have required that the omission be very closely connected to the harm that has resulted.

Action Offences

Most of the offences in the *Criminal Code* are action offences: offences that require the accused to commit a certain act (striking, stealing, counterfeiting, and so on) in order to be convicted. An action offence may also include a requirement that the action of the accused caused a certain result (for example, the offence of assault causing bodily harm). This brings up the issue of causation.

Causation

Causation is an important element of proof in any offence that requires evidence of the consequences of an accused's action. Causation can be divided into two types: factual causation and legal causation.

Factual causation is established when it is shown that a consequence would not have resulted *but for* the actions of the accused. For example, a victim would not have died if the accused had not struck the victim with a tire iron.

Legal causation is a more complicated issue. The purpose of determining legal causation is to attribute fault as among more than one alleged cause. In determining legal causation, the court must measure the importance of one factual cause against all other factual causes of the same consequence. For example, if the victim was hit by a car, struck by lightning, and suffered from an incurable disease at the time the accused struck him or her, any of which could have led to the victim's death, the court has to determine which of the causes was the legal cause of the victim's death.

The *Criminal Code* provides guidance for resolving some common instances in which legal causation is at issue, but novel issues are resolved by referring to the common law concepts of foreseeability of consequences and culpable intervention by a third party.

Foreseeability, which will be discussed in Chapter 10, is a test to determine whether a reasonable person could expect that a certain result may follow from his or her act. For example, it is foreseeable that someone may get shot if a person enters a bank with a gun.

reasonable person
a hypothetical person on which a standard of behaviour is based for comparison with someone's actual behaviour

causation
the element of an offence that involves whether an act or omission of one party resulted directly in the injury to the other party

factual causation
the situation where a certain result would not exist if a specific action or event had not occurred

legal causation
the situation where one or more actions could have caused a certain result and, for the purposes of a legal decision, the action that was most responsible for the result must be determined

foreseeability
a test to determine whether a reasonable person could expect that a certain result may follow from his or her act

Culpable intervention by a third party occurs when someone unexpectedly does some improper act that contributes to or causes the result or changes the chain of events or causation. For example, Uriah stabs Rhodida and Rhodida is taken to a hospital. Her injuries are not life-threatening, but at the hospital Doctor Patel makes a mistake and gives Rhodida the wrong medication. She dies. Whether Uriah will be charged with murder will depend on whether Doctor Patel's act altered the chain of causation. In a case like this, the question may be left for the trier of fact (the judge or jury) to determine whether the doctor's act caused Rhodida's death or whether it was simply incidental to the chain of events that foreseeably resulted from Uriah's actions.

culpable intervention
an unexpected action, often by a third party, that contributes to or causes a chain of events

Mens Rea

Imposing criminal sanctions in the Canadian legal system depends on a legal finding of moral guilt. To determine fault, the court examines evidence of the accused's state of mind at the time of committing the alleged offence. To be found guilty of a true criminal offence, the accused person must have

- made a choice to do something wrong,
- made the choice voluntarily or with free will, and
- known that the act was wrong.

If all of these elements are proven, then the accused is said to have the requisite *mens rea*, or "guilty mind." Most *Criminal Code* sections describe not only physical acts but also the mindset of the accused at the time of committing those acts, using modifying words to define the criminal behaviour. Offences may depend not only on the action committed but also on how it is committed—for example, "wilfully," "recklessly," or "with intent to injure."

The modifiers chosen to define offences often bring public policy considerations into the criminal law, reflecting societal norms and expectations. Most *Criminal Code* offences require only proof of a **general intent** to commit a crime. However, offences such as break-and-enter with intent to commit an indictable offence (s 348), wilfully obstructing a peace officer (s 129), and first- or second-degree murder (s 229) require proof of **specific intent** because of the language in the section of the Code.

general intent
a level of *mens rea* where the accused need not have intended to commit the offence or cause certain results but must have intended to act in a way that resulted in the offence occurring

specific intent
a level of *mens rea* that requires the prosecution to prove that the accused meant to commit the offence or to cause the harm that resulted

Intent

Intent is key to *mens rea*. The law recognizes degrees of intent, which range from **direct intent** (the most serious in a criminal offence) to **negligence** (the least serious). There are many different degrees in between, and it is important to understand what degree of intent has to be proven to obtain a conviction for each specific *Criminal Code* offence. In general, offences that carry more serious penalties require a higher level of intent. One form of first-degree murder, for example, requires not only a specific intent to kill but also evidence of planning and deliberation on the part of the accused. Second-degree murder requires proof of the specific intent to kill. Manslaughter simply requires a general intent to injure the victim without any particular thought as to whether the victim will die as a result.

Intent is sometimes confused with **motive**. Motive is the "why" that explains the reason behind the accused's actions. The two concepts are related, but while proof of intent is necessary to establish *mens rea*, motive may be relevant only as evidence of intent (an

direct intent
a level of intent (*mens rea*) where the accused has a clear intent to commit the offence or to cause certain results

negligence
the failure of a person to respect or carry out a duty of care owed to another

motive
the reason a person committed an offence

element of proof of the crime) and as a factor to be considered for sentencing purposes. In fact, motive need only be proven if it is an *actus reus* element; for example, possession for the purpose of trafficking in an illegal substance is a more serious offence than simple possession.

Lower Levels of Intent

At the lower end of the range of intent are issues of recklessness, wilful blindness, carelessness, and negligence. These lower levels of *mens rea* may be said to describe unjustifiable risk-taking.

recklessness
a level of intent (*mens rea*) where the accused knows the potential consequences of his or her action and takes an unjustifiable risk despite that knowledge

Recklessness describes a level of *mens rea* where the accused is aware of the potential harmful consequences of his or her action but takes an unjustifiable risk in the face of that knowledge, perhaps hoping that nothing bad will happen. The prosecution must prove that the accused appreciated the risk he or she was taking and that a reasonable person in similar circumstances would not have taken the risk given the potential consequences.

Wilful blindness is similar to recklessness except, instead of knowing of the risk, the accused needs to have refused to consider the possibility that the risk existed. Wilful blindness also applies where an accused suspected criminal consequences but did not confirm them and closed his or her mind to them. Possession of stolen property, contrary to section 354 of the *Criminal Code*, is an offence where wilful blindness is the level of *mens rea* required.

carelessness
a level of intent (*mens rea*) where a person fails to appreciate a risk that a reasonable person would have foreseen

Carelessness is an even lower level of intent. An accused is careless when he or she fails to appreciate a risk that a reasonable person would have appreciated and avoided. The prosecution is not required to prove that the accused understood the risk he or she was taking.

Negligence is the failure to take the care that a reasonable person would use in the same circumstances. It does not involve any particular intent at all. Negligence as such has not traditionally been a part of the criminal law because of the absence of a *mens rea* element; however, some case law suggests that failing to take the precautions that a reasonable person would take in a similar situation may be the basis for criminal liability under some circumstances. Dangerous driving (s 249), failing to provide the necessaries of life (s 215), and careless use of a firearm (s 86) are all *Criminal Code* offences where negligence can be the required *mens rea*.

criminal negligence
actions that are defined as criminal under the *Criminal Code* even though they incorporate a level of *mens rea* falling below conscious intent—for example, indifference

Criminal negligence differs from ordinary or civil negligence in that it generally requires some level of *mens rea*, such as wanton and reckless disregard for the lives and safety of others. The offence of criminal negligence is established by proof of the accused's indifference to the consequences of this act. Table 5.1 shows a *mens rea* continuum—various levels of intent involved in *Criminal Code* offences, ranging from the highest level to lower levels.

Arguments Against Intent

It is possible for the accused to argue that he or she did not intend to commit an offence.

factual mistake
an error made about the truth of a fact or the existence of a condition

One argument against intent is **factual mistake**. If a person accused of possessing a narcotic honestly believed that the substance was baking powder, the person cannot be said to have the intent to possess a narcotic. It would then be up to the prosecution to prove that either the accused was wilfully blind to the fact that the substance was in fact cocaine, or the accused's belief was unreasonable given the circumstances. If the prosecution fails to prove this, it can still obtain a conviction if it can convince the judge or jury that the accused's mistake was not material to the offence. For example, an accused's mistaken belief that his or her victim wished to be killed is not material to the offence of murder, since the law does not allow a person to consent to his or her own murder.

Several years ago, the issue of factual mistake was a hot topic in the law of sexual assault. Sexual assault requires proof that the sexual contact occurred without the consent of the victim. For a time, the common law allowed the accused to argue that he should be acquitted because he had an honest but mistaken belief that the victim had consented based on her failure to protest, her earlier behaviour, or even her choice of clothing. When the law was amended to eliminate this defence, defence lawyers argued that the level of intent was changed, creating an offence that attracted very serious penalties while requiring only a very low level of intent: negligence or recklessness.

TABLE 5.1   Mens Rea Continuum: From Proof of Higher Levels of Intent to Lower Levels

Level of Mens Rea	Definition	Wording in the Offence Section*	Example
Direct intent†	Accused fully intends to commit the *actus reus*. In other words, the accused foresees it and desires it.	"intentionally," "with intent," "wilfully," "purposely"	Vinh plans to go to a bar where Amit will be present so that Vinh can punch Amit.
Knowledge	Accused must have knowledge of certain facts in order to have the requisite *mens rea*.	"knowingly," "with knowledge"	Sally was caught by the police with a baggie of marijuana. The Crown must prove that Sally knew that the baggie contained marijuana.
Wilful blindness	Accused knows about the illegal act but deliberately chooses not to investigate or inquire any further.	"wilfully," "knowingly," "with knowledge," "deliberately"	Mario is walking through a park at midnight and is approached by someone who wants to sell a box of ten brand new iPhones, still in their packaging, for $200.
Recklessness	Accused is aware of a *danger* or *risk* in an action and persists in doing it anyway.	"reckless," "recklessly," "disregarding"	Preet throws an empty beer bottle toward his neighbour's house, which shatters the window.
Criminal negligence/ Carelessness	Accused does not realize the consequences of his or her actions, but a reasonable person would have.	"with negligence," "negligently," "neglectfully"	Magda is driving 20 km/h over the speed limit in a rainstorm, fiddling with her CD player, and talking on a cellphone. She hits a pedestrian, instantly killing him.

* Even without the use of these words, the offence may include acts that involve the requisite level of *mens rea*. It is not necessary that offences include specific words describing the level of *mens rea*.

† Intention should not be confused with premeditation—it is not a requirement that the accused plan the *actus reus* ahead of time.

Another argument against intent is that the accused is suffering from a mental disorder at the time of committing the offence and is unable to appreciate the nature and quality of his or her actions. The defence of mental disorder is discussed in greater detail in Chapter 8.

Sometimes it is difficult to determine whether a particular defence diminishes the *mens rea* or *actus reus* component of an offence. For example, in *R v Parks*,[13] a case in which a sleepwalker killed one person and injured another while asleep, the Supreme Court of Canada found that the accused did not have control over his physical movements. Being in a sleepwalking state affected the accused's *actus reus* of committing the killing. Since the *Parks* decision in 1992, the courts have limited the scope of this defence.

No-Intent Offences

Almost all offences in the *Criminal Code* and other, similar statutes require proving some form of intent on the part of the accused. In general terms, society believes that a person should not be sent to prison or face serious punishment unless he or she is morally guilty—that is, he or she acted with intent in committing an offence.

However, some quasi-criminal offences (created mostly by provincial statutes or by regulations) require little or no mental element for a conviction. In general, these offences attract only fines or other punishments not involving imprisonment. The two types of these offences are absolute liability offences and strict liability offences.

Absolute Liability Offences

absolute liability offence
an offence that permits a conviction on proof of the physical elements of the offence (*actus reus*), with no proof of intention to commit the offence (*mens rea*) required

Absolute liability offences permit immediate conviction where the accused has committed the physical aspect of the offence. The prosecution has to prove only that the accused committed the prohibited act. The prosecution does not have to prove a guilty mind, fault, or negligence on the part of the accused. A person may be convicted of an absolute liability offence even if a reasonable person would have behaved in exactly the same way.

Once the *actus reus* of the offence is proven, the accused person's arguments and explanations have no effect. Examples of absolute liability offences can be found in the Ontario *Highway Traffic Act*. For example, the Act makes it an offence for a driver to drive his or her vehicle through a stop sign without stopping. If the prosecution proves that the driver did not stop at the stop sign, it does not matter if the driver did not know that the stop sign was there, if the driver was rushing to the hospital to deliver a baby, or even if the driver was trying to escape another vehicle that was chasing him or her. The driver failed to stop and so is guilty.

In *Re BC Motor Vehicle Act*,[14] the Supreme Court of Canada decided that, on their face, absolute liability offences violate the principles of section 7 of the *Charter of Rights and Freedoms* because they allow for the conviction of people without guilty minds. However, the court also held (para 75) that an absolute liability offence would violate the Charter "only if and to the extent that it has the potential of depriving [the accused] of life, liberty, or security of the person" as guaranteed by section 7. Because failing to stop at a stop sign is punishable only by a fine and demerit points, the section of the *Highway Traffic Act* is not nullified by the Charter. For a detailed discussion of the Charter and the criminal law, see Chapter 6.

Strict Liability Offences

strict liability offence
an offence that depends for conviction only on proof of the physical element of the offence; a court will assume that the accused was negligent unless he or she can prove otherwise

For **strict liability offences**, the prosecution needs to prove only that the accused committed the *actus reus* of the offence; the court will assume, unless the accused can prove otherwise, that he or she was negligent in committing the act.

Does Characterizing Extreme Speeding as "Stunt Driving" Create an Unconstitutional Offence?

In January 2010, the Ontario Court of Appeal considered the case of *R v Raham*, which involved a conviction under section 172(1) of the Ontario *Highway Traffic Act*. This section prohibits the operation of a motor vehicle on a highway in a race or contest, while performing a stunt, or on a bet or wager.

At her trial before a justice of the peace in the Ontario Court of Justice, Jane Raham was convicted under section 172(1). Raham was radar-clocked driving 131 km/h on a highway with an 80 km/h speed limit. She appealed the conviction to the Ontario Court of Justice.

The basis of Raham's appeal was that the offence with which she was charged was an absolute liability offence and that, because imprisonment was a possible punishment for this offence, section 172(1) violated her constitutional rights under section 7 of the Charter. It is an accepted principle of law that to send a person to prison for committing an offence for which there is no *mens rea* is unconstitutional (against the Constitution) because it is an unjustifiable interference with a person's right to liberty as guaranteed by section 7 of the Charter. (This principle comes from *Re BC Motor Vehicle Act*.)

The provision that Raham was challenging reads as follows:

> 172(1) No person shall drive a motor vehicle on a highway in a race or contest, while performing a stunt or on a bet or wager.
>
> (2) Every person who contravenes subsection (1) is guilty of an offence and on conviction is liable to a fine of not less than $2,000 and not more than $10,000 or to imprisonment for a term of not more than six months, or to both, and in addition his or her driver's licence may be suspended,
>
>> (a) on a first conviction under this section, for not more than two years; or
>>
>> (b) on a subsequent conviction under this section, for not more than 10 years.

At her appeal, Raham successfully argued that since speeding is considered an absolute liability offence, the legislature cannot get around the constitutional limitation on imprisonment for these offences just by recharacterizing *extreme speeding* (50 km/h over the limit) as "stunt driving."

Stunt driving is defined in Ontario Regulation 455/07 as including "[d]riving a motor vehicle at a rate of speed that is 50 kilometres per hour or more over the speed limit."

Raham succeeded in her appeal, and her conviction was overturned. The prosecution appealed further, to the Ontario Court of Appeal.

At the Court of Appeal, the prosecution argued that section 172(1) creates not an absolute liability offence, but rather a strict liability offence. In making this argument, the prosecution relied on a number of factors identified in *R v Sault Ste Marie*, a case that considered the importance of government motives, such as the protection of the public, in imposing penalties of imprisonment. The prosecution also argued that because it is possible for a person who is charged with a strict liability offence to argue a defence at trial (the usual defence used in these cases is called the defence of "due diligence"), strict liability offences have an intention component that at least approaches the concept of *mens rea*. This intention component is what separates strict liability from absolute liability, and is what supports the constitutionality of prison sentences for strict liability offences.

The Court of Appeal agreed with the prosecution's arguments, and ruled that section 172(1) creates not an absolute liability offence, but a strict liability offence. Raham's case was sent back to the Ontario Court of Justice for a new trial.

Questions for Discussion

1. The stunt driving offence had to be created by the legislature because speeding had been interpreted, by the courts, as an absolute liability offence. Do you agree that extreme speeding (50 km/h over the limit) can, as a practical matter, occur without intent?

2. Besides defining extreme speeding as stunt driving, what other options might have been open to a legislature that wished, for policy reasons, to make extreme speeding an offence attracting a potential prison term?

Sources: *R v Raham*, 2010 ONCA 206; *Re BC Motor Vehicle Act*, [1985] 2 SCR 486; *Races, Contests and Stunts*, O Reg 455/07; and *R v Sault Ste Marie*, [1978] 2 SCR 1299.

Strict liability offences differ from absolute liability offences in that an accused can provide explanations or defences to strict liability charges. If the accused can convince the judge that a reasonable person would have committed the *actus reus* of the offence under the circumstances, an acquittal will follow. In other words, the accused can prove that he or she was not negligent in doing what he or she did.

Examples of strict liability offences include polluting the environment and corporate violations of health, licensing, and safety requirements.

Attempts and Offences Involving Indirect Involvement

Attempts to Commit Crimes

attempt
a criminal offence in which the offender took steps toward committing a crime but failed to complete it

Attempts to commit certain crimes are punishable. Section 24 of the *Criminal Code* states:

> 24. Every one who, having an intent to commit an offence, does or omits to do anything for the purpose of carrying out the intention is guilty of an attempt to commit the offence whether or not it was possible under the circumstances to commit the offence.

The section also states that an attempt is an act that goes beyond "mere preparation" to commit the offence. The *actus reus* for an attempt does not depend on the proof of consequences. However, establishing intent alone (the *mens rea*) is not enough to convict without evidence of an act committed for the purpose of carrying out the intended objective. For example, Frank decides to deface a school with graffiti. If all he does is pick a date and time and buy spray paint, this is not enough to convict him of an attempt, since these acts amount only to mere preparation. However, if Frank is caught in the schoolyard with a spray can in his hand, but he has not yet defaced the building, he could be convicted of the offence of mischief.

inchoate crime
a crime that is incomplete or attempted

Attempted crimes, often called **inchoate** (incomplete) **crimes**, are usually subject to less severe punishments than completed crimes. The three essential elements of an attempt are (1) intent, (2) some act or omission toward committing the offence, and (3) non-completion of the criminal act.

Parties to an Offence

party
a person who has involvement in the commission of an offence, whether direct or indirect

It is possible for a person to be charged, tried, and convicted of a serious criminal offence even if that person was not the main actor who actually committed the crime. Driving a getaway car, allowing a person who commits a crime to hide from police at your house, or helping someone plan a crime are all offences that are punishable by law if they are done willingly and knowingly.

principal
a person who is directly involved in committing an offence

The main **parties** that commit a crime are often called **principals** to the offence. Forms of secondary involvement in offences that are recognized in the *Criminal Code* include aiding, abetting, counselling, and being an accessory after the fact. People who engage in these activities will have their liability judged independently of the actions of the principals based on individual findings of *actus reus* and *mens rea*. If they are found guilty, secondary participants may be convicted of the same criminal offence as the principal offender and sentenced accordingly.

aid
knowingly assist the commission of a crime

Aiding and Abetting

abet
intentionally encourage the commission of a crime

Aiding means knowingly assisting the commission of a crime in any way. The *actus reus* of aiding is material facilitation (helping) for a specified illegal purpose. **Abetting** means intentionally encouraging the principal to commit a crime.

Aiding and abetting, set out in section 21(1) of the *Criminal Code*, are often charged together, and both offences require proof of direct or indirect intent. As a general rule, a person who is simply present and doesn't object to the crime being committed won't be convicted as an aider and abettor. If the person is under a duty to act and does nothing to stop the commission of a crime, he or she can be convicted of aiding or abetting by omission. For example, in *R v Nixon*[15] a senior police officer who was in charge of a lockup was found to have aided and abetted an assault on a prisoner by failing to act under his statutory duty to protect a prisoner in his care.

Counselling

Counselling is charged where a person advises, recommends, procures, solicits, or incites another person to be a party to an offence. There are two types of counselling offences. The first is counselling a crime that is never committed, contrary to section 464 of the Code. This offence is subject to a lesser punishment, similar to an attempted but incomplete offence. The other type of counselling is a more serious offence and is set out in section 22 of the Code. This offence involves being a party to an actual crime that is committed. The counsellor becomes a party to an offence and is subject to the same punishments faced by the principal actors.

counsel
advise another person to be a party to an offence

Accessory After the Fact

An **accessory after the fact** is, according to section 23 of the *Criminal Code*, a person who, knowing that another person has committed an offence, "receives, comforts or assists" that person for the purpose of helping him or her to escape. There are two clear mental elements to this offence. First, the accused must know that the person he or she is assisting has been a party to an offence, and second, the accused must knowingly provide the assistance for the purpose of helping the party escape. A person who is an accessory after the fact is not considered a party to the offence, but he or she can be tried and sentenced under section 463 of the Code as if guilty of attempting the offence.

accessory after the fact
a person who, knowing that another person has committed an offence, helps that person to commit a related offence (for example, converting stolen goods) or to escape prosecution

CHAPTER SUMMARY

The Canadian *Criminal Code* is a detailed statute containing the majority of the criminal offences chargeable in Canada and the procedures for investigating and prosecuting those offences. (Procedures for dealing with youth charged with crimes are contained in the *Youth Criminal Justice Act*.) Other criminal offences are found in other federal statutes such as the *Controlled Drugs and Substances Act*; quasi-criminal offences are found in provincial statutes such as the Ontario *Highway Traffic Act*.

While all offences share certain similarities, the serious consequences associated with criminal offences warrant special procedures and protections for offenders.

A careful study of *Criminal Code* provisions reveals that offences generally contain a substantive part (which describes the acts and intention that must be proven), a procedural part (which explains how the offence will be prosecuted), and a penalty part (which explains the sentences available should an accused be convicted of the offence). The substantive part of many offences allows aggravating factors (bodily harm, use of a weapon, specific intents) to be layered into an offence, creating a system of included offences.

Besides these three structural components, criminal offences also incorporate two essential elements: an *actus reus* (culpable act or omission), and a *mens rea* (intention or mental state). Each must be proven in order to support a conviction.

Finally, the criminal law addresses situations in which a person intends but does not complete a crime (attempts, or inchoate offences), or does not commit a crime herself, but rather supports another or others in committing a crime (aiding, abetting, or counselling) or helps them escape (being an accessory after the fact).

KEY TERMS

abet, 76
absolute liability offence, 74
accessory after the fact, 77
act, 65
actus reus, 67
aid, 76
attempt, 76
carelessness, 72
causation, 70
consent, 69
conviction, 65
counsel, 77
criminal negligence, 72
culpable intervention, 71
direct intent, 71
element, 67
evidence, 65

factual causation, 70
factual mistake, 72
foreseeability, 70
general intent, 71
hybrid offence, 66
inchoate crime, 76
included offence, 68
indictable offence, 66
intent, 65
legal causation, 70
mens rea, 67
motive, 71
negligence, 71
offence, 62
offence grid, 63
omission, 65
oral testimony, 67

party, 76
penalty part (of an offence), 66
physical evidence, 67
possession, 69
principal, 76
procedural part (of an offence), 66
quasi-criminal, 65
reasonable person, 70
recklessness, 72
sentence, 64
specific intent, 71
strict liability offence, 74
substantive part
  (of an offence), 66
summary conviction offence, 66

NOTES

1   *Constitution Act, 1867* (UK), 30 & 31 Vict, c 3, reprinted in RSC 1985, Appendix II, No 5.

2   *Mental Health Act*, RSO 1990, c M.7.

3   *Criminal Code*, RSC 1985, c C-46, as amended.

4   *Highway Traffic Act*, RSO 1990, c H.8.

5   *Controlled Drugs and Substances Act*, SC 1996, c 19.

6   *Crimes Against Humanity and War Crimes Act*, SC 2000, c 24.

7 *Compulsory Automobile Insurance Act*, RSO 1990, c C.25.

8 *Canadian Charter of Rights and Freedoms*, Part I of the *Constitution Act, 1982*, being Schedule B to the *Canada Act 1982* (UK), 1982, c 11.

9 *Canada Evidence Act*, RSC 1985, c C-5.

10 *Youth Criminal Justice Act*, SC 2002, c 1.

11 *R v Marshall* (1986), 25 CCC (3d) 151 (NSCA).

12 *Supra* note 4.

13 *R v Parks*, [1992] 2 SCR 871.

14 *Re BC Motor Vehicle Act*, [1985] 2 SCR 486.

15 *R v Nixon* (1990), 57 CCC (3d) 97, [1990] 6 WWR 253 (BCCA).

EXERCISES

Multiple Choice

1. Criminal offences that are listed in the *Criminal Code* are created by
    a. the federal government
    b. provincial governments
    c. municipal governments
    d. all of the above

2. Which of the following statutes is not generally included in an annotated edition of the *Criminal Code*?
    a. *Canada Evidence Act*
    b. *Highway Traffic Act*
    c. *Youth Criminal Justice Act*
    d. *Crimes Against Humanity and War Crimes Act*

3. The difference between negligence and criminal negligence is that criminal negligence has
    a. a *mens rea* component
    b. an *actus reus* component
    c. a due diligence component
    d. no defence available in court

4. What term describes the situation where a person is aware of the potentially harmful consequences of an act but acts anyway?
    a. mistake
    b. wilful blindness
    c. carelessness
    d. recklessness

5. What term describes provincial or municipal offences that are similar in nature to *Criminal Code* offences?
    a. no-intent offences
    b. quasi-criminal offences
    c. absolute liability offences
    d. strict liability offences
    e. included offences

True or False?

_____ **1.** Quasi-criminal provincial offences can be found in the *Criminal Code*.

_____ **2.** The *Highway Traffic Act* is an example of provincial legislation.

_____ **3.** A person charged with any offence, whether criminal or quasi-criminal, must have intended to commit the offence in order to be convicted.

_____ **4.** The common law, in the form of court decisions, must be consulted when interpreting *Criminal Code* provisions.

_____ **5.** The *actus reus* is the physical component of a crime.

_____ **6.** An accused may, in some cases, be convicted of a lesser, included offence if the prosecution fails to prove an aggravating element (for example, the use of a firearm).

_____ **7.** Aiding means intentionally encouraging the commission of a criminal act.

_____ **8.** A counsellor to an offence can actually be charged as a party to an offence under the *Criminal Code*.

_____ **9.** A person must be charged with an included offence in order to be convicted of it.

_____**10.** Negligence is the most serious level of intent for criminal offences.

Short Answer

1. Consider section 245 of the Code: Administering Noxious Thing. Which terms or phrases in this offence will you need to research further to understand the offence properly?

2. Explain the main differences between criminal offences and quasi-criminal offences.

3. In what part of the *Criminal Code* would you expect to find the following offences?

   a. assault

   b. arson

   c. carrying concealed weapon

4. Write a scenario that demonstrates specific intent and one that demonstrates general intent.

5. Explain the differences among recklessness, carelessness, and negligence.

6. Describe the difference between aiding and abetting.

Activity

For each act described in the chart, mark whether the person has the *mens rea* and/or *actus reus* necessary to be found guilty of an offence.

Act	Mens Rea	Actus Reus
1. Jacquie picks up and babysits her neighbour's kids after school, sometimes running errands while they are with her. One day, she decides to run into the store to pick up a few grocery items. She leaves the kids inside her car with the ignition turned off for ten minutes, even though it is 35 degrees outside. Before she comes out of the store, someone walks by, notices the kids, and calls the police.		

Act	Mens Rea	Actus Reus
2. In line at a concert, a friend asks Jade to hold her bag while she goes to the bathroom. A drug dog stops in front of Jade. The police search the friend's bag and find a few marijuana joints. Jade is charged with possession of a narcotic.		
3. Amar is charged with assault after he loses his temper in a bar. He feels that the bar tab is unfair. Amar kicks a nearby stool, knocking over a glass which strikes another customer in the face, cutting her.		
4. While browsing in a bookstore, Amy runs into an old friend. They decide to get a coffee. As they leave the store, Amy forgets that she has a book that she had been considering buying under her arm. She is stopped by store security.		
5. Antonio comes to work on Monday, while feeling sick. He's recovering from the flu and has taken cold medication. After a few hours, Antonio decides to drive home, because he is feeling very tired. Antonio starts driving but is having a hard time focusing on the road. A police officer observes him weaving across several lanes. Just before Antonio is pulled over, he drives into a ditch. Fortunately for him, no one is seriously injured.		
6. During a particularly heated junior hockey game, Lance is looking to get back at Vinh, a player on the opposing team, for a dirty bodycheck during their last game. After a brief verbal exchange, the two players drop their gloves and start punching each other. Neither are seriously injured and both are asked to sit out during the rest of the game.		

Investigation of Crime, Police Powers, and the Canadian Charter of Rights and Freedoms

6

LEARNING OUTCOMES

After completing this chapter, you should be able to:

■ Describe and explain the test for a reasonable search.

■ Explain the process for obtaining a search warrant.

■ Understand the requirements for arresting an individual.

■ Identify the major individual rights protected by the *Canadian Charter of Rights and Freedoms*.

■ Explain how the Charter affects crime investigations.

■ Understand the test for excluding tainted evidence from trial.

Investigating Crime

person of interest
a person the police wish to speak to in order to obtain further information

suspect
a person the police are actively investigating with regard to an offence but who has not yet been charged

accused
a person against whom a criminal or quasi-criminal charge has been laid, but who has not yet been convicted

excluded
barred by a judge's order from being used as evidence at trial, often as a result of a breach of a Charter right in producing the evidence

Once a crime has been committed, it is up to the police to investigate it, collecting evidence to prove who committed the crime and how. The goal is to collect enough evidence to prove that a person is in fact guilty of the crime to the satisfaction of a judge or jury in court. To use the terminology from Chapter 5, the police must find evidence to prove that the person is guilty of each element that makes up the equation of the offence.

When the police wish to speak to a person in order to obtain information about the offence, this person may be referred to as a **person of interest**. While a person is being investigated under suspicion of committing the crime, he or she is referred to as a **suspect**. Once charges have been laid, the person becomes the **accused**.

Much of the investigation process is not governed by any law or statute; the police officer simply follows the guidelines for investigations produced by the police force. However, once the investigation begins to focus on a specific person, with the potential for infringing on his or her rights, the officer's actions are governed—and, in many ways, limited—by the rules set out in the *Criminal Code*[1] (specifically part XV), the *Canadian Charter of Rights and Freedoms*,[2] and the common law.

Evidence that is discovered or obtained in a manner that is contrary to the Code, the Charter, or common law may be **excluded** from consideration in a trial. The decision to exclude evidence is made by the judge. In general, the defence will "move" (ask) to exclude the evidence; the judge will then send the jury, if any, out of the courtroom, listen to the arguments of both the prosecution and the defence, and decide whether the evidence can be considered or not.

Evidence that is excluded cannot be considered by the decision-maker (the judge or the jury) in making a finding of guilt or innocence. If, in a trial by judge alone, the judge has heard the evidence in the course of the exclusion hearing, he or she must be careful to ignore the evidence when making the final decision. Even if the "tainted" evidence clearly suggests that a person committed a certain crime, the judge may rule that the prosecution is barred from using it at trial because it was obtained improperly.

As a result, it is very important that police officers understand what they can and cannot do when investigating a crime. This chapter discusses the rules governing the power of police to investigate crime and gather evidence against a suspect. The rules discussed here deal with the police powers of **search and seizure**, the proper procedure for arresting a suspect, and the various Charter rights that the officer must be aware of in conducting an investigation. Because the rights of individuals are considered of paramount importance in Canada, the Charter plays a role in all discussions of police investigative powers.

search and seizure
part of investigating offences, where the police inspect people or places and take into custody any physical evidence of crime that is found

The Canadian Charter of Rights and Freedoms

The *Charter of Rights and Freedoms* (see Chapter 4) sets out those individual rights that Canadians believe are fundamental to a free and democratic society. In broad language, the Charter establishes rules that all levels of government must follow in their efforts to regulate the lives of citizens and other persons living in Canada. These rules have been extensively challenged in the courts, and the common law surrounding each section of the Charter is already complex and well developed.

Among other things, the Charter protects the individual's right to freedom of expression and association; to be free from unreasonable search and seizure and from arbitrary detention; and to enjoy life, liberty, and security of the person.

The Charter applies equally to laws (both statute law and common law) and to the actions of the government and its representatives. In stating that the Charter applies to laws and government actions, we mean that a law that infringes on the rights and freedoms of individuals can be struck down unless that law represents a reasonable limit "prescribed by law as can be demonstrably justified in a free and democratic society" (s 1). Government action that infringes a Charter right will attract "such remedy as the court considers appropriate and just in the circumstances" (s 24(1)).

Any discussion at trial of how the Charter applies to a section of the *Criminal Code* or an action of a police officer will first involve establishing that a right has been infringed (or breached), then determining whether the infringement is sufficient to attract a **remedy**, and then determining what that remedy will be. For example, evidence collected as the result of a breach of a right may be excluded from use at trial.

remedy
an award or order provided by the court to compensate a victim for the commission of a legal wrong, such as a tort or a breach of contract

The Charter and the Criminal Code

The *Charter of Rights and Freedoms* and the *Criminal Code* often conflict. The Charter, which is part of the Constitution of Canada and therefore paramount (above all other statutes), protects the legitimate interests of individuals to be protected from unreasonable actions of the state. The Code, a federal statute, protects the legitimate interests of society to be protected from crime and the people who commit crime.

Because the Charter is a constitutional document, it overrides the Code at every turn—no section of the Code that contravenes the Charter is lawful. If a section of the Code is found to be unlawful under the Charter (often called "unconstitutional"), that section may be struck down by a judge and declared to be of no force or effect. Unless the decision of the judge is later overturned, a law or part of a law that has been struck down cannot be enforced in any situation, not just in the case in which it was found to be unconstitutional. This process was discussed in Chapter 4.

The actions of police officers, correctional officers, Crown attorneys, and other government agents are also subject to the Charter. As agents of the government, the police are required to behave at all times in a way that does not infringe on the Charter rights of individuals. This is particularly true when the police investigate crimes. As discussed above, if evidence of a crime is obtained in a manner that infringes the Charter rights of the accused, that evidence may be excluded from the trial of the accused. The authority for excluding evidence is found in section 24(2) of the Charter.

What follows is a discussion of the various sections of the Charter that apply to criminal investigations.

Search and Seizure (Section 8 of the Charter)

Both statute law and common law give certain investigative powers to police officers. One of the most important investigative tools available to police is the ability to search private property and seize evidence, but this police power has limits. Section 8 of the Charter states, "Everyone has the right to be secure against unreasonable search or seizure." This section begs the question, "What is **reasonable**?" In the case *R v Collins*,[3] the Supreme Court of Canada determined that a search will be reasonable if

reasonable
a subjective standard, used in the Charter or common law rules, of what is acceptable to society under the circumstances

- it is authorized by law,
- the law itself is reasonable, and
- the manner in which the search is carried out is reasonable.

Authorized by Law

A search is **authorized by law** if a statute exists that specifically allows the police to conduct the search in question or if the police officers obtain judicial authorization for the search before they conduct it. Examples of *Criminal Code* provisions that allow police to obtain a **search warrant**—a written authorization to conduct a search—include:

- section 487—basic search warrant
- section 164—warrant for seizure of obscene materials
- section 186—authorization to obtain wiretap evidence
- section 256—warrant to obtain blood samples for impaired driving
- section 492.2—authorization to obtain telephone records

A warrant sets out the offence being investigated, the place that may be searched, the items that may be searched for, who may attend at the search, and when the search may be conducted. Failing to follow the terms of the warrant carefully may lead to the search being declared unlawful or without due authorization. For example, if the warrant allows officers to search a specific car and they search not only the car but also the garage in which it is found, they have overstepped the legal authority of the warrant. Any evidence they find in the garage may be excluded by the court as a result of having been obtained unreasonably.

The common law rule is that the warrant itself must be obtained legally and according to specific requirements; otherwise, the warrant is improper and the search is illegal. The usual procedure for obtaining a search warrant is for a police officer (the **informant**) to appear before a justice of the peace. The officer swears to the truth of an affidavit, which the Code calls an **information to obtain a search warrant**, that sets out the grounds for believing that the items sought in a search warrant will result in discovering evidence of the commission of a crime. Sometimes, if the officer can't personally go to the courthouse, the justice of the peace issues a **telewarrant** under section 487.1.

The issue of what constitutes reasonable and probable grounds for police action is a very important one. Law enforcement officers will encounter this issue in many facets of their work, not only with respect to search and seizure.

"Grounds" refers to the evidence on which an officer bases his or her desire to conduct the search. This evidence can come in many forms: verbal evidence from a third party (for example, a tip from an informer); eyewitness evidence (for example, observations that the officer has made in the course of surveillance of the outside of the building sought to be searched); or physical or documentary evidence (for example, a printed invitation to a film screening of what sounds, from the description, like child pornography).

"Reasonable" and "probable" are adjectives used to describe the quality and reliability of the evidence. Assessing the quality and reliability of an officer's grounds, and the degree to which they suggest that an offence has been or will be committed, is up to the justice of the peace.

In general, before issuing a warrant, the justice of the peace will look for specificity in the evidence, as well as credibility on the part of third-party sources. In *Hunter et al v Southam Inc*,[4] the Supreme Court of Canada held that, to be constitutional (consistent with a person's Charter rights), a search warrant must set out the reasonable grounds to believe that an offence has been committed and that the particular items to search for in a certain location will likely yield evidence of a crime. The description of the items must be detailed enough to allow the officers to identify the items and link them to the offence described in the search warrant; a search is not permitted to be what is commonly described as "a fishing expedition." There must also be a nexus (connection) between the location to be searched and the items being sought. The minimum requirements for issuing a search warrant are

- a description of the offence, including the name of the accused if known, the section of the Code that creates the offence being investigated, the identity of the victim, the date of the crime, the circumstances of the offence, and so on;
- a list of the items to be seized;
- the location to be searched; and
- the informant's reasonable grounds (reasons, and evidence supporting those reasons) for believing that the evidence will be found in the specified location.

If the proper procedures are not followed to obtain the warrant, or if the warrant is issued without sufficient grounds, it is considered invalid and the search that it authorizes is considered unlawful. As a result, any evidence discovered through the search may be excluded from the trial of the accused.

CASE IN POINT

Do Warrantless Cellphone Searches Violate an Accused's Rights Under the Charter?

In 2009, two men were arrested after an armed robbery of a jewellery merchant at a market. Upon arrest, the police searched and found a cellphone in the pocket of one of the suspects. While looking through the phone, which was not password protected, the police found photographs of a handgun, as well as an unsent text message to a third person. This suggested that the two suspects were involved in the armed robbery. The cellphone was searched once more at the police station.

The accused were both convicted. At the trial and appeal, one of the accused challenged the warrantless search of the cellphone, arguing that it was an unreasonable search and seizure under the Charter. The case was ultimately appealed to the Supreme Court of Canada in *R v Fearon*.

The majority of the Supreme Court ruled that warrantless cellphone searches are fair game after a lawful arrest, and if conducted properly, they do not violate an accused person's rights under the Charter. The Supreme Court outlined four conditions that must be met in order for the search of a cellphone (or other similar device) incidental to arrest to be valid:

1. the arrest must be lawful;
2. the search must truly be incidental to the arrest—meaning that the police must have a reason based on a valid law enforcement purpose to carry out the search;
3. the nature and extent of the search must be tailored to the purpose of the search (limited to areas where evi-

dence is likely to be found—text messages, emails, and call logs); and

4. police must record detailed notes about what they examined on the device and what procedures were used to do so.

Justice Cromwell stated that law enforcement and privacy concerns may be balanced in many ways—beyond those suggested in the case.

Questions for Discussion

1. In another case, *R v Morelli*, the Supreme Court of Canada held that privacy interests outweigh law enforcement objectives in circumstances where evidence is obtained from an accused's personal computer. Given that technology has progressed to the point where computers and cellphones have similar data-processing and storage capabilities, perform similar functions, and contain delicate and personal information, do you think the court in *R v Fearon* should have taken this into account? Why or why not?

2. The Supreme Court found that it did not make a difference whether or not the cellphone was password protected. Do you think that an individual's expectation of privacy is greater when he or she decides to use a password? In other words, if someone decides not to use password protection, does he or she abandon the right to privacy?

Sources: *R v Fearon*, 2014 SCC 77; *R v Morelli*, 2010 SCC 8.

Section 489 of the Code does allow for "plain-view" seizures of items that are not named in a search warrant if the items are found during a lawful search and are in plain view of the police officers. To seize these items, the officers must have reasonable and probable grounds to suspect that they may be evidence of an offence. For example, if police officers are searching a house for stolen jewellery and they look in the freezer and find, instead of jewellery, neatly bundled hundred-dollar bills, they may be justified in seizing the cash as evidence of the sale of stolen goods. However, the police would not likely be able to support the seizure of $36.71 in mixed bills and change from the pocket of a parka in the accused's hall closet.

The Law Is Reasonable

For a search to be reasonable under section 8 of the Charter, the law that authorizes the search must be reasonable. This requirement applies to two different kinds of law: the statute that authorizes the search or the search warrant, and the statute that specifies the way the warrant is obtained.

For example, the courts have found section 254 of the *Criminal Code*, which allows for warrantless demands for breath samples, to be reasonable. Ordinarily, this kind of random search would not be allowed; however, an exception has been made to permit it on the basis of society's interest in reducing drunk driving and improving public safety on the roads. This balance between individual rights and social interests was discussed in Chapter 4, where we examined how the courts analyze laws to determine whether they are consistent with the Charter.

The procedure prescribed by law for obtaining the warrant must be reasonable. For example, the information form provided to the justice of the peace to obtain the warrant must require a written summary of the informant's reasonable and probable grounds. The law must require that a justice of the peace decline to issue a warrant if the form lacks the required written summary, or if the summary fails to disclose reasonable grounds for a search.

The Manner of the Search Is Reasonable

Even if a search is lawful and the law permitting that search is reasonable, the evidence obtained as a result of the search may be excluded from trial if the manner in which the police conducted the search was unreasonable. It is not reasonable, for example, for police who are looking for stolen vehicles in a garage to rip out the garage walls or dismantle the plumbing. Police must consider whether less intrusive alternatives exist. Figure 6.1 summarizes the requirements for a reasonable search and seizure.

Common Law Powers to Search and Seize

Even without a warrant or a specific statutory authorization, the common law provides that the police may, in certain narrow circumstances, conduct a search. All of the search powers described below, for which the police are not required to obtain a warrant, are derived from common law. The six types of searches that do not require the police to obtain a warrant are shown in Table 6.1.

The common law allows a police officer to search without a warrant during an investigative detention and as incident to a lawful arrest. If a police officer has a legal right to arrest a person, that officer also has a common law right to search the person, for the safety of both the officer and the person. The common law recognizes that police officers must be able to assure themselves that the arrested person will not be in a position to harm them or to escape custody. A reasonable search for weapons or other dangerous items may be conducted at the time of the arrest—the officer does not have the right to conduct a full cavity search of the person, to take blood or DNA samples, or to search the person's house.

In conducting a search incidental to arrest, the police can take only those actions that are consistent with the purpose of the search—namely, ensuring personal safety or securing and preserving any evidence found on the suspect. The nature of the search must directly relate to the purpose of the arrest. In general, this amounts to a pat-down of the suspect's body through clothing.

It is important to maintain a distinction, however, between a search incidental to arrest, and a search *during* an investigative detention. During an investigative detention, the police do not have reasonable and probable grounds to arrest the detainee. They have a reasonable suspicion that the detainee is involved in some way to the offence. As such, the power to search a detainee is also significantly limited. The police must believe on reasonable grounds that officer safety, or the safety of others, is at risk before a search will be justified. A mere hunch or intuition will not be sufficient to warrant a search.

This was confirmed by the Supreme Court of Canada in the case of *R v Mann*,[5] a police officer conducting a pat-down felt a soft bulge in a suspect's sweatshirt pocket. Upon reaching into the pocket, the officer found illegal drugs. The drugs seized were later excluded from evidence because the court decided that reaching into the pocket for something soft (that is, something that did not appear to pose a threat to safety) amounted to an illegal search and seizure.

FIGURE 6.1   Requirements for Reasonable Search and Seizure

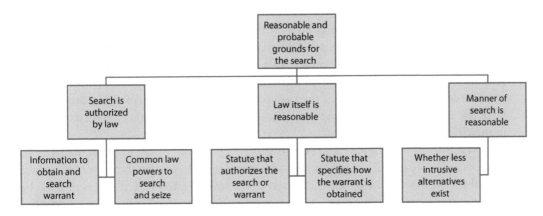

TABLE 6.1   Common Law Searches

Type of Search	Description
Consent search	when police request permission to search from the owner or occupier of the premises, and permission is granted
Search incident to arrest	police may search the person under arrest and the immediate area surrounding the person for weapons and/or destruction of evidence
Inventory search	police may conduct a search of a person being placed in custody in order to secure his or her personal possessions
Search to protect the safety of the public	police may search an area if there is a reasonable fear that there is an imminent threat to public safety
Search necessary to prevent destruction of evidence	police may search an area where there is imminent danger that evidence will be lost, removed, or destroyed, or will disappear if the search is delayed (these are known as "exigent circumstances")*
"Hot pursuit" search	when the police enter a dwelling-house to apprehend a person when they believe that entry is necessary in order to prevent imminent bodily harm or death to any person, or to prevent the imminent loss or destruction of evidence

* When exigent circumstances do not exist, police are required to obtain a warrant to arrest a person in a dwelling-house (*R v Feeney*, [1997] 2 SCR 13).

Consent to a search is another complicated matter. The police must take steps to ensure that the consent is informed and voluntary—that the person who consents understands what he or she is consenting to and is not feeling threatened by the officer making the request. The officer must also ensure that the person consenting to the search of a building actually has the legal right to give such consent. The person must be the owner or occupier of the place to be searched and not just a guest.

Programs like RIDE or even routine roadside checks for seat belt use, licence and registration, or insurance are constantly being challenged under the Charter. Police are, in general, not allowed to simply conduct random checks of people's virtue. Absent a legally recognized exception, they must have reasonable grounds to suspect that an offence is being committed before beginning an investigation. The RIDE program has been allowed by courts because it fulfills a pressing social need (reducing drunk driving) but interferes in only a minimal way with the rights of the drivers who are stopped.

The related issue of "investigative detention," whereby the police randomly detain a person, even briefly, on a hunch (less than reasonable grounds) is discussed below, in the section on arbitrary detention.

Arrest and Investigation

Arrest is one of the most complex and important issues for a police officer. In all cases, officers should refer to the rules for arrest set out in the *Criminal Code*.

arrest
the act of taking a suspect into police custody

Arrest is the lawful restriction of liberty that consists of words of arrest and a physical demonstration of detention. In other words, a police officer arrests a person when the officer makes a statement like "You're under arrest" and then puts the person in the back seat of a police cruiser. Stopping an individual to ask for identification is not generally considered an arrest. However, if the person is given reason to form the impression that he or she is not free to go, the stop may amount to investigative detention (discussed later in the chapter).

Arrest is dealt with in part XVI (Compelling Appearance of Accused) of the *Criminal Code*. Arrests are usually made for one of four reasons: to ensure that a person appears at trial for crimes that he or she is accused of committing, to prevent a person from beginning to commit an offence, to stop a person in the process of committing a crime, or to preserve evidence that would likely be destroyed or lost if a person were not arrested. If a person is suspected of committing an offence that is not serious and there is no reason to believe that the person will not appear in court when required, the police officer need not arrest the person but may simply issue a document called an **appearance notice** to the person, which directs the accused to be at a certain court at a certain date and time.

appearance notice
a formal document, given to a person before a charge is laid, that sets out the requirement to attend court for trial at a certain date and time

Arrests may be made either with an arrest warrant or without one. The process for obtaining an arrest warrant is described in sections 504 to 514 of the Code. As with a search warrant, an arrest warrant is obtained by applying to a justice of the peace or a provincial court (for example, Ontario Court of Justice) judge. An informant (usually a police officer) must appear before a justice of the peace and swear an information that identifies the person involved, alleges that the person has committed an indictable offence, and states that the person is or is believed to be located within the jurisdiction of the justice of the peace. The justice will review the adequacy and form of the information, and, if it is proper, the justice must then decide whether issuing a summons is enough or whether an arrest warrant is necessary.

summons
a document that may be delivered to a person accused of a crime requiring that person to be in court at a certain date and time to answer the charges

A **summons** is simply an order that the accused person appear in court at a certain date and time to answer the charge made against him or her. No arrest is involved.

Warrantless Search Justified in the Interest of Public Safety

The police were called about a noise complaint at the home of the accused, MacDonald. When MacDonald opened his front door, the officer noticed that he had an object in his hand hidden behind his leg. The officer twice asked MacDonald what was in his hand. When the accused did not answer, the officer pushed the door slightly further open in order to see. MacDonald and the officer engaged in a struggle, and MacDonald was disarmed of a loaded handgun.

MacDonald was charged with several firearms-related offences and was convicted at trial. The Court of Appeal upheld most of the convictions but reduced MacDonald's sentence. Both the accused and the Crown appealed to the Supreme Court of Canada.

The officer's action of pushing the door further open did invade the accused's reasonable expectation of privacy and constituted a breach of section 8 of the Charter. However, the warrantless search fell under the common law police duty to protect the lives and safety of the public and constituted a "safety search," which may justify a Charter breach if it is found to be reasonably necessary. In determining whether the search was reasonably necessary, the Supreme Court considered several factors and balanced the duty of the police to protect the public against the accused's liberty interests. These factors included "the importance of the duty to the public good; the necessity of the infringement for the performance of the duty; and the extent of the infringement."

In this case, the officer had reasonable grounds to believe that there was an imminent threat to public and police safety. The door was pushed open a few inches further only after the accused was asked what he had behind his leg and had failed to answer. Furthermore, the search itself was minimally intrusive. In the result, the Supreme Court held that the section 8 Charter breach was justified and dismissed the accused's appeal.

Question for Discussion

Although the decision of the Supreme Court of Canada was unanimous in this case, the court was divided as to whether the police require (1) reasonable grounds to *believe* an individual is armed and dangerous in order to conduct a safety search or (2) reasonable grounds to *suspect* an individual is armed and dangerous in order to conduct a safety search. Explain the difference between these two standards. Which do you think ought to apply and why?

Source: *R v MacDonald*, 2014 SCC 3.

If, however, the justice of the peace decides, on the basis of the offence alleged against the accused person or the evidence produced at the warrant hearing, that the public interest requires that the accused be arrested, then the justice may issue a warrant for the arrest of the accused.

According to section 495(1) of the Code, with certain exceptions, a police officer may lawfully arrest a person without a warrant if that person has committed an indictable offence, or the officer has reasonable grounds to assume that the person is about to commit an indictable offence, or the person is found committing a criminal offence of any kind.

To ensure that a person who has been placed under arrest knows that he is a suspect, and that his arrest has triggered certain Charter rights, the police generally administer a **caution** to the suspect. The wording of police cautions varies, but they generally include a warning to the suspect that any statements he makes may be used against him in a criminal prosecution, and advise the suspect that he has the right to instruct and retain counsel.[6]

caution
a statement made by a peace officer to a person who is detained, advising that person of his or her right to remain silent and to hire a lawyer

Arbitrary Detention (Section 9 of the Charter)

Section 9 of the Charter protects an individual's right not to be arbitrarily detained. In addition, section 10(a) guarantees the individual's right to be informed of the reason for the arrest or detention.

Detention by the police for the purposes of these sections involves restraining a person's liberty. Detention occurs when the conduct of the police physically or psychologically deprives a person of his or her choice to simply walk away.[7] Whether a person's liberty has been restrained is treated, by judges, as a question of fact, which means that it depends on the particular circumstances of each case. Judges have ruled, for example, that a police officer at the scene of a car accident has detained people simply by telling them to sit in the back seat of a police cruiser. In that instance, the police officer, in directing the people to enter the cruiser, assumed control over people's movements in a circumstance where they believed that they would face serious legal consequences if they did not obey.

The common law test for determining whether a detention is arbitrary involves considering the following factors:

- whether there is an articulable cause for the detention,
- the extent and duration of the detention, and
- the conduct of the police.

Articulable cause means a reason for detaining someone that arises out of information known to the police officer that indicates that detention is necessary or justified. For example, if a police officer receives a report that a crime is in progress at a certain store and, on approaching the store, sees two people running from it, that officer has articulable cause to stop and detain them, if only to get information on what the people may have seen in the store before leaving.

For a detention to be lawful, police must have some reason, beyond simple suspicion, to detain a person. In recent years, the issue of "investigative detention" has attracted attention. Investigative detention is a practice that has no express basis in law (no statutory provision allows it), and the term has come to describe the practice of detaining a person for the purpose of gathering information. In those situations where police detain a suspect on a hunch to obtain information—rather than act on the basis of known information—this generally amounts to detention without articulable cause.

In the case of *R v Mann*, discussed above, Mr. Mann was stopped in the street by police who were cruising the area after reports of a break-in. The police knew the name of the break-in suspect, but even though Mr. Mann gave a different name (his own) when he was questioned, the police detained and searched him, discovering marijuana, which led to his arrest.

Although the *Mann* case turned not on the issue of investigative detention, but rather on the issue of search incidental to detention, the Supreme Court made some comments about investigative detention—namely, that it is not specifically provided for by law. However, the court opted not to take a hard-line approach against investigative detention.

In 2009, the Supreme Court examined the issue of investigative detention again, this time in the case of *R v Suberu*.[8] In that case, two men attempted to buy liquor from an LCBO store using a gift certificate purchased with a stolen credit card. The cashier phoned police. When the police arrived, one officer followed one of the two men, Suberu, to his vehicle, and ultimately searched the vehicle (and found the stolen credit card) without offering Suberu the opportunity to contact counsel. At trial and in the Ontario Court of Appeal, the police successfully argued that Suberu's right to counsel had not arisen at the time he was accompanied to his car, because he had merely been investigatively detained; and that his right to counsel did not arise until he was arrested after the stolen goods were found. The Supreme Court, however, found that Suberu's right to counsel arose as soon as he was detained next to the vehicle.

In making that finding, however, the court reaffirmed its tolerance for investigative detention by stating:

> [N]ot every interaction between the police and members of the public, even for investigative purposes, constitutes a detention within the meaning of the *Charter*.

Section 9 of the *Charter* does not dictate that police abstain from interacting with members of the public until they have specific grounds to connect the individual to the commission of a crime. …

To simply assume that a detention occurs every time a person is delayed from going on his or her way because of the police accosting him or her during the course of an investigation, without considering whether or not the interaction involved a significant deprivation of liberty, would overshoot the purpose of the *Charter*.

The *Mann* and *Suberu* decisions suggest that the actions of police in stopping people in suspicious circumstances will be tolerated by the court, at least to a narrow degree, but clear violations of arrest and seizure rules will lead to Charter remedies.

Right to Counsel (Section 10(b) of the Charter)

When people are detained or arrested by the police for any reason, section 10(b) of the Charter protects their right to

1. instruct counsel (a lawyer) without delay, and
2. be informed of that right upon arrest or detention.

A person's right to retain counsel includes the right to do so in private and to be informed of the availability of legal aid and duty counsel services.

The police also have a duty to refrain from questioning people until they have either exercised or waived (given up) their right to counsel. This is subject to the requirement that people exercise their right to counsel (for example, by calling a lawyer) within a reasonable time. A person is not able to put off being questioned indefinitely simply by refusing to call a lawyer.

The information about right to counsel must be given in a timely and comprehensible manner. If the police are aware of any language difficulties, intoxication, or mental disability on the part of the suspect, they must take appropriate steps to enable comprehension.

To **waive** the right to counsel, the individual must make a clear statement that he or she understands the right to counsel and does not wish to exercise that right. Judges generally don't want to accept a waiver of the right to counsel unless it is made in clear, unambiguous terms. Some people hesitate to call a lawyer because they feel they cannot afford one. For this reason, good police practice means not only advising suspects of the existence of legal aid and duty counsel, but also providing relevant phone numbers so that the suspect knows how to access these services.

If the police fail to inform the person of the right to counsel or fail to allow the person to exercise the right (for example, by not providing a private room and a phone) prior to questioning him or her, any answers that the individual gives to police questions may be ruled **inadmissible** at trial as a result of this Charter breach.

waive
give up a legal right

inadmissible
refers to evidence that was obtained in a manner that breached a Charter right and is disallowed by a trial judge so that the prosecution cannot use it as part of its case against the accused

Deprivation of Life, Liberty, and Security of the Person (Section 7 of the Charter)

Section 7 of the Charter states clearly that the government may not take away the life, liberty, or security of a person, except in accordance with the principles of fundamental justice.

In some ways, section 7 is a general statement that serves as the basis for the rights that follow in sections 8 through 14 of the Charter. Each of those sections establishes a specific right that can be seen as an aspect of the right to life, liberty, and security of the person.

fundamental justice
the basic tenet of the
Canadian system of
rights and freedoms
that requires that all
persons investigated
for and accused of a
crime receive procedural
protections to ensure
that they are treated fairly
throughout the process

Fundamental justice is a broad concept that includes the right to remain silent when detained by the authorities. Police officers violate this right if their conduct effectively or unfairly deprives someone of the right to choose whether to speak to police. Police should not assume that people are guilty when they assert their right to silence.

Right to Silence (Sections 7 and 11(c) of the Charter)

The right to silence includes the right to make a free and meaningful choice as to whether to speak or remain silent. However, when an accused person has chosen to exercise the right to remain silent, the right is not absolute. It does not prevent the police from questioning an accused in the absence of counsel retained by the accused. The police may use persuasion to question an accused as long as it does not deny the accused the freedom to choose whether to remain silent or not.

The Supreme Court of Canada, in the case of *R v Singh*,[9] reiterated that the right to silence includes the right of the detainee to make a meaningful choice as to whether or not to speak to the police. However, the court also stated that it is inappropriate to impose a rigid requirement on the police that they refrain from questioning a suspect who has indicated that he or she does not wish to speak to the police. In *Singh*, the accused asserted his right to silence 18 times throughout police interviews. On each occasion, the interviewing officer either affirmed that Singh had the right to not say anything or explained that he (the officer) had a duty to present the evidence to the accused. The officer continued on with the interview. The Supreme Court of Canada upheld Singh's conviction, stating that the right to remain silent does not mean that a person has the right not to be spoken to by the police. Questioning a suspect is vital to the investigative role of the police. At the same time, the court noted that where the police persist in continued questioning despite repeated assertions from the accused that he wishes to remain silent, this may lead to the conclusion that the subsequent statement was not given out of the accused's own free will, depending on the circumstances of the case.

In *R v Liew*,[10] the Supreme Court held that the police may use undercover agents to observe the accused. However, the court drew a distinction between the use of undercover agents to observe the accused and the use of agents to actively elicit information from the accused. The common law holds that it does not matter if a police agent (whether undercover or not) lies to the accused, permits himself or herself to be misidentified, or engages in subterfuge, as long as the accused's responses are not actively elicited or result from interrogation during which the accused has chosen to exercise his or her right to remain silent.

Where the accused exercises his or her right to remain silent in the face of accusations made by the police, no inferences may be drawn at trial from an accused's decision to remain silent.

Right to Be Tried Within a Reasonable Time (Section 11(b) of the Charter)

The right to be tried within a reasonable time is protected by section 11(b) of the Charter. The inclusion of this right in the Charter led, in the years following its proclamation, to the dropping of hundreds of charges because of excessive delays between the time of arrest and the time of trial.

In the twin cases of *R v Jordan*[11] and *R v Williamson*,[12] the Supreme Court of Canada set out a presumptive ceiling beyond which delay is presumed to be unreasonable. Delay is considered from the laying of the charge to the actual or anticipated end of the trial. The presumptive ceiling is 18 months for cases heard in the provincial court, and 30 months for cases heard in superior court. Where the defence has caused the delay or has waived the delay, this time is not included in the calculation of the presumptive ceiling. Once this time-line is exceeded, the burden is on the Crown to rebut the presumption of unreasonableness.

The Crown may rebut the presumption on the basis of exceptional circumstances, or circumstances that lie outside of the Crown's control in that (1) they are reasonably unfore-seen or reasonably unavoidable, and (2) they cannot reasonably be remedied. These excep-tional circumstances fall under two main categories: discrete events and particularly complex cases. Examples of discrete events include illness of a witness or an unexpected event at trial. If the case is so complex that it requires extensive preparation or multiple court appearances, this may result in more delay than would be typical. If the Crown is able to prove that exceptional circumstances exist, then this period of time will be sub-tracted from the total delay. It should be noted that the seriousness of the offence and a lack of institutional resources are not reasons that fall under exceptional circumstances.

The remedy for a breach of the right to be tried within a reasonable time is a **stay of proceedings**, meaning the charges are dropped and the accused person is free to go.

Remedies for Infringement of Charter Rights (Section 24 of the Charter)

If the actions of the police are found to have infringed the Charter rights of a person ac-cused of an offence, section 24 of the Charter provides options to the judge for providing redress to the accused.

Section 24 is divided into two parts: section 24(1) allows the judge to award "such rem-edy as the court considers appropriate and just in the circumstances"; section 24(2) allows the judge to exclude from the trial any evidence that is found to have been obtained in a manner that infringed a Charter right if "it is established that, having regard to all the cir-cumstances, the admission of [the tainted evidence] in the proceedings would bring the administration of justice into disrepute."

In criminal trials, the second part of the section is used most often. The person alleging the Charter breach and requesting that the evidence be excluded from the trial must estab-lish for the judge that the requirements of section 24(2) have been met.

Once it has been established that the police have infringed on the rights of the accused in obtaining evidence, the accused must establish that the evidence was obtained as a re-sult of the Charter breach. For example, if the police conduct an illegal search of the home of the accused and find a blood-stained shirt, it seems clear that the evidence (the shirt) would not have been found had the police not conducted the illegal search. On the other hand, if the police conduct an illegal search of the home of the accused and, during the search, the accused enters with his or her lawyer and admits to having committed the crime, there does not appear to be a connection between the Charter breach and securing the evidence (the admission of guilt).

The final question to be asked under section 24(2) (once the breach of the right and its connection to finding the evidence are established) is whether admitting the tainted evi-dence in the trial will result in an unfair trial. The common law test for excluding evidence under section 24(2) has three elements:

1. assessing the seriousness of the Charter violation;
2. assessing the impact of the Charter violation on the accused person's protected interests; and
3. assessing the societal interest in adjudication on the merits of the case.

stay of proceedings
a decision by a judge to drop the charges against an accused; usually the result of improper actions on the part of the police or the prosecution

Each of these elements is subjective in nature. The judge must first consider the severity of the Charter breach. If it is a minor breach—a small defect in the form of the search warrant, for example—or if the police officer committed the breach unintentionally and in good faith, the evidence will not likely be excluded. A major breach, on the other hand, or a breach conducted knowingly and in a high-handed way by the police officer (for example, entrapment—where the accused is set up to commit a crime by the police), will generally lead to the exclusion of the evidence.

The judge must then consider the seriousness of the impact of the Charter breach. The more intrusive the violation, the less likely the court will be willing to admit evidence stemming from it.

The final element involves consideration of the reliability of the evidence and the value of it in proving the allegations against the accused person. If the evidence is essential to adjudication and is reliable, then exclusion of it may undermine the truth-seeking function of the criminal justice system.

After applying this three-part test to the facts of a case, the judge will decide whether to admit the tainted evidence and allow the prosecution to use it in its case against the accused. The decision can have a major impact on the outcome of the trial.

Police officers who know and understand how the Charter affects police investigations take pains to always act in a way that ensures that the evidence they discover will not be excluded from trial.

CHAPTER SUMMARY

Before a person can be convicted of a crime, the prosecution must prove all of the elements of the crime beyond a reasonable doubt in criminal court. The evidence needed for this task is collected by the police, who have the power to investigate crime. While many aspects of police investigations are regulated only by police policy, once a suspect has been identified, the police are constrained in how they must deal with that suspect by certain provisions of the *Criminal Code*, the Charter, and the common law.

Police activities regulated by law include the search of persons and places and the seizure of evidence. Police searches, to be valid, must meet three conditions: they must be authorized by law, the authorizing law must be reasonable, and the manner in which the search is conducted must be reasonable.

A suspect also has Charter rights that relate to arrest and detention. A person cannot be arbitrarily detained. A person cannot be deprived of liberty except in accordance with fundamental justice, and a person who has been arrested has the right to know the reasons why, the right to refrain from speaking to police until he or she has had a chance to speak with counsel (for example, a lawyer), and the right to contact counsel without delay.

An accused has the right to make a free and meaningful choice as to whether to speak to the police. Finally, an accused has a right to a trial within a reasonable time after being charged. This right is guaranteed by section 11(b) of the Charter.

Where a person has been searched, detained, or arrested unreasonably, or has been denied a trial within a reasonable time in violation of his or her Charter rights, that person may be entitled to a legal remedy, such as exclusion of the offending evidence at trial or a stay of proceedings.

KEY TERMS

accused, 84
appearance notice, 90
arrest, 90
authorized by law, 86
caution, 91
excluded, 84
fundamental justice, 94

inadmissible, 93
informant, 86
information to obtain a search warrant, 86
person of interest, 84
reasonable, 85
remedy, 85

search and seizure, 84
search warrant, 86
stay of proceedings, 95
summons, 90
suspect, 84
telewarrant, 86
waive, 93

NOTES

1 *Criminal Code*, RSC 1985, c C-46, as amended.

2 *Canadian Charter of Rights and Freedoms*, Part I of the *Constitution Act, 1982*, being Schedule B to the *Canada Act 1982* (UK), 1982, c 11.

3 *R v Collins*, [1987] 1 SCR 265.

4 *Hunter et al v Southam Inc*, [1984] 2 SCR 145.

5 *R v Mann*, 2004 SCC 52, [2004] 3 SCR 59.

6 For a study on suspects' ability to understand cautions, see Joseph Eastwood & Brent Snook, "Comprehending Canadian Police Cautions: Are the Rights to Silence and Legal Counsel Understandable?" (2010) 28:3 Behav Sci & L 366, online: <http://www.mun.ca/psychology/brl/publications/Eastwood__Snook_2009_BSL>.

7 *R v Grant*, 2009 SCC 32.

8 *R v Suberu*, 2009 SCC 33.

9 *R v Singh*, 2007 SCC 48.

10   *R v Liew*, [1999] 3 SCR 227.

11   *R v Jordan*, 2016 SCC 27.

12   *R v Williamson*, 2016 SCC 28.

EXERCISES

Multiple Choice

1. Which of the following is not a requirement of a valid search warrant?

    a. the accused's criminal record

    b. a description of the offence

    c. the location to be searched

    d. the items to be seized

    e. when the search may be conducted

2. The *Charter of Rights and Freedoms* guarantees which of the following rights?

    a. the right of the accused to remain silent

    b. the right of the accused to be advised by a lawyer

    c. the right of all people to earn a living

    d. the right of all people to be free from unreasonable search and seizure

    e. a, b, and d

3. For a police search to be reasonable,

    a. the law that authorizes the search must be reasonable

    b. the way the search is conducted must be reasonable

    c. the procedure for obtaining the search warrant must be followed exactly

    d. all of the above

    e. none of the above

4. Police may conduct a search without a warrant or legal authorization if

    a. the search is incidental to the arrest of a person

    b. the search is consented to by the person searched

    c. the search is consented to by the person in possession of the premises being searched

    d. a and b

    e. a, b, and c

5. The legal right of a police officer to search someone who has been arrested is based in

    a. the common law

    b. the *Charter of Rights and Freedoms*

    c. the *Criminal Code*

    d. a and c

    e. none of the above

True or False?

_____ 1. Items that are not specifically named in a search warrant may be seized if they are in plain view and the officer has reasonable grounds to suspect that they are evidence of the commission of an offence.

_____ 2. The law does not permit police to arrest a suspect without a warrant.

_____ **3.** Section 11(b) of the Charter guarantees an individual's right to counsel upon arrest or detention.

_____ **4.** The Code and the Charter have equal importance and neither has authority over the other.

_____ **5.** Failing to inform an arrested person of his or her rights is a breach of the Charter.

_____ **6.** Even where the police have just arrested an accused person, they must obtain a search warrant to search him or her.

_____ **7.** Detention only occurs where the police physically deprive a suspect of the choice to walk away.

_____ **8.** Articulable cause refers to a reason to stop someone based on information known to the police that indicates that detention is necessary or justified.

_____ **9.** The use of an undercover police officer to observe the accused person's demeanour while the person is in custody is contrary to the Charter.

_____**10.** Where an accused person has chosen to remain silent, the police may use persuasion to attempt to change the person's mind.

Short Answer

1. List three circumstances when police may conduct a search according to the common law.

2. Describe the process by which a judge must decide to admit or exclude evidence that has been obtained in a manner that contravenes the Charter.

3. When is a search considered lawful?

4. What is the common law test for arbitrary detention?

5. What are the factors in determining whether a period of delay is reasonable or not?

Criminal Pre-Trial Issues

7

LEARNING OUTCOMES

After completing this chapter, you should be able to:

- Discuss the difference between section 469 offences (more serious offences) and non–section 469 offences (less serious offences) in the context of bail hearings.

- Identify the issues relevant to the decision to grant or refuse pre-trial release.

- Understand the reasons why an accused may be found mentally unfit to stand trial.

- Describe the different pleas available to an accused and discuss how plea bargains are made.

- Explain the rationale for the Crown's obligation to disclose its evidence to the defence.

Introduction

Canada's justice system requires that any person charged with an offence (whether criminal, quasi-criminal, or other) should have the right to be tried for that offence in a court of law. The person charged with the offence has the right to require the Crown attorney (the prosecutor in a criminal case, who represents the state) to **prove beyond a reasonable doubt** that the accused has in fact committed the offence and that the accused is guilty of the *actus reus* and *mens rea* of the offence. Accused people are also entitled to have a lawyer represent them in the trial to help them defend against the charges.

However, the trial can't be held as soon as the accused is arrested and charged with the offence. It often takes several months, and sometimes several years, before the trial is held. There are many reasons for this delay: the accused and his or her lawyer must have time to prepare for the trial, the police must be allowed to complete their investigation of the offence, time must be found in the court's already busy schedule to conduct the trial, and so on. In fact, our court system is often so overburdened and the delays before trials so long that under the *Canadian Charter of Rights and Freedoms*,[1] protection of an accused's right to be tried within a reasonable time of the laying of charges (s 11(b)) is often invoked by accused people and their lawyers in an effort to have the charges dismissed in court. The right to a trial within a reasonable time was discussed in Chapter 6.

The length of the pre-trial period raises an important question: what do we do with accused people between the time they are arrested and charged and the time they are actually tried? The pre-trial period also allows for other issues and procedural matters to be dealt with before the trial starts. This chapter will discuss some of the pre-trial issues.

Pre-Trial Detention and Bail

As mentioned above, the period of time between the arrest of the accused and the trial is often several months or even a year or more. What is done with the accused during that time? Section 11(d) of the Charter states that the accused has the right "to be presumed innocent until proven guilty according to law in a fair and public hearing." If he or she is presumed innocent, we cannot simply leave the person in prison until the trial; the accused must, in most cases, be set free to await trial. Otherwise, we are presuming his or her guilt before a trial has taken place, given that imprisonment is one of our most serious forms of punishment for those found guilty of an offence.

On the other hand, there are public interest reasons to hold certain accused people in prison pending trial. They may have been charged with a particularly serious crime, they may be likely to commit further serious crimes if released, or they may be likely to flee rather than appear to attend their trial if they are released.

The *Criminal Code*[2] and the common law attempt to balance the interest of the public to be protected from the accused with the accused's right to be presumed innocent and to be protected from arbitrary detention. The Code and the common law do this by creating procedures by which a justice (either a judge or a justice of the peace) decides whether the accused should be released or kept in custody while awaiting the trial.

These procedures are divided into two categories, depending on the seriousness of the offence. For less serious charges (those not listed in s 469 of the Code), the accused must be granted a bail hearing at which he or she must be granted an unconditional release unless the Crown can **show cause** for detaining the accused or for placing conditions on his or her release. For serious charges (those listed in s 469 of the Code: treason, alarming Her Majesty, intimidating Parliament, inciting to mutiny, sedition, piracy, piratical acts, or murder), the accused is held in prison pending trial unless he or she makes an application to be released.

The following is a brief discussion of these two procedures.

Bail and Less Serious Offences

For charges based on less serious or **non–section 469 offences**, section 503 of the *Criminal Code* provides that the accused is entitled to be brought in front of a justice of the peace within 24 hours of the initial arrest and detention. This section describes the responsibilities of police officers to ensure that individuals arrested either with or without a warrant be brought before a justice and dealt with according to the law. Failure to do this may be considered a violation of a person's right to be free from arbitrary detention (s 9 of the Charter).

It may, however, not be practical for a bail hearing (which is described in s 515 of the Code) to proceed right away. The accused's lawyer, for example, may need time to assemble the evidence and witnesses they need to persuade the justice to release the accused. Under section 516 of the Code, the justice presiding over the **bail** (or **judicial interim release**) hearing may grant an adjournment (postponement), of no more than three days, at the request of either the defence or the prosecution. The justice may grant a longer adjournment, but only with the consent of the accused.

non–section 469 offence
a less serious *Criminal Code* offence for which, at a bail hearing, the onus is on the prosecution to show cause why the accused should not be released pending trial

bail
the release of a person accused of a crime before trial, with or without conditions

judicial interim release
bail; also known as pre-trial release

CASE IN POINT

Can Police Delay a Bail Hearing to Prolong Interrogation?

In 2006, the Ontario Court of Appeal, considering the trial decision in *R v Mangat*, agreed that an investigating officer's decision to keep an accused from a prompt bail hearing in order to obtain an inculpatory statement violated section 9 of the Charter, which guarantees the right to be free from arbitrary detention.

Mangat was arrested as an accessory to a robbery. It was alleged that he masterminded, though didn't physically participate in, a scheme to steal the bank deposit bag from a fellow Rogers Video store employee while the employee walked to the bank.

Mangat was arrested at 7:10 a.m. on October 19, 2001, which would have meant that the outer limit of acceptable delay, before he could be brought before a bail court, would have been 7:10 a.m. on October 20. He was taken before the bail judge at 8:30 a.m. on October 20 instead.

The trial judge ruled that the reason for the delay was that investigators were determined to get Mangat to make an inculpatory statement (admission of guilt) before he was granted bail. The investigators interrogated Mangat all day on the 19th and did in fact get him to make an inculpatory statement.

The trial judge awarded Mangat a stay of proceedings as a remedy for the Charter breach. Normally, an order excluding

evidence is the more appropriate choice of remedy in this type of case; however, excluding the inculpatory statement as a Charter remedy would have been redundant in Mangat's case, because the court had already excluded the statement on the basis that it was not voluntary. For this reason, the trial judge awarded Mangat a stay of proceedings (an order that ends the trial with no conviction).

The Court of Appeal, though it agreed that the 80-minute excessive delay did amount to a Charter breach, overturned the stay of proceedings remedy and awarded the (redundant) exclusion-of-evidence order instead, saying it was an adequate remedy.

Questions for Discussion

1. What do you think of this decision generally? Do you believe that the decision represents a fair balance between the accused's right to freedom and the investigative powers and duties of the police? Why or why not?

2. Why did the trial judge order a remedy that precludes the conviction of the accused? Do you think this remedy was chosen for any purpose *other* than to compensate Mangat for the delayed bail hearing? Discuss.

Source: *R v Mangat* (2006), 209 CCC (3d) 225 (Ont CA).

Onus at the Hearing

onus
burden of proof;
the necessity for a
certain party to prove
a certain fact

condition
a requirement that limits
the freedom of an accused
who has been released
on bail or on parole

recognizance
a promise; in the context
of a bail hearing, a promise
to return for trial

reverse onus
a situation where, instead
of the prosecution being
required to prove all
aspects of an offence
(which is the norm),
the accused bears the
burden of proving a
fact or allegation

primary ground
a ground for ordering
detention of an accused
at a bail hearing for a
non–section 469 offence;
based on the judge's belief
that the accused is unlikely
to appear at trial if released

secondary ground
a ground for ordering
detention of an accused
at a bail hearing for a
non–section 469 offence;
based on the judge's belief
that the accused poses
a danger to the public

tertiary ground
a ground for ordering
detention of an accused
at a bail hearing for a
non–section 469 offence;
based on the judge's
belief that detention is
necessary to maintain
confidence in the
administration of justice

At the hearing, the **onus**, or burden of proof, is on the Crown to prove, on a balance of probabilities, that the accused either should not be released at all pending trial or should be released on certain **conditions**. If the Crown fails to meet this onus, the accused must be released on his or her own **recognizance** (promise to return for the trial). This is covered by section 515 of the Code.

Section 515(6), however, describes certain situations where the onus to demonstrate why the accused should be released shifts to the accused, even though he or she is charged with a less serious (non–s 469) offence. This is called a **reverse onus** because it reverses the general rule that, because of the presumption of innocence, the prosecution is required to prove the accused's guilt rather than the accused being required to prove his or her own innocence. The reverse-onus situations are as follows:

1. The accused is charged with committing a non–section 469 indictable offence while on bail for another indictable offence.

2. The accused is charged with committing a non–section 469 indictable offence under section 467.11, 467.111, 467.12, or 467.13 (in connection with organized crime).

3. The accused is charged with an offence relating to terrorism, such as those in sections 83.02 to 83.04, and 83.18 to 83.23.

4. The accused is charged with an offence under the *Security of Information Act*[3] (see s 515(6) for the specific list of offences).

5. The accused is charged with a non–section 469 indictable offence and does not ordinarily live in Canada (s 515(6)(b)).

6. The accused is charged with committing an offence under sections 145(2) to (5) while the accused was free after being released in respect of another offence under section 679, 680, or 816 (s 515(6)(c)).

7. The accused is charged with committing an offence punishable by life imprisonment under sections 5 to 7 of the *Controlled Drugs and Substances Act*[4] or is charged with conspiring to commit such an offence (s 515(6)(d)).

8. The accused is charged with an offence under section 99, 100, or 103 (weapons trafficking), or an offence under section 239, 272, 273, 279(1), 279.1, 344, or 346 when that offence is alleged to have been committed using a firearm or, where the accused is under a weapons prohibition order relating to certain weapons listed in section 515(6), with a weapon covered by the prohibition order.

This last reverse-onus category was created in 2006, as part of a government initiative to crack down on gun crime in the wake of a gun-crime peak in Ontario in 2005—a year that became known in the media as the "Year of the Gun."

In these situations, the accused must show why he or she should not be detained.

Grounds for Ordering Detention

At the end of the show cause hearing, the justice may order detention, release without conditions, or release with conditions. Detention may be ordered on any of three grounds:

1. the **primary ground** that detention is necessary to ensure that the accused appears in court (s 515(10)(a)),

2. the **secondary ground** that detention is necessary to protect the public (s 515(10)(b)), or

3. the **tertiary ground** that detention is necessary to maintain confidence in the administration of justice (s 515(10)(c)).

The justice must consider each ground on its own merit, and it may be the case that concerns exist on more than one ground. Figure 7.1 demonstrates the justice's considerations upon deciding whether or not to release an accused person on bail. Note that not all considerations may apply in a particular case.

Under section 515(10)(c), the justice may consider a number of factors, including: the strength of the Crown's case, the seriousness of the offence, the circumstances surrounding how the offence was committed—including the use of a firearm, and whether the accused is facing the potential of a lengthy term of imprisonment, or where there is a minimum term of imprisonment of three years for a firearms-related offence. The constitutionality of section 515(10)(c) was challenged in the case of *R v Hall*.

Evidence at the Hearing

Section 518 sets out the evidence that may be presented at a show cause hearing. As in a trial, the prosecution can present evidence at the bail hearing that tends to prove that the accused committed the offence. The rules of evidence for bail hearings are, however, much more open than they are for a trial.

To prove that the accused should not be released, for example, the Crown may present evidence that the accused has a criminal record or that the accused is, at that time, charged with other offences. At the trial, the Crown generally can't present evidence of the accused's criminal record, since this evidence is considered too prejudicial to the accused.

FIGURE 7.1   Justice Considerations on Bail

Charter Challenge of the Tertiary Ground

The accused, David Scott Hall, was charged with first-degree murder in the death of his cousin's wife. The victim had been stabbed 37 times in her neck, face, shoulders, arms, and back. Her neck had been cut to the vertebrae. The Crown's case against Hall was strong: there were traces of his blood in the victim's home, footprint impressions with the victim's blood and matching the type of shoes worn by the accused were found in the kitchen, and a surveillance photo showed the accused wearing those shoes on the night of the murder. A police officer testified that there was a general sense of fear that the killer was at large.

The accused applied for judicial interim release, and the judge denied bail on the tertiary ground. Neither the primary nor the secondary grounds were of concern, given that the accused had community and family ties, sufficient sureties were proposed, and there were no reasons to believe that the accused would commit another offence if released on bail with the proper conditions. However, the judge felt that the accused's detention was justified on the tertiary ground—to maintain confidence in the administration of justice, in light of the aftermath of the murder and the strength of the evidence against the accused.

The judge's decision to deny bail was upheld by the Superior Court and the Ontario Court of Appeal. The accused appealed to the Supreme Court of Canada, arguing that section 515(10)(c) should be declared unconstitutional because it violated the presumption of innocence and the right not to be denied reasonable bail except for just cause, as guaranteed under the Charter.

Source: *R v Hall*, 2002 SCC 64.

The Supreme Court of Canada held that the specific provision under section 515(10)(c) permitting detention "on any other just cause being shown" was unconstitutional because it allowed for an open-ended judicial discretion to refuse bail. The provision was too vague and imprecise. However, the balance of section 515(10)(c) was held to be valid. This section provided a basis for denial of bail not covered by the primary and secondary grounds. It may not have been used frequently, but it did provide a means to deny bail where public confidence was essential to the proper functioning of the judicial system. There was a proper balance between the rights of the accused and the need to maintain justice in the community.

In dismissing the appeal, the Supreme Court held that the offending phrase "on any other just cause being shown" ought to be severed from section 515(10)(c), and that the remainder of the provision was constitutionally valid.

Questions for Discussion

1. Locate and read section 515(10)(c). Are the factors listed under the tertiary ground simply a means of satisfying the public, or are these valid considerations in determining whether or not an accused person should be released on bail?

2. Do factors such as the strength of the Crown's case and the seriousness of the offence have an impact on whether the accused person is a suitable candidate for bail, if he or she does not pose a risk on the primary or secondary grounds?

---

hearsay evidence
information that comes from a source that does not have direct knowledge of the truth of the information

Other forms of evidence that may not be admissible at trial may be presented at the show cause hearing. **Hearsay evidence**—where one person gives evidence as to what another person said outside of court—is generally admissible at the bail hearing but not at trial. This often takes the form of "will say" evidence, where a police officer testifies at the bail hearing as to what various witnesses will say at trial. At the bail hearing, for example, a police officer may give evidence as simple as "Raj Singh will say at trial that he saw Bob Jones stab the victim." At trial, Raj Singh will be required to appear and give this evidence himself so that the defence lawyers can cross-examine him and test his evidence.

Forms of Release

The forms of release set out under sections 515(1) and (2) of the *Criminal Code* are similar to rungs on a ladder: the court must consider whether the least onerous form of release is justified under the circumstances, as illustrated in the diagram below.

Figure 7.2 outlines the forms of release that a justice may consider, from the least oner-ous at the bottom, to an order of detention (where the accused remains in custody until the trial).

For less serious offences, our justice system assumes that the accused will be released on his or her own undertaking at the bail hearing. If the Crown has shown cause, how-ever, the justice may order other bail conditions or order that the accused be detained in jail.

Bail with conditions means that the accused is released as long as he or she complies with certain requirements as set out by the justice. The conditions that may be imposed are set out in section 515(2) of the *Criminal Code*. They include giving an **undertaking** (promise) and entering into a recognizance with or without **sureties** (money guarantees) and with or without a **deposit**. If, after bail has been granted, the justice is satisfied that the accused has contravened or is about to contravene any summons or appearance notices or has committed an indictable offence, the justice can revoke or cancel bail and issue an ar-rest warrant, as described in section 524 of the Code.

undertaking
a promise or monetary payment made as security for a recognizance

sureties
monetary guarantees that a person will appear at court to answer the charges against him or her; this money is forfeited if the accused does not appear as required

deposit
partial payment of a surety

FIGURE 7.2   Forms of Release or Order of Detention by a Justice

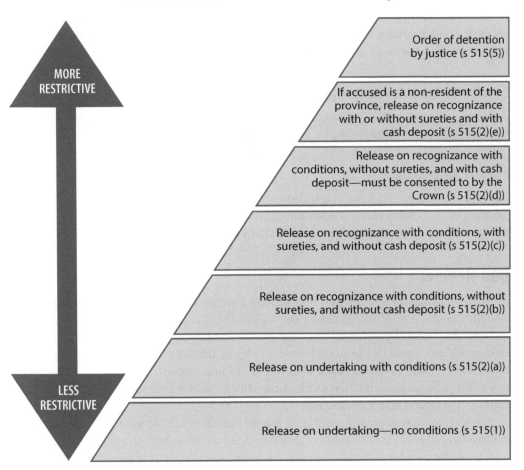

Forms of Release or Order of Detention by a Justice

MORE RESTRICTIVE

LESS RESTRICTIVE

Order of detention by justice (s 515(5))

If accused is a non-resident of the province, release on recognizance with or without sureties and with cash deposit (s 515(2)(e))

Release on recognizance with conditions, without sureties, and with cash deposit—must be consented to by the Crown (s 515(2)(d))

Release on recognizance with conditions, with sureties, and without cash deposit (s 515(2)(c))

Release on recognizance with conditions, without sureties, and without cash deposit (s 515(2)(b))

Release on undertaking with conditions (s 515(2)(a))

Release on undertaking—no conditions (s 515(1))

Bail and More Serious Offences

Whereas bail hearings may be held by judges or justices of the peace for less serious offences, bail hearings for **section 469 offences** fall within the jurisdiction of a superior court judge (Superior Court of Justice, in Ontario). The rules governing release hearings for persons charged with section 469 crimes are set out in section 522 of the Code.

Onus at the Hearing

People who are accused of a section 469 offence do not have an automatic right to a bail hearing. They must apply to the superior court judge to be granted such a hearing. Because they are accused of serious offences, once they have applied for a hearing they face the onus of proving to the judge, on a **balance of probabilities**, that they should be released. If they fail to do so, they must be detained until the trial. Proving something on a balance of probabilities means proving that it is more likely to be true than not true. This is a lower standard of proof than the "beyond a reasonable doubt" standard that must be achieved to support a conviction at trial.

Grounds for Ordering Release

The judge must have grounds for ordering that a person accused of a section 469 offence be released. These grounds are, in general, the reverse of the grounds for detention listed above for bail hearings involving less serious offences. To be released, accused persons must prove that they will appear at the trial and that they are not a threat to the public.

Evidence at the Hearing

According to section 522(5), the rules of evidence at the bail hearing for a section 469 offence are similar to those for the bail hearing for a non–section 469 offence.

Forms of Release

It is rare for a person accused of a section 469 offence to be granted unconditional release pending trial. In most cases, if release is granted, it will be subject to some fairly serious conditions, including the posting of significant sureties.

Bail Review

An accused person or a prosecutor may request a review of a detention or release order (or a condition of either of them) before the trial starts. The review provisions are found in section 520 (review by accused) and section 521 (review by prosecutor). In Ontario, review applications must be brought before a judge of the Superior Court of Justice. These reviews apply only to orders made with respect to non–section 469 charges; a release or detention order made in relation to a section 469 charge is reviewable only by the court of appeal, as provided under section 680.

The accused may apply for a bail review either to allow him or her to be released from detention, or to remove or change conditions placed on his or her release. The prosecution may apply for a bail review to convince the judge that the accused should in fact be detained or should face more onerous conditions upon release.

New evidence may be introduced at a bail review hearing, including evidence of the behaviour of the accused since the original bail hearing. The judge may decide simply to dismiss the review application and leave the bail order as is or modify the order, as long as the modifications still comply with the law of bail.

Post-trial bail—bail granted to a person awaiting the appeal of a conviction—will not be dealt with here.

Fitness to Stand Trial

The mental condition and cognitive capacity of the accused always play a role in a criminal trial. As discussed in Chapter 5, most offences include a mental element (the *mens rea*), without which the accused cannot be found guilty. So, the mental condition of the accused at the time the offence took place is a very important issue. If, because of some form of **mental disorder**, the accused was incapable of having the mental intent required for the offence, he or she cannot be found guilty of the offence.

The mental condition of the accused at the time of the trial is also important. For a trial to be fair, the accused must be cognitively and psychologically capable of understanding what is going on; of understanding the consequences he or she faces as a result of the trial; and of understanding, instructing, and receiving advice from his or her lawyer. If the accused is cognitively or psychologically incapable of these things, the trial cannot proceed.

Defence counsel, the prosecutor, or the court may bring an application under section 672.23(1) of the *Criminal Code* to determine the accused's **fitness to stand trial**. A person is deemed "unfit to stand trial," as defined under section 2, if he or she is

> unable on account of mental disorder to conduct a defence at any stage of the proceedings before a verdict is rendered or to instruct counsel to do so, and, in particular, unable on account of mental disorder to
> (a) understand the nature or object of the proceedings,
> (b) understand the possible consequences of the proceedings, or
> (c) communicate with counsel.

A person who is found to be unfit to stand trial may be committed to a mental health care facility until either he or she is fit to stand trial or he or she is acquitted because the Crown cannot establish a *prima facie* case against the accused. Being unfit to stand trial does not save the accused from facing the charges, and perhaps being convicted of them— it simply delays the trial.

It is important to note that an accused's mental condition can change over time. The person may be capable of forming the intent required for an offence at the time of committing it but may not be capable of standing trial several months later. On the other hand, the accused may not be cognitively or psychologically capable of forming the requisite intent at the time of committing the offence, yet be capable of standing trial when the trial date arrives.

Disclosure

The police investigate the commission of offences. From their investigations, they determine who they believe committed a particular offence and provide evidence to the prosecution that tends to prove that the accused committed the offence. The prosecution uses this evidence at trial.

Accused people do not have a police force working for them to prove their innocence. In almost all cases, they do not have the resources to conduct an independent investigation

mental disorder
a disease or condition of the mind under section 16 of the *Criminal Code* that results in the accused lacking the mental ability to intend to commit a crime

fitness to stand trial
the accused's mental competence, at the time of trial, to understand the trial and what is at stake and to communicate with counsel

of the offence to check the work of the police and to discover evidence the police may have missed that might prove that someone else committed the crime.

Since our criminal justice system is based on the presumption of innocence, and since the common law (arising out of s 7 of the Charter) has determined that accused people have a right to know the case that will be made against them and to make full answer and defence to that case, we have developed a system of **disclosure** that requires the police to provide all evidence to the Crown, and the Crown to provide to accused people and their lawyers all evidence in its possession related to the particular offence. This is often called Crown disclosure.

The accused's right to be able to make **full answer and defence** is at the core of our notion of fundamental justice, as set out in section 7 of the Charter. Full answer and defence involves not only the opportunity for the accused to present his or her case at trial but also the accused's right to know what evidence the Crown has against him or her, to have an opportunity to contest and refute that evidence, and to know of any evidence that the police have found that may tend to prove that the accused did not, in fact, commit the offence or that another person did.

This introduces the issue of **culpability**. Culpability means guilt or responsibility. A culpable person is responsible for or guilty of an offence. Evidence is **inculpatory** if it tends to prove that the accused committed the offence; evidence is **exculpatory** if it tends to prove that the accused did not commit the offence.

So, the accused and his or her lawyers have the right to request that *all* relevant evidence be disclosed to them by the Crown before the trial begins so that they have the opportunity to prepare for the trial. All relevant evidence must be disclosed, whether the material is inculpatory or exculpatory, and regardless of whether the Crown intends to introduce the evidence at trial or rely on it as part of the Crown's case.

The initial disclosure should be provided before the accused is asked to choose a mode of trial (by judge or by judge and jury) or to plead (guilty or not guilty; see below). There is also a continuing obligation on the Crown to disclose new information and evidence, as it is uncovered or discovered, to the accused. These disclosure obligations are not reciprocal; the defendant is not obliged to disclose his or her own evidence (with a single exception, discussed in Chapter 8) to the Crown. This apparent imbalance is intended to address the imbalance in power between the accused (an individual, often with no resources) and the Crown (a government agency, with an entire police force providing it with investigative resources).

The disclosure requirement extends through the Crown prosecutors to the investigating police officers themselves. The police have a statutory and common law duty to disclose to the Crown prosecutor all relevant information that has been discovered during an investigation, even if that evidence tends to prove the innocence of the person the police believe committed the offence. If the police fail to do this, the accused is entitled to a remedy. If evidence has been lost or destroyed either by the police or by the prosecution and this loss affects an accused person's ability to make full answer and defence, the charges may be stayed.

A judicial stay of proceedings is a ruling that stops the prosecution altogether. To be granted a stay, the defence must establish that the accused's right to a fair trial has been denied or irreparably harmed, or that the non-disclosure was in bad faith (motivated by improper reasons) or constitutes an **abuse of process**—an improper action or series of actions on the part of the police that undermines the fairness of the criminal procedure.

Police officers must also provide a copy of their notes as part of disclosure. They also have a duty to prepare accurate, detailed, and comprehensive notes as soon as practicable after an offence has been committed. This duty was mentioned by the Supreme Court of Canada in the case of *Wood v Schaeffer*.[5]

disclosure
the requirement that the prosecution provide to the defence any and all evidence relevant to the charges against an accused

full answer and defence
a principle of fundamental justice whereby the accused person must be provided with the information and the means to have the opportunity to defend against the charges

culpability
guilt or responsibility

inculpatory
proving guilt; of evidence, tending to show that a person committed an offence

exculpatory
proving innocence; of evidence, tending to show that a person did not commit an offence

abuse of process
a course of action on the part of the police or the prosecution that misuses court process or ignores the spirit of that process and interferes with the accused's ability to make full answer and defence, threatening to bring the administration of justice into disrepute

CASE IN POINT

Charges Against the Arresting Officer—the Accused's Business?

In general, most people hold the view that a person is entitled to privacy about his or her criminal record—as long as that record doesn't affect others. But would we let a cocaine-buying police officer investigate a cocaine trafficker?

The 2007 Ontario Court of Appeal decision in *R v McNeil* focused on the issue of whether an accused in a drug-trafficking case was entitled to disclosure of the fact that the officer that had arrested him was himself facing drug charges.

McNeil, the accused, was arrested by members of the Barrie Police Service, charged with possession of marijuana and cocaine for the purpose of trafficking, and convicted. Constable Rodney Hackett, one of the arresting officers, was the main witness for the prosecution at trial.

After his conviction but before he was sentenced, McNeil learned that Constable Hackett had himself run into drug trouble. At the time McNeil was awaiting sentencing, Hackett, who lived in the same municipality, was subject to both a police disciplinary proceeding and a set of criminal charges relating to cocaine possession and abuse.

McNeil brought a motion requesting full disclosure, from the Crown, of the information related to Hackett's charges, to assist him in preparing for an appeal. After considering the law relating to "third party records," the court ordered the third parties to produce the criminal investigation files in their possession related to the charges against Hackett to the federal Crown prosecuting McNeil's case.

Constable Hackett pleaded guilty to one of the charges against him. The admission about Hackett's conviction was admitted into the record at McNeil's appeal. As a result, McNeil's convictions were set aside. The Crown chose not to undertake a new trial against McNeil. In its written endorsement of the appeal decision, the Court of Appeal noted:

We ... agree that the proposed fresh evidence could well have affected the verdict, not only because it would have affected the trial judge's assessment of the arresting officer's credibility but also his assessment of the officer's motive for approaching the appellant. As was already noted by Simmons JA in the original decision on this motion regarding disclosure of documents (*R v McNeil*, [2006] OJ No. 4746), because of Constable Hackett's cocaine habit, "there is a reasonable possibility that evidence of the underlying misconduct would be admissible to support an inference that the arresting officer had an ulterior motive for approaching the appellant."

The *McNeil* case ultimately went before the Supreme Court of Canada to resolve a technical disclosure issue; the Supreme Court did not disturb (change) the Court of Appeal's finding that McNeil was entitled to early and voluntary disclosure, from the Crown, of the information about Constable Hackett's drug charges and conviction.

Questions for Discussion

1. It is not clear, from this summary, how the accused came to learn of the charges against the investigating officer. Do you believe that police and Crown personnel should be subject to a duty to volunteer information about their criminal records, or criminal charges pending against them?

2. What are the "risks" (practical, constitutional, administrative) associated with the court's finding that accused are entitled to disclosure relating to the personal lives of investigative personnel? Where would you draw the line with respect to this disclosure?

Source: *R v McNeil*, 2009 SCC 3, 2007 ONCA 646.

Remedies for Non-Disclosure

If the Crown does not make full disclosure to the defence, several remedies can be granted by the court. The court grants a remedy by making an order—a formal decision bearing the seal of the court.

- The court can grant an **adjournment** (postponement of the trial to a later date) to allow the defence to incorporate previously undisclosed evidence into their case.

- A **mistrial** can be declared. A mistrial ends the trial without imposing a conviction (or granting an acquittal) and it forces the Crown to begin its case again with a new jury, giving the accused more time to prepare.

- A judicial stay of proceedings can be granted, meaning the accused is free to go, although it is possible that the Crown will lay the charge again.

adjournment
postponement of a trial

mistrial
a declaration by a judge that the trial of an accused cannot be allowed to continue because of unfairness to the accused, and that a new trial must be conducted

- The judge may disregard the evidence that was not disclosed and withhold it from the jury in a jury trial, forcing the Crown to prove that the accused is guilty without having the benefit of the tainted evidence.
- The Crown may be ordered to pay the accused's legal costs incurred as a result of the Crown's failure to disclose the evidence.

Diversion Programs

diversion program
an alternative to a criminal proceeding; typically available to an accused person who does not have a criminal record and who is charged with a very minor offence

Diversion programs are an alternative to prosecution. The rationale behind diversion is that not all criminal charges need to be dealt with through the court process and a criminal prosecution. The Crown determines which cases are eligible for diversion since it is up to the Crown to make decisions regarding the prosecution of a case. Diversion is usually considered where an accused person has a minimal or no criminal record, and the offence is very minor in nature.

Cases may be pre-approved for diversion by the Crown even before the information is laid. In other situations, the **charge screening form** may indicate that the case has been pre-approved for diversion.

charge screening form
a form filled in by Crown counsel that sets out the charge(s) the Crown will be proceeding on and the penalty the Crown will be seeking upon a guilty plea or upon conviction after trial

The accused must either accept or reject the offer of diversion. Agreeing to diversion does not involve an admission of guilt regarding the offence. However, there are consequences that stem from it. An accused person must accept responsibility for the charge and must be willing to comply with the terms of the program. Each courthouse or jurisdiction may offer slightly different programs, depending on the location and availability. Examples of diversion programs include community service work, counselling sessions for anger management or addictions, or making a charitable donation to a non-profit community or charitable organization.

Some courthouses have direct accountability programs, which are available to adults who have had limited or no prior involvement in the criminal justice system and who have been charged with a minor criminal offence. Direct accountability programs involve a **community justice worker**, who assists the accused in setting up counselling sessions or in finding a suitable placement for community service hours. The community justice worker also verifies with the Crown that the conditions of diversion have been satisfied.

community justice worker
person who attends court on a regular basis, receives referrals from the Crown for diversion, and assists the accused in registering for and fulfilling the conditions

Once the conditions have been satisfied, the Crown may stay the charge or withdraw the charge. Once the charge is stayed or withdrawn, it does not result in a criminal conviction on the accused's record. Therefore, participating in and completing a diversion program is beneficial to the accused.

Pleas and Plea Bargaining

plea
a statement of a legal position (guilty or not guilty); a legal argument or basis for a claim

The first step in the trial process is entering the accused's **plea** into the trial record. However, before a plea is entered, the prosecution and the accused may choose to negotiate a plea bargain.

Plea Bargains

plea bargain
an agreement between the defence and the prosecution as to how the accused will plead and what punishment the prosecution will seek

A **plea bargain** is a negotiated agreement between the prosecution and the accused as to how to settle one or more charges against the accused. The purpose of a plea bargain is either to narrow the scope of the trial, so that it focuses only on the best-founded charge(s) (which saves trial costs and the justice system's time), or to avoid a trial altogether. In general, in negotiating a plea bargain, the Crown is looking to gain a guaranteed conviction or to obtain a conviction to a lesser charge when the evidence does not support the original charge; and the accused is asking, in exchange, for leniency when it comes to sentencing. Because avoiding an unnecessary trial saves the public money, the court has a public policy interest in supporting plea bargaining. The judge is not obligated to accept the sentencing suggestions put forward by the parties as part of a plea bargain, but he or she is motivated to do so, based on public policy.

The bargain may include the accused agreeing to plead guilty to one charge and the prosecution agreeing to withdraw another. It may involve the accused and the prosecution agreeing to a guilty plea on a lesser but included offence (see s 662)—for example, a plea of guilty to assault when the accused is charged with assault causing bodily harm. A plea bargain may also include both the Crown and defence making a joint submission to the judge that a particular sentence ought to be imposed on the accused.

Plea bargains struck between the Crown prosecutors and the lawyers for the defence are discussed before the judge only when an agreement is reached. If an accused offers to plead guilty to a lesser but included offence and the Crown prosecutor refuses to accept the offer, the Crown may not then attempt to use the accused's offer to plead guilty to the lesser offence as evidence to prove that the accused is guilty of the original offence. Plea discussions are made in confidence that they will not be repeated in court if the matter does not resolve in a guilty plea.

Section 606(4) allows the court, with the consent of the prosecution, to accept a guilty plea for another offence arising out of the same circumstances without drafting a new information. The other offence is not necessarily included in the offence charged, but it must arise out of the same incident. For example, a person charged with attempted murder may plead guilty to assault. The facts supporting attempted murder (an attack on the victim) also support assault. This saves a great deal of time and resources, since the Crown does not have to go through the whole process of laying a new charge when a plea bargain is made.

Plea bargains are considered essential to an efficient justice system because they encourage guilty pleas and reduce the number of cases that actually go to trial.

Plea Options

According to sections 606 and 607 of the Code, the accused person has four plea options. He or she can

1. plead guilty,
2. plead not guilty,
3. plead not guilty as charged but guilty to a lesser, included offence or other offence, or
4. enter a special plea.

Guilty Plea

If the accused pleads guilty to the charges, there is no need for a trial, and the court proceeds directly to the step of sentencing. Sentencing is discussed in greater detail in Chapter 9.

Not Guilty Plea

If the accused pleads not guilty, the Crown must prove beyond a reasonable doubt at trial that the accused committed the offence. If the accused does not enter a plea, he or she is deemed to have pleaded not guilty.

Not Guilty as Charged but Guilty of Lesser or Other Offence

As noted in the discussion of plea bargains above, the accused may reach an agreement with the prosecution to plead not guilty as charged but guilty to a lesser offence or to another offence arising out of the same incident.

Special Plea

special plea
a statement, other than guilty or not guilty, made by an accused when he or she is required to enter a plea to the charges

A **special plea**, described under section 607 of the Code, is one that does not depend on the question of guilt or innocence. Instead, it invokes the common law principle of *res judicata*. If the accused has already been charged with and tried for an offence (has gone through a trial), he or she cannot be retried for the same crime arising out of the same circumstances. Often called "double jeopardy," this situation is prohibited by the principle of **res judicata** (Latin, meaning "the issue has already been decided"). Where an accused believes that the prosecution is seeking to retry him or her for a crime that has already been addressed by the court system, the accused can enter a special plea of either *autrefois acquit* or *autrefois convict*. These pleas arise in very specific and rare situations and are governed by sections 607 to 611 of the Code.

res judicata
Latin for "already decided"; a special plea with which the accused argues that the charges against him or her have already been dealt with in a court of law

Autrefois Acquit

acquit
find an accused not guilty of an offence

If the accused has already been tried and **acquitted**, he or she cannot be retried for the same offence but may enter the special plea of **autrefois acquit** (French, meaning "previously acquitted") under section 607(1)(a) of the Code. This plea is not generally available where the accused has been tried but the trial has ended in a stay of proceedings or other outcome that does not result in an acquittal.

autrefois acquit
French for "previously acquitted"; a special plea by which the accused alleges that he or she has already been charged, tried, and acquitted of the offence that is currently being charged

Autrefois Convict

If the Crown tries to initiate the same charge after having obtained a conviction of the accused for the charge in the past, the accused can enter the special plea of **autrefois convict** (French, meaning "previously convicted") under section 607(1)(b). If the Crown can distinguish between the charges (prove that the new charge arises out of different circumstances than did the first), the multiple convictions may survive.

autrefois convict
French for "previously convicted"; a special plea by which the accused states that he or she has already been charged, tried, and convicted of the offence that is currently being charged

Elections

election
choice

As discussed in Chapter 5, the way a charge is to be tried—by way of summary conviction or by way of indictment—has an impact on the court in which the trial will be held and who the trier of fact will be. If the offence charged is a hybrid offence, the prosecution makes the first **election**: whether it wishes to try the accused by way of summary conviction or indictment.

Trial by summary conviction involves no preliminary hearing. The trial is held in the provincial court (for example, in the Ontario Court of Justice) before a judge alone. No jury is involved.

Trial by indictment gives the accused the right to a preliminary hearing (also called a preliminary inquiry; see below) unless the accused waives the right, either by

- electing to be tried by a provincial court judge (without a jury), or
- waiving the preliminary hearing while still electing to proceed in the superior court (in Ontario, the Superior Court of Justice).

In some cases, a preliminary hearing will also be dispensed with when the attorney general for the province takes the unusual step of preferring the indictment (forcing the matter to trial without holding a preliminary hearing). For more information on preferred indictments, see section 574 of the Code.

Trial by indictment also gives the accused the right to elect the mode of trial: (1) in front of a provincial court judge alone, (2) in front of a judge of the superior court alone, or (3) in superior court with a judge and jury.

Once the accused has made his or her election, the accused has only limited rights to change his or her mind, or to re-elect. If the initial election was to proceed in the provincial court, the accused has until 14 days before the scheduled start date for the trial to re-elect to have the trial in the superior court (in front of a judge or a judge and jury).

If the initial election was to proceed in the superior court with a judge alone, the accused has until 15 days after the end of the preliminary hearing to re-elect either to proceed in the superior court by judge and jury or to proceed in the provincial court before a judge.

If the initial election was to proceed in the superior court with a judge and jury, the accused has until 15 days after the end of the preliminary hearing to re-elect either to proceed in the superior court by judge alone or to proceed in the provincial court before a judge.

If the accused wants to re-elect and change his or her mind at any other time, he or she must obtain the consent of the prosecution to the re-election.

The choice of mode of trial can be a very important tactical one. The provincial court route is often faster. The choice between a superior court judge alone and a judge and jury may depend on the complexity of the evidence, on the seriousness of the offence, or on many other factors. If the prosecution is proposing to introduce certain kinds of evidence that may have a tendency to make the accused "look bad," the accused and his or her lawyers may feel that a judge alone, who may be accustomed to considering such evidence, will be more likely to return a fair verdict than a jury would be.

For example, a judge who is used to hearing the evidence of young children may be better able to focus on the content of the evidence rather than on his or her feelings of sympathy for the child witness. Or, where the prosecution will be introducing evidence of past behaviour (called "similar fact evidence"), which is admissible only to prove or disprove one aspect of the offence, an experienced judge may be better able to avoid coming to the conclusion that, for example, "once a violent drunk, always a violent drunk." The general belief is that members of the public on a jury are more likely to be improperly influenced against the accused upon hearing sensitive evidence and therefore less likely to accept technical defences in such cases than a judge might be.

Preliminary Inquiry

In the following discussion, keep in mind that preliminary inquiries are available only for indictable offences tried in the superior court and that an accused can waive his or her right to a preliminary inquiry.

Once a not-guilty plea has been entered for an indictable offence, a **preliminary inquiry**, or "prelim," will usually be conducted before the trial in accordance with part XVIII of the *Criminal Code*. The purpose of the prelim is to force the Crown to prove to a judge that the available evidence is sufficient to require the accused to stand trial for the offence charged. This inquiry is often called a **charge screening device**.

preliminary inquiry
a judicial hearing where the prosecution must demonstrate that it has enough evidence to prove, if uncontested and accepted by the trier of fact, that the accused is guilty of the charges against him or her

charge screening device
see preliminary inquiry

As provided in section 548, before trials of certain offences, provincial court judges will hold a hearing to inquire into the charge and determine whether there is sufficient evidence to warrant placing the accused on trial (often called "committing" the accused to trial). On hearing the evidence, the judge will either order the accused to stand trial or discharge the accused.

The test at the preliminary inquiry is whether there is sufficient evidence that, if believed, could result in a conviction. The test must be met with respect to each offence (count) charged. Where an accused is charged with more than one offence, the judge may find that there is sufficient evidence to support a trial on some of the charges but not others. In this case, the judge will **commit** the accused to stand trial only on those supported charges. Where the evidence at the preliminary hearing warrants, the judge can also commit the accused to trial for new offences or counts that were not part of the original set of charges. If an accused is not committed on any of the charges, he or she is discharged. This means the accused is free to go.

commit
declare an accused ready to stand trial after the preliminary inquiry, if any, has been completed, and the accused's not-guilty plea has been accepted by the court and entered into the trial record; this act is known as the "committal"

CHAPTER SUMMARY

There is generally a delay between the time of the charges being laid and the date of the trial because time must be found in the court's busy schedule to conduct the trial and because considerable preparation, on the parts of both the accused and the prosecution, is required.

During this delay, a number of pre-trial issues must be addressed. The first of these is pre-trial release (sometimes called bail), which is determined at a bail hearing. In most cases, the accused's right to be presumed innocent until proven guilty means that the accused should not be deprived of freedom while waiting for trial. In other cases, including where the accused has been charged with a more serious crime, the accused is held prior to trial unless he or she can prove to a judge that release is appropriate.

Another issue to be determined is the accused's fitness to stand trial. If the accused is not capable of understanding the nature or consequences of the proceedings, or of advising counsel, he or she will be found to be unfit to stand trial, and the trial will be postponed. Some accused spend the duration of the resulting postponement in a mental health care facility.

Before the accused is required to enter a plea, he or she is entitled to receive disclosure from the prosecution of all inculpatory and exculpatory evidence about the case that the Crown has in its possession, whether or not the Crown intends to rely on that evidence at trial. Where the Crown is found to have failed to make appropriate disclosure, the court can order a remedy.

Depending on the nature of the offence and his or her previous criminal record, an accused person may be eligible for a diversion program. The accused must accept responsibility for the offence and be willing to fulfill the requirements of the program. Once the conditions are satisfied, the charge is stayed or withdrawn by the Crown and will not result in a criminal conviction.

Before entering a plea, many accused choose to negotiate with the prosecution in an attempt to make a plea bargain. Most plea bargains involve the accused entering a guilty plea, or a guilty plea to a lesser or other offence, in exchange for the prosecution's pursuit of a more lenient sentence.

An accused has four plea options: (1) plead guilty to the charges, in which case the proceedings go directly to the sentencing stage; (2) plead not guilty, in which case a trial is held; (3) plead not guilty as charged but guilty to a lesser or other offence, which also results in a trial; or (4) enter a special plea of *autrefois acquit* or *autrefois convict* based on the doctrine of *res judicata* (double jeopardy).

Finally, there may be some elections to be made about the manner in which the trial will proceed. If the offence charged is a hybrid offence, the prosecution chooses whether to try the accused by way of summary conviction or indictment. If the indictment route is chosen, the accused has the right to a preliminary hearing, where the judge either commits the accused to trial or discharges him or her.

KEY TERMS

abuse of process, 110

acquit, 114

adjournment, 111

autrefois acquit, 114

autrefois convict, 114

bail, 103

charge screening device, 115

charge screening form, 112

commit, 116

community justice worker, 112

condition, 104

culpability, 110

deposit, 107

disclosure, 110

diversion program, 112

election, 114

exculpatory, 110

fitness to stand trial, 109

full answer and defence, 110

hearsay evidence, 106

inculpatory, 110

judicial interim release, 103

mental disorder, 109

mistrial, 111

non–section 469 offence, 103

onus, 104

plea, 112

plea bargain, 112

preliminary inquiry, 115

primary ground, 104

proof beyond a reasonable doubt, 102

proof on a balance of probabilities, 108

recognizance, 104

res judicata, 114

reverse onus, 104

secondary ground, 104

section 469 offence, 108

show cause, 102

special plea, 114

sureties, 107

tertiary ground, 104

undertaking, 107

NOTES

1   *Canadian Charter of Rights and Freedoms*, Part I of the *Constitution Act, 1982*, being Schedule B to the *Canada Act 1982* (UK), 1982, c 11.

2   *Criminal Code*, RSC 1985, c C-46, as amended.

3   *Security of Information Act*, RSC 1985, c O-5.

4   *Controlled Drugs and Substances Act*, SC 1996, c 19.

5   *Wood v Schaeffer*, 2013 SCC 71.

EXERCISES

Multiple Choice

1. Which of the following is not a recognized remedy for non-disclosure of relevant state evidence to the defence?

   a. a judicial stay of proceedings

   b. costs against the state

   c. an apology from the Crown or police

   d. a mistrial

2. Which of the following is considered a special plea?

   a. *autrefois acquit*

   b. *quid pro quo*

   c. not criminally responsible

   d. guilty with an explanation

3. People who are accused of committing a section 469 offence

   a. have an automatic right to a bail hearing

   b. must apply to a superior court judge to be granted a bail hearing

   c. have no right to a bail hearing

   d. a and b

   e. none of the above

4. The mental condition of an accused at the time the offence took place

   a. always plays a role in a criminal trial

   b. never plays a role in a criminal trial

   c. is an important issue in a criminal trial

   d. affects the *mens rea* element

   e. a, c, and d

5. The principle of disclosure requires

   a. the Crown prosecutors to disclose to the defence all evidence in their possession

   b. the police to disclose to the prosecution all evidence in their possession

   c. the accused and his or her lawyers to disclose to the prosecution all evidence in their possession

   d. a and b

   e. a and c

True or False?

_____ **1.** Fitness to stand trial is determined by the accused's mental state and cognitive capacity at the time the offence was committed.

_____ **2.** In a show cause hearing, the Crown bears the burden of proving why an accused should be detained in custody pending trial when the accused is charged with assaulting a peace officer contrary to section 270 of the Code.

_____ **3.** Evidence of a previous criminal record would be considered part of the primary ground for detention in a bail hearing.

_____ **4.** A person charged with treason must make an application to have a bail hearing before a superior court judge.

_____ **5.** A mistrial can be declared if the defence does not make full disclosure to the Crown.

_____ **6.** The accused must plead guilty to the offence in order to be eligible for a diversion program.

_____ **7.** Both inculpatory and exculpatory evidence must be disclosed to an accused person.

_____ **8.** Types of evidence which are not admissible at a trial may be admissible at a show cause hearing.

_____ **9.** For a non–section 469 offence, the onus is on the accused to show cause why he or she should be released from custody.

_____**10.** Either the accused or the Crown may request a review of a detention or release order.

Short Answer

1. Do you agree with the rules governing the onus of proof at show cause hearings? Why or why not?

2. What are sureties?

3. Why is it important for investigating officers to turn over to the Crown all material that is relevant to a crime?

4. Explain the benefits of plea bargaining in our judicial system.

5. When is a person deemed unfit to stand trial?

Criminal Trial Issues and Defences

8

LEARNING OUTCOMES

After completing this chapter, you should be able to:

- Describe the basic process of a criminal trial.

- Differentiate between an information and an indictment and explain the elements required for both.

- Explain the difference between a peremptory juror challenge and a challenge for cause.

- Understand the three standards of proof and explain the meaning of reverse onus.

- Identify the two types of defence and the major subcategories under each type.

Introduction to the Criminal Trial

Once a person has been accused of a crime, charges have been laid, and the pre-trial issues discussed in Chapter 7 have been dealt with, the accused person is brought to trial.

People Involved in the Trial

In general terms, a criminal trial involves five different parties: the trier of fact, the trier of law, the prosecution, the defence, and the witnesses.

The **trier of fact** is either the judge (in a trial by judge alone) or the **jury** (in a trial by judge and jury). The trier of fact is the party that will make final decisions, based on the evidence, about what is true and what is not true. For example, the trier of fact will decide whether or not the accused was the person who pulled the trigger.

The **trier of law** is always the judge. It is the judge's job in every trial to interpret the law and apply it to the proven facts of the case. The judge, for example, decides the legal question whether a specific piece of evidence should be admitted into the trial. If the trial is by judge alone, the judge will act as both trier of fact and trier of law. In trials by judge and jury, the judge will interpret the applicable law for the jury and, once all the evidence has been presented, will instruct the jury on how it must apply the law to the evidence presented at trial.

The **prosecution** refers to the Crown attorney or attorneys, who are representatives of the attorney general and present the evidence and arguments to prove that the accused is guilty of the offence.

The **defence** refers to the accused and the lawyer or lawyers whom the accused has hired to help defend him or her. The job of the defence is to refute (counter and raise doubts about) the evidence presented by the prosecution and to produce evidence of its own that will cause the trier of fact to doubt that the accused is guilty of the offence.

The witnesses are people who appear at the trial to tell the court what they know about the offence or the accused. Witnesses may be brought to court by the prosecution or by the defence and are required to swear or affirm that their testimony will be true.

Both the prosecution and the defence may also introduce physical evidence at the trial such as a weapon, a photograph, or the results of DNA tests. This physical evidence plays a role, along with the verbal evidence of the witnesses, in convincing the trier of fact of the guilt or innocence of the accused.

The Trial Process

The trial process is a formal one. Trials can be as short as a few hours or as long as several months. The following is a brief overview of the stages in a normal jury trial after the charges have been laid, the bail hearing has been held, the accused has made his or her plea, and the committal and/or elections, if applicable, have been made. Each stage will be discussed in greater detail below, with the exception of sentencing, which is covered in Chapter 9.

The typical stages of a jury trial are as follows:

- The jury is selected.
- Any pre-trial applications are heard.
- The charges are read and the plea is entered into the trial record.
- The prosecution makes its opening statement.
- The defence makes its opening statement.

trier of fact
the person or people who must decide what facts have been proven at a criminal trial (either the judge or the jury)

jury
a group of 12 citizens who are chosen to act as the trier of fact in a criminal trial

trier of law
the judge who interprets the law and applies it to the facts as found by the trier of fact at a criminal trial

prosecution
the Crown attorney or attorneys who are given the task of proving an accused guilty of an offence

defence
the person accused of an offence in a criminal trial and his or her lawyer(s)

- The prosecution presents its evidence.
- The defence presents its evidence.
- The judge instructs the jury on how to apply the law.
- The jury deliberates and delivers its verdict.
- The judge listens to submissions from both sides and renders a sentence.

First, the jury is selected. This will be dealt with in greater depth later in this chapter. Once a jury has been selected, the trial itself may begin.

The second step is hearing any pre-trial applications. Pre-trial applications are brief hearings on a specific issue that needs to be addressed before the trial itself can proceed. For example, if the defence feels that certain pieces of evidence have been obtained in a way that contravened the rights of the accused under the *Canadian Charter of Rights and Freedoms*,[1] the defence may bring an application to exclude that evidence from trial. Applications are brought before the judge alone, since they concern questions of law. If the judge rules that the evidence should not be admitted into the trial under section 24(2) of the Charter, the jury will never know that that piece of evidence existed.

The first two steps—selecting the jury and hearing pre-trial applications—may take place in reverse order if, in the opinion of the parties and the judge, the applications will take several days or weeks. This is done to avoid bringing the jurors to the courthouse and disrupting their lives and then making them wait through several days of applications that they cannot attend.

Once the pre-trial applications are completed, the trial begins. The charges against the accused and the accused's plea in response to those charges are read for the benefit of the judge and/or jury, and so that they can be entered into the trial record. The two sides (the prosecution and the defence) are given the opportunity to make opening statements to the jury about what they intend to prove at the trial.

The prosecution is then required to present its evidence against the accused. Any witnesses presented by the prosecution may be cross-examined by the defence to test the trustworthiness of their evidence. As discussed in Chapter 5, the prosecution must be very careful to present evidence to prove each element of the offence with which the accused is charged. Failure to do so will result in a failure of the prosecution and the acquittal of the accused.

After the prosecution finishes presenting its case to the jury, the defence usually (but not always) presents evidence of its own. Once again, any witnesses called to testify by the defence may be cross-examined by the prosecutors. The defence may simply try to present evidence that undermines the evidence presented by the prosecution, or it may attempt to prove certain recognized defences that, if accepted by the jury, may lead to the acquittal of the accused. Defences will be explained in more detail later in this chapter.

Once all the evidence has been presented, the judge reviews the evidence for the jury, providing them with **instructions** on how to apply the law to the facts as they may find them. For example, the judge may say to the jury, "If you find as a fact that the accused intended to cause the death of the victim when she struck him with the baseball bat, then you must find the accused guilty of murder. If, on the other hand, you find that the accused had no such intention, you must find her guilty of manslaughter."

The jury is then asked to consider all the evidence, along with the instructions given to it by the judge, before rendering a **verdict**. The jury members are escorted to a private room to discuss the evidence and to reach a consensus with respect to a verdict. The jury then re-enters the courtroom and returns its verdict: guilty of the offence charged, guilty of a lesser but included offence, or not guilty.

instructions
directions given to the jury by the judge at the end of a trial advising it on how to apply the law to the facts of the case

verdict
the decision as to the guilt or innocence of the accused

Once the jury's verdict has been delivered, the trial is over. Chapter 9 will discuss sentencing and appeals.

Informations and Indictments

charging document
a written document, either an information or an indictment, that sets out the charges against a person accused of an offence

count
a single charge on a charging document

information
a form of charging document used for less serious offences

indictment
a form of charging document used for serious (indictable) offences

pre-enquete hearing
a hearing that is not open to the public

Two types of **charging documents** are used in criminal law. The charging document is what brings the criminal charges against the accused and begins the process toward trial. It contains individual charges or offences (known as **counts**) that the accused is alleged to have committed.

The first type of charging document is an **information**. It is usually sworn by a police officer, and contains a criminal charge against an accused. It is used only for offences tried in provincial court (in Ontario, the Ontario Court of Justice) or youth court. The other kind of charging document is an **indictment**. An indictment is usually signed by the prosecutor and is used for offences tried in superior court (in Ontario, the Superior Court of Justice).

The Information

An informant, who is typically a police officer, swears to a justice of the peace that he or she has knowledge or reasonable and probable grounds to believe that the accused committed the offence in question. For hybrid and indictable offences, if the accused has not yet been arrested, the justice must hear and consider the allegations at a **pre-enquete hearing**. Added to the information later are a list of all court appearances and the purpose for each, the names of all court officials present, all elections made by both the prosecution and the accused, any detention orders, the outcome of a preliminary inquiry if one has been held, and any adjournments.

The *Criminal Code*[2] requires that a document called a Form 2 be prepared by the informant. Police departments have copies of this form for common offences so that the officers have to fill in only the accused person's name and the place and date of the alleged crime. Note that some offences—for example, public nudity (s 174) and distributing hate propaganda (s 319)—require the consent of the attorney general before an information can be sworn. These are exceptions to the general rule that a police officer alone can bring a sworn information before a justice.

An important difference between informations and indictments (discussed below) is that the prosecution faces certain timing restrictions with respect to certain informations. Section 786 of the *Criminal Code* provides that where the offence charged is a summary conviction offence, the information creating the charge must be sworn no later than six months from "the time when the subject-matter of the proceedings arose," which usually means the date the alleged crime was committed. This limitation can mean that, should the court rule that there is a problem with the information, the prosecution may not be able to re-swear the information in time to prosecute the charge.

The Indictment

The indictment is the charging document that is used when the case progresses to superior court. The document used for the indictment is a Form 4 regardless of whether the accused has elected trial by judge and jury or by judge alone. The indictment sets out the history of the case in the same way the information does.

The meaning of the word "indictment" is tricky in criminal law because it has more than one definition. It can refer to the charging document used in superior court. However, the word "indictment" can also refer to the nature of the procedures in superior court (sometimes called "the indictable procedure"), in the sense that, by choosing to proceed more formally, the Crown has elected to prosecute a hybrid offence "by way of indictment" (that is, as an indictable offence).

Challenging the Charging Document

Informations and indictments must follow five principles:

- Each count must relate to a single transaction (s 581(1)).
- Each count must charge an offence known to law (s 581(1)).
- Each count must charge only one offence (duplicity rule—see below).
- Each count must identify the act or omission alleged to be an offence (s 581(3)).
- Each count must identify the transaction (s 581(3)).

FIGURE 8.1   Five Principles for Informations and Indictments

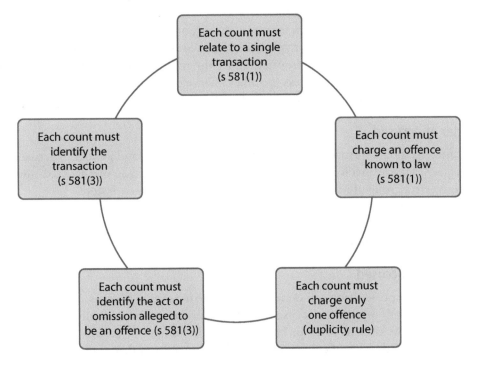

The information or indictment may be challenged by the defence if there are any deficiencies. Common types of deficiencies are discussed below.

Insufficiency

Under sections 581 and 583 of the *Criminal Code*, the charging document may be challenged for **insufficiency** if any crucial information that is necessary to give the accused adequate notice of the crime for which he or she is being charged is missing. In *R v Côté*,[3] the Supreme Court of Canada held that the "golden rule" with respect to sufficiency is that the accused should be reasonably informed of the transaction alleged against him so that he can make full answer and defence of it at trial.

Duplicity

The common law rule against **duplicity** prohibits the listing of two separate charges or offences in a single count on the charging document. Basically, it does not allow the informant

insufficiency
a flaw in a charging document that causes it to fail to contain the required information to sustain the charge

duplicity
a flaw in a charging document where a single count contains two or more alternative offences so that the accused does not know against which offence to defend

to charge the accused with one offence and a second offence as an alternative for the same actions. For example, a single count cannot state that, on or about the 12th of June 2016, the accused committed assault causing bodily harm or murder. If such a count was allowed, the defence would not know which offence the prosecution would proceed with, and this would reduce its ability to defend the accused against the charges. If the charging document is unclear about what charges the accused will face at trial, it is improper.

Improper Joinder of Charges

joinder
where two or more charges or two or more accused persons are tried together in the same trial

In many cases, it is easier and more efficient to bring an accused to trial at the same time for all offences he or she is accused of having committed, even if they do not arise out of the same incidents or circumstances. This is called **joinder** of charges.

Joinder of charges, however, can result in prejudice to the accused in that a jury may be more inclined to believe that a person charged with assault causing bodily harm is also guilty of shoplifting. If a person is charged and tried with a whole series of offences, all arising out of different incidents, the jury may also be more inclined to believe that the accused is guilty of at least some of the charges.

Therefore, to avoid unfairness to the accused, there are clear rules about which offences may be joined and which offences may not be joined. Sections 589 and 590 of the *Criminal Code* set out when joinder is inappropriate. Most important, a charge of murder cannot be joined with any other offence unless the other offence arises out of the same situation as the charge of murder or the accused consents to the joinder.

Joinder of Accused

A distinction should be made here between joinder of charges and joinder of accused. In many cases, a crime involves the alleged participation of more than one accused—for example, where a group of robbers work together to rob a convenience store.

In cases of this nature, there are compelling reasons to conduct a single trial for all of the accused (called "joinder of accused"), because to try them separately would involve the need to repeat the same evidence in multiple different trials.

Severance of Accused

Strategically, the prosecution will sometimes prefer to have separate trials, especially where it will be necessary to have the accused provide evidence against each other. The defence may also have its reasons for wanting to "sever" the joinder of accused—for example, where one accused's level of culpability is much different from that of the other accused, and the culpability of the most "guilty" accused would colour the jury's opinion of the less culpable accused. (Consider, for example, a case in which a little brother of one of the robbers in the gang simply holds the convenience store door open, but another of the robbers commits a murder during the robbery.)

While there are fewer legal restrictions on the joinder of accused, it is not uncommon for the defence to bring a motion, under section 593 of the *Criminal Code*, requesting severance of the accused for the purposes of trial.

Saving Devices or Remedies

particulars
details of a count

Two saving devices are available to the court to remedy the above deficiencies: (1) the judge may order that the prosecution give the defence **particulars** of the unclear counts, or (2) the judge can amend the charging document to rectify the deficiency.

According to section 587 of the *Criminal Code*, the judge can order the prosecution to give the accused more information and details (particulars) of the accusation so that he or she can make full answer and defence and facilitate the administration of justice. This is a common remedy for insufficiency.

The court also has wide discretion to amend an indictment or information, as set out in sections 601 and 795 of the *Criminal Code*. This is a common remedy for duplicity.

According to section 601(4), in determining whether an amendment should be made to a count in the information, the court must take into account:

- the matters disclosed by the evidence taken at the preliminary inquiry;
- the evidence taken at trial;
- the circumstances of the case;
- whether the accused has been misled or prejudiced in his or her defence by any variance, error, or omission; and
- with regard to the merits of the case, whether an amendment may be made without injustice occurring.

Under section 601(5), if the court is of the view that the accused has been misled or prejudiced by the amendment, the accused may be entitled to an adjournment of the proceeding.

If an information or indictment is so deficient that it cannot be remedied, the judge may **quash** (overthrow or void) the charging document. The prosecution may still be able to appeal the order to quash the charging document, or if time permits, the prosecution may simply lay the charges again in proper form.

quash
overthrow or void

Juries

A jury in a criminal case typically includes 12 people. Jurors must decide unanimously on a conviction or an acquittal. The jury is involved only in determining guilt—it is not involved in sentencing. The one exception is that the jury may make recommendations about parole eligibility in second-degree murder cases. Rules relating to juries are found in sections 626 to 644 of the *Criminal Code*.

If the accused elects to proceed to trial before a judge and jury, selecting the jury can become a long and contentious process. The jury is, after all, the trier of fact and as such has the ability to decide the fate of the accused.

Jury selection begins when prospective jurors are asked to appear at the local courthouse. One at a time, each person steps forward and the defence and the prosecution are asked whether they want to challenge the juror or are content with the juror. If the defence and the prosecution are satisfied with the juror, he or she is sworn and seated in the jury box. Both sides are entitled to a certain number of challenges of the jury pool.

Peremptory Challenges

Each side is allowed to exclude a certain number of potential jurors with no explanation. These are called **peremptory challenges**.

Where the accused is charged with an offence that is punishable by more than five years of imprisonment, each side has 12 peremptory challenges (except for cases that involve first-degree murder or treason, where both the prosecution and the defence are entitled to 20 challenges). Where the offence is punishable by five or less years of imprisonment, each side has only 4 peremptory challenges.

peremptory challenge
the right of either party to a criminal jury trial to reject a prospective juror without giving a reason

Challenges for Cause

Before jury selection begins, both the prosecution and the defence have the opportunity under section 629 of the *Criminal Code* to request of the judge that every member of the jury panel (the group of citizens from which the jury is selected) be challenged or questioned regarding his or her feelings on certain subjects related to the accused or the offence. The goal is to screen out people who might allow their personal feelings to affect their impartiality. An Asian accused, for example, should not be tried by jurors who have expressed prejudices against Asians; a homosexual accused should not be tried by jurors who are homophobic.

If the judge agrees that a proposed concern is legitimate, a question is formulated to deal with the concern and asked of each prospective juror. This question is called a **challenge for cause**. If a potential juror's response indicates a lack of impartiality, that person will not be permitted to join the jury.

Proof of Facts

The Canadian criminal legal system has adopted the **presumption of innocence** as the basis for its procedure and its rules of evidence. The presumption of innocence means that a person who has been accused of a crime will be considered innocent until proven guilty by the trier of fact in a court of law. The presumption of innocence is a principle of fundamental justice (discussed in Chapter 6) and is guaranteed by section 11(d) of the *Canadian Charter of Rights and Freedoms*.

At trial, the prosecution must prove that the accused committed the offence. This proof is created through the use of evidence, which can take the form of either the oral testimony of witnesses or physical items.

The **burden of proof**, or onus, refers to the requirement that a certain party has to provide proof of a given fact or theory. In most cases, the prosecution has the burden of proof: it bears the burden of proving the elements of the offence and, therefore, the guilt of the accused. Situations that require the accused to prove a particular fact are called reverse-onus situations.

The **standard of proof** is the level or degree of proof that the party must produce to be successful. In other words, the standard of proof refers to how convincing the proof must be. In general terms, there are three standards or levels of proof, each more difficult or strict than the last:

1. the **evidentiary standard**, meaning that the party must simply provide some evidence of the truth of the fact;

2. the **civil standard** (also known as the "balance of probabilities"), meaning that the party must prove that it is more likely than not that the fact is true; and

3. the **criminal standard** (also known as "proof beyond a reasonable doubt"), meaning that the party must prove the guilt of the accused to such a high degree that no reasonable person would have a real doubt as to its truth.

The Prosecution's Burden of Proof—Proof Beyond a Reasonable Doubt

The prosecution bears the burden of proving an accused person's guilt at trial to the criminal standard of proof: proof beyond a reasonable doubt. The fact that the prosecution's burden of proof must meet the highest standard results from the fact that, if found guilty of the offence, the accused faces the most serious punishment our justice system allows: imprisonment.

The key word in the criminal standard of proof is "reasonable." The prosecution does not have to eliminate *all* doubt to obtain a conviction—it simply has to provide proof

challenge for cause
the right of either party in a criminal jury trial to require that prospective jurors be questioned about certain aspects of the offence or the accused that may result in bias on the part of the jurors

presumption of innocence
the basis of criminal legal procedure and rules of evidence—that an accused person is considered innocent until proven guilty

burden of proof
the requirement that a certain party prove a particular fact at trial

standard of proof
the level to which a party must convince the trier of fact of a given allegation

evidentiary standard
a basic level of proof; an alleged fact meets the evidentiary standard when there is at least some evidence that the allegation might be true

civil standard
the level of proof that a party must achieve in a civil trial to be successful—proof on a balance of probabilities

criminal standard
the level of proof that the prosecution must provide in a criminal trial to obtain a conviction—proof beyond a reasonable doubt

beyond a reasonable doubt that is based on the evidence or the lack of evidence against the accused.

The trier of fact must be convinced beyond a reasonable doubt, on all the evidence, that the accused is guilty of the offence in order for a conviction to result. Note, however, that the prosecution does not have to prove each piece of evidence beyond a reasonable doubt. It is enough for the sum of the evidence to convince the trier of fact that the accused is guilty of the offence beyond a reasonable doubt.

The Defence's Burden of Proof

The burden of proof in criminal trials falls on the prosecution. The defence is not required to present any evidence, and there is no obligation on the accused to prove his or her innocence or even to raise a doubt.

In some cases, however, the defence may choose to present evidence, if only in an attempt to create a reasonable doubt about the evidence presented by the prosecution. It is sufficient for the defence to meet the very low evidentiary standard of proof: to produce some evidence of facts alleged in its attempt to combat the prosecution's case. The defence does not have to prove its position beyond a reasonable doubt or even on a balance of probabilities; it only needs to cast doubt on the case presented by the prosecution.

Defences

The accused and his or her lawyers have many options when it comes to attempting to obtain an acquittal at trial. These options are called **defences**. In most cases, the accused will simply try to create a reasonable doubt as to the prosecution's case. This may be referred to as a **passive defence**, since it goes no further than refuting the allegations against the accused.

However, a number of other defences involve the accused and his or her lawyers attempting to prove that circumstances existed that negate the guilt of the accused, in most cases by proving that the accused did not have the required intent (*mens rea*) to commit the offence. These can be referred to as **positive (or affirmative) defences**.

Passive Defences

The simplest way to defend an accused against criminal charges is to assert that the prosecution has failed to establish proof beyond a reasonable doubt of an essential element of the offence—usually either the *mens rea* (mental element) or the *actus reus* (physical element). In such a case, the accused often does not call any witnesses (though Crown witnesses may be cross-examined), nor does he or she testify or present an affirmative defence. Indeed, at the end of the presentation of the prosecution's case, the accused asks the judge (by bringing a motion) to rule that the prosecution has failed to provide sufficient evidence that, if accepted completely by the trier of fact, proves the accused's guilt. The judge may, at that point, rule that the prosecution has failed to meet its standard of proof and acquit the accused without requiring any evidence from the defence, even if a jury is involved in the trial. This is called a **directed verdict**.

In most cases, therefore, the defence lawyers will cross-examine the witnesses presented by the prosecution in an effort to create doubt in the mind of the trier of fact. They may try to prompt an eyewitness to the offence to admit that he is not absolutely certain it was the accused he saw committing the offence because, for example, he was not wearing his glasses at the time; they may attempt to prove that a witness has a motive for wanting the

defences
the arguments that the defence uses to contradict the prosecution's evidence against the accused

passive defence
a defence by which the accused and his or her lawyers simply assert (through cross-examination or in closing arguments by counsel) that the prosecution has failed to prove the accused's guilt beyond a reasonable doubt

positive (or affirmative) defence
a trial defence where the accused and his or her lawyers actively attempt to refute the evidence of the prosecution and perhaps introduce evidence of their own to clear the accused

directed verdict
an early verdict of acquittal based on the prosecution's failure to meet its standard of proof

accused to be convicted of the crime even if he or she is innocent; they may even attempt to prove that the witness herself is unreliable as a result of her mental condition, abuse of alcohol or drugs, or history of lying in other circumstances.

In these situations, the defence is not attempting to prove anything new, but simply trying to undermine the credibility of the prosecution's evidence to create a reasonable doubt. Finally, the defence may enter exculpatory physical or documentary evidence into the trial record.

Positive, Affirmative, or "True" Defences

True defences are those that involve the defence lawyers attempting to prove a new fact or facts that tend to negate the existence of one or more of the elements of the offence or tend to attack the charges themselves. These defences may be subdivided into four categories: justification, excuse, entrapment, and alibi.

Defences in criminal law are extremely complex and can't be dealt with adequately in the context of this chapter. What follows is simply a brief discussion of the basics of each defence.

Justification

justification
a rare defence that negates the objective wrongfulness of an act and exempts the accused from the application of the *Criminal Code*

Defences of **justification** are rare, but when proven, they negate the objective wrongfulness of the act and exempt the accused from the application of the *Criminal Code*. An example of using a justification defence is the medical use of marijuana. Although the *Controlled Drugs and Substances Act* states that using marijuana is an offence, the common law has developed to allow people suffering from painful medical conditions the right to use marijuana for therapeutic purposes. The use of the drug is not for a purpose that is wrong and, in the opinion of judges who create the common law, should not be punishable as a criminal offence. The accused may be justified, as a result of the medical condition, in using marijuana.

Self-Defence

self-defence
a defence that can be used against assault if the force used was no more than was necessary to protect against the assault

Self-defence can be a defence against assault if the force used was no more than was necessary to protect against the assault. The judge will consider the accused's subjective perceptions of the situation and the reasonableness of those perceptions. The rules governing self-defence are set out in section 34(1) of the *Criminal Code*, which reads as follows:

> 34(1) A person is not guilty of an offence if
> (a) they believe on reasonable grounds that force is being used against them or another person or that a threat of force is being made against them or another person;
> (b) the act that constitutes the offence is committed for the purpose of defending or protecting themselves or the other person from that use or threat of force; and
> (c) the act committed is reasonable in the circumstances.

Pursuant to section 34(2), there are a number of factors that must be considered by the court in determining whether the act is reasonable, including:

- the nature of the force or threat;
- whether the use of force was imminent or whether there were other options available;

- the person's role in the incident;
- whether any party to the incident used or threatened to use a weapon;
- the size, age, gender, and physical capabilities of the parties;
- the nature, duration, and history of the relationship between the parties, including any prior use of force and the nature of that threat or force;
- any history of interaction or communication between the parties;
- the nature and proportionality of the person's response to the use of or threat of force; and
- whether the act committed was in response to a use or threat of force that the person knew was lawful.

Defence of Property

A similar provision, section 35 of the *Criminal Code*, permits an accused person to protect his or her property if he or she is in peaceable possession of it and someone else either is about to enter the property, is entering the property, or has already entered the property without being entitled by law to do so. This provision also applies if someone is about to take property, is taking property, has already taken property, or is about to damage or destroy property. Under these circumstances, the accused may be found not guilty of committing an act to protect the property in order to prevent someone from coming in, taking, or damaging the property.

When this occurs, the defender of the property is entitled to use a reasonable amount of force, subject to the rules of self-defence, to prevent the offence. For example, if Jim tries to steal Kim's purse, Kim is entitled to defend her purse by grasping Jim's wrist and wrenching it away from her purse. The fact that Jim was trying to steal Kim's property justifies Kim's assault on Jim. Kim is not entitled to beat Jim unconscious with a baseball bat, however.

Finally, in order for the defence to apply, the conduct must be reasonable under the circumstances.

The use of excessive force is prohibited under section 26 of the *Criminal Code*, even where the person is authorized by law to use force. Section 25(1) of the *Criminal Code* specifies that if a police officer acts on reasonable grounds to administer or enforce the law, he or she may use as much force as is necessary for that purpose. This is limited to a reasonable use of force.

However, force that is intended or is likely to cause death or grievous bodily harm may be justified where all of the following conditions are met:

- the suspect is fleeing from police,
- the police are attempting to arrest the suspect, and
- force is necessary for the safety of the officer or others.

Where these conditions are not met, the use of excessive force on the part of law enforcement authorities may result in criminal charges as well as disciplinary proceedings under the *Police Services Act*. Furthermore, where the accused believes on reasonable grounds that a police officer is acting unlawfully, he or she may act in self-defence, pursuant to section 34(3) of the *Criminal Code*.

In *R v Nasogaluak*, although no criminal charges were laid against the officers involved, the court found that they had used excessive force.

Police Use of Excessive Force

The RCMP received a tip about an intoxicated driver and were involved in a high-speed pursuit of the accused, Lyle Nasogaluak. When the accused came to a stop, officers had to use force to remove him from his vehicle. He resisted, and one officer punched him twice in the head while wrestling him out of the car. Nasogaluak continued to resist and the officer yelled at him to stop resisting before punching him in the head again. The accused was then pinned face down on the ground with one officer straddling his back and another officer kneeling on his thigh. After Nasogaluak refused to put his hands up to be handcuffed, a second officer punched him twice in the back, breaking his ribs. This ultimately resulted in the accused suffering from a punctured lung.

While at the RCMP detachment, the accused provided breath samples that placed him over the legal blood alcohol limit. He did not have any obvious signs of injury and did not request any medical assistance, and no attempts were made to get him any medical attention. However, Nasogaluak told an officer that he was hurt and could not breathe, and he was also observed to be crying, leaning over, and moaning. When he was released the next morning, the accused went to the hospital. He was diagnosed as having broken ribs and a collapsed lung that required emergency surgery.

The officers did not report the force that they had used during the arrest and provided very little information about the circumstances leading up to the arrest. The accused pleaded guilty to charges of impaired driving and flight from police officers. During the sentencing, the judge found that the officers used excessive force during the arrest and breached the accused's rights under section 7 of the Charter. The judge reduced the accused's sentence to a 12-month conditional discharge on each count, even though there is a statutorily mandated minimum fine for a first offence of impaired driving.

The Court of Appeal agreed that there was sufficient evidence to support the trial judge's finding as to the excessive force used by the officers, but set aside the conditional sentence discharge on the impaired driving offence and imposed the mandatory minimum fine. The court did not interfere with the sentence imposed for the flight from police offence. Both the Crown and the accused appealed to the Supreme Court of Canada.

The appeal and cross-appeal were dismissed. The Supreme Court of Canada stated that the conduct of the RCMP officers was a substantial interference with the accused's physical and psychological integrity and security of the person, and it was a clear breach of section 7 of the Charter. Section 25(1) of the *Criminal Code* permits use of force to effect an arrest, but only to the extent that it is reasonably necessary. Under section 25(3), force intended or likely to cause death or grievous bodily harm is prohibited unless the officer has reason to believe that the amount of force used is necessary to protect himself or herself or another person from death or grievous bodily harm. The allowable degree of force is constrained by the principles of proportionality, necessity, and reasonableness.

However, the court went on to say that the sentencing judge's discretion in crafting the appropriate sentence is limited by case law and statute. A sentencing judge cannot reduce a sentence below a statutorily mandated minimum unless the provision is unconstitutional. There was no need for the sentencing judge to turn to section 24(1) of the Charter in order to reduce the sentence. Sentencing provisions in the *Criminal Code* provide adequate remedial protections to accused persons whose rights have been infringed, whether these rights are Charter-related or not.

Questions for Discussion

1. Should sentencing judges have residual discretion to override otherwise constitutional mandatory minimum sentences in situations in which police officers use excessive force?

2. When an accused person pleads guilty to an offence, how much weight should the court place on a breach of a Charter right in crafting an appropriate sentence?

Source: *R v Nasogaluak*, 2010 SCC 6, [2010] 1 SCR 206.

Consent

consent
a defence that arises when the accused has an honest yet mistaken belief in the complainant's consent to an action

Consent, or the accused's honest but mistaken belief in consent, is a common defence to the offences of assault and sexual assault. The offence of assault, pursuant to section 265(1)(a) of the *Criminal Code*, is defined as the application of intentional force on another person—either directly or indirectly— without the other person's consent. Therefore, it is a defence to assault that the accused had an honest yet mistaken belief that the complainant or victim consented to the application of force.

If the victim does not resist or submits to the assault, the accused may rely on the defence of consent. However, the defence is limited by section 265(3), which indicates that no consent is obtained when the complainant does not resist or submits to the assault because of the application of force to the complainant or another person, or because of threats made to the complainant or another person, or by reason of fraud or the exercise of authority. Additionally, consent may be apprehended, meaning that as long as there is some evidence that the defendant held an honest belief that the victim consented, he or she may rely on the defence of consent.

It should be noted that the defence of consent does not apply to assault resulting in bodily harm or aggravated assault. In the case of *R v Jobidon*,[4] the accused and the victim got into a consensual bar fight. The accused struck the victim once and the victim was knocked unconscious. The accused continued to strike the victim even after he became unconscious, and the victim died as a result of his injuries. The Supreme Court of Canada ruled that consent is not a defence when bodily harm results or when excessive force is used.

In these situations, consent is vitiated because the application of force is intended to cause harm to the complainant.

Excuse

Defences of **excuse** concede that an accused's actions were wrong but claim that external or internal forces influenced the accused so that the mental element required to establish the offence was not present. These defences usually depend on physical involuntariness (drunkenness) or mental impairment (mental defect, disease, or infancy). The Crown must prove both the *actus reus* and *mens rea* of an offence beyond a reasonable doubt before the accused considers whether to put forth a legal excuse as a defence.

excuse
a defence that concedes that the accused's actions were wrong but claims that external or internal forces influenced the accused

Necessity

Necessity is a type of a defence of excuse. It asserts that the accused had no real opportunity to avoid breaking the law. The defence of necessity depends on proving three elements: (1) an urgent peril, (2) no reasonable legal alternative to the criminal action taken, and (3) a reasonable proportionality between the peril avoided and the crime committed. Simply stated, the accused could avoid some imminent disaster, calamity, or serious harm only by breaking the law.

For example, imagine that Karen was snowmobiling and fell through the ice in a remote area of Algonquin Park. To avoid freezing to death, she broke into a nearby cottage to warm and dry herself. It appears obvious that Karen committed both the *actus reus* and *mens rea* of the indictable offence of breaking and entering under section 348 of the *Criminal Code*. The circumstances—the fact that she would likely have died if she had not committed the offence—would probably provide her with the excuse of necessity and lead to an acquittal.

Once the accused has raised some evidence of the defence of necessity, the onus falls on the prosecution to prove that necessity did not exist.

Duress

The defence of **duress** is closely related to necessity since it involves committing an offence to avoid some threatened harm. Duress itself is any unlawful threat or coercion used by one person to induce another person to act or yield in a different way than he or she would if operating under his or her own free will. The defence of duress is very complicated, partly because it is both a *Criminal Code* defence and (with different requirements) a common law defence.

duress
a defence that allows the accused to be acquitted if he or she committed the offence under threat of immediate death or bodily harm

Section 17 of the Code states that an accused may be acquitted if he or she committed the offence under threat of immediate death or bodily harm by a person who is present at the time of the offence. The person who commits the offence must hold an actual subjective belief that the threat will be carried out in order to use the defence of duress. The defence of duress does not apply to all offences under the *Criminal Code*.

Mental Disorder

The defence of mental disorder is dealt with under section 16 of the Code. If the accused suffers from some form of mental disorder, he or she is not considered capable of the *mens rea* of most offences.

An accused who uses the defence of mental disorder must give evidence of a disease or disorder that rendered him or her incapable of either appreciating the nature and quality of the impugned act or understanding the moral wrongfulness of the act. A successful defence of not guilty by reason of mental disorder (also called "not criminally responsible," or "NCR-MD") may result in detention for treatment if the accused is found to be a danger to society.

People may be found to be suffering from a mental disorder if they meet one of two tests. The mental disorder must have made them incapable (1) of appreciating the nature and quality of the act or omission or (2) of knowing that the act or omission is morally wrong. In general, the case law has determined that the term "disease of the mind" includes any abnormal condition, disorder, or illness that impairs the functioning of the human mind. However, mental disorder excludes self-induced states caused by alcohol or drugs, as well as temporary mental states such as hysteria or concussion.

It is important to know, and the case law reinforces the principle, that the analysis of what constitutes a mental disorder for the purpose of determining guilt is a legal, not a medical, analysis. The legal definition of "mental disorder" is *not* the same thing as a medical diagnosis of mental illness. The purposes and goals of a medical diagnosis of mental illness and a legal determination of *mens rea* are very different, and many individuals found to have a mental disorder for the purpose of the law do not have a medically recognized mental illness.

The word "appreciating" in section 16 has been defined to mean that the accused had an understanding beyond mere knowledge of the physical quality of the act.

Automatism

Automatism is similar to the defence of mental disorder because both defences flow from the idea that the accused cannot be held criminally responsible because of a mental deficiency. **Automatism** is involuntary or unconscious behaviour. In *R v Rabey*,[5] the court expanded on the definition by writing that automatism is an "unconscious, involuntary behaviour, the state of a person who, though capable of action, is not conscious of what he is doing. It means an unconscious, involuntary act, where the mind does not go with what is being done."

A distinction has been drawn, in the case law, between "insane" and "non-insane" automatism. Insane automatism is said to flow from an internal cause (a mental disorder), and an accused who is found to suffer from insane automatism is treated like any other accused with a mental disorder: he or she may be found not criminally responsible on account of mental disorder and may be committed to a health care facility.

Non-insane automatism, by contrast, is said to flow from an external cause. An accused who attributes his or her behaviour to non-insane automatism alleges that he or she acted while suffering from an externally provoked condition leading to involuntary action that

automatism
involuntary or unconscious behaviour

negated the *mens rea* of the offence charged. Accused typically frame their defences in non-insane automatism to avoid involuntary committal, because an accused found to have acted while in the throes of non-insane automatism will not be found NCR-MD, but rather, will be acquitted. However, as noted in the Case in Point below, the distinction between the two forms of automatism may be eroding: the current trend is to increasingly interpret most instances of automatism as mental disorder.

In alleging automatism, there is an onus on the defence to provide at least some evidence of the accused's suffering from this unusual condition. With respect to non-insane automatism, *R v Parks*[6] is an interesting case. In *Parks*, the Supreme Court unanimously upheld the trial court's ruling that the accused's sleepwalking (also called somnambulism) was not a "disease of the mind" and only the defence of non-insane automatism should be put to the jury.

Provocation

Provocation is a defence that is available only to persons charged with murder. A successful provocation defence does not lead to the acquittal of the accused, however; it just serves to reduce the offence from murder to manslaughter on the basis that a provoked person does not form the required intent to murder someone.

To be successful, the defence must provide evidence that the actions of the victim constituted a serious criminal offence and were of such a nature as to deprive a reasonable person of self-control. The accused must also act on this suddenly, before any time for reasoned reflection. Provocation is codified in section 232 of the *Criminal Code*:

> 232(1) Culpable homicide that otherwise would be murder may be reduced to manslaughter if the person who committed it did so in the heat of passion caused by sudden provocation.
>
> (2) Conduct of the victim that would constitute an indictable offence under this Act that is punishable by five or more years of imprisonment and that is of such a nature as to be sufficient to deprive an ordinary person of the power of self-control is provocation for the purposes of this section, if the accused acted on it on the sudden and before there was time for their passion to cool.
>
> (3) For the purposes of this section, the questions
>
> (a) whether the conduct of the victim amounted to provocation under subsection (2), and
>
> (b) whether the accused was deprived of the power of self-control by the provocation that he alleges he received,
>
> are questions of fact, but no one shall be deemed to have given provocation to another by doing anything that he had a legal right to do, or by doing anything that the accused incited him to do in order to provide the accused with an excuse for causing death or bodily harm to any human being.
>
> (4) Culpable homicide that otherwise would be murder is not necessarily manslaughter by reason only that it was committed by a person who was being arrested illegally, but the fact that the illegality of the arrest was known to the accused may be evidence of provocation for the purpose of this section.

The wording of section 232 shows that there are both objective and subjective elements to the defence of provocation. The objective component is whether the wrongful act was serious enough to take away an ordinary person's self-control. The subjective component of the test is whether the accused acted on the provocation and did so before his or her passion cooled.

Restrictions on the defence of provocation are detailed in section 232 and the case law:

- Generally, the provoking act must come from the victim and not from a third party.
- The provoking act must be a serious indictable offence punishable by at least five years of incarceration.
- The act and the reaction must both be sudden.
- Provocation does not exist when the accused has incited the other person to react.
- Provocation does not exist where the victim was doing anything he or she had a legal right to do.

CASE IN POINT

Reconciling Luedecke and Parks

In the *Parks* case mentioned just above and also in Chapter 5, the defendant, while sleepwalking, injured one person and killed another. After presenting a defence based on non-insane automatism, he was acquitted.

In the case of *R v Luedecke*, the trial court found that the defendant Luedecke, while asleep, committed a sexual assault by engaging in non-consensual sex with the victim. At his trial, Luedecke acknowledged that he had committed the assault (performed the *actus reus*), but denied having had the requisite *mens rea*. He raised the same defence as had Mr. Parks: non-insane automatism. The trial court, following the precedent set in *Parks*, acquitted Luedecke.

The Crown appealed Luedecke's acquittal on the basis that Luedecke's parasomnia (sleep disorder) should be treated not as non-insane automatism, but rather as a mental disorder, and that instead of being acquitted, Luedecke should be made subject to a verdict of "NCR-MD" (not criminally responsible on account of mental disorder), a finding that permits the court to conduct a hearing to consider the danger that the accused poses to the public, and that can lead, in some cases, to having the accused involuntarily committed to a treatment facility.

In making this order, Justice Doherty of the Court of Appeal wrote:

> The respondent personifies one of the most difficult problems encountered in the criminal law. As a result of his parasomnia, he did a terrible thing, he sexually assaulted a defenceless, young victim. The reason for his conduct—automatism brought on by parasomnia—renders his actions non-culpable in the eyes of the criminal law. That very same explanation, however, makes his behaviour potentially dangerous and raises legitimate public safety concerns. An outright acquittal reflects the non-culpable nature of the conduct but does nothing to address the potential danger posed by the respondent's condition. ... On a proper application of the principles developed in the Canadian case law, the respondent's automatism is

properly characterized as a mental disorder and should have led to an NCR-MD verdict.

Parks, while sleepwalking, injured one person and killed another; Luedecke committed a sexual assault. How can we reconcile seeing Parks acquitted and Luedecke found NCR-MD?

The answer is that our courts' analysis of the issue of automatism has increasingly incorporated elements of public policy. Although it was true that Parks stabbed his in-laws without any knowledge of what he was doing, his acts—and the potential ongoing danger to society that they pose—were alarming. If parasomniacs (sleepwalkers) truly have no control over their actions, must we simply tolerate their violent acts, or does our justice system have responsibility for imposing appropriate controls on these individuals?

After the *Parks* case, the Canadian Psychiatric Association recommended to a committee of the House of Commons that all automatism claims should be treated as mental disorder claims. After that, Justice Bastarache of the Supreme Court of Canada, giving the reasons in another automatism case called *R v Stone*, created a controversial five-part test for establishing non-insane automatism that greatly restricted the use of the defence. Finally, the *Parks* case was decided at a time where being found NCR-MD could result in a person being detained indefinitely in a mental health care facility, a practice that was greatly restricted after the introduction of part XX.1 of the *Criminal Code*.

The Court of Appeal in *Luedecke* characterized the *Stone* case as a "high-water mark" in the rejection of non-insane automatism defences (this is usually "judge code" for saying the case goes too far). However, Justice Doherty accepted that the *Stone* case requires that trial judges "examine the risk of the recurrence of the factors or events that triggered the accused's automatistic state." Because the assault leading to the charge in *Luedecke* did not represent the first time that Luedecke had engaged in sexual intercourse with someone while asleep but at least the fourth time (the first three times, the other party was a girlfriend, not a stranger), and because the possibility that Luedecke would assault another person in future existed, it was clearly possible that Luedecke represented a danger to society. The court therefore allowed the appeal and ordered a new trial.

The new trial ended in May 2009 with a verdict of NCR-MD. The verdict triggered a hearing to determine whether Luedecke was a danger to the public, and Luedecke, who from the beginning was remorseful about what he did and cooperative with the police, was granted an absolute discharge. This means he has no criminal record and has his freedom. Although the Crown applied for an order forcing Luedecke to comply with the *Sex Offender Information Registration Act*, that

application failed on a technical basis. There is no evidence that Luedecke has ever reoffended.

Questions for Discussion

1. The *Parks* and *Luedecke* cases pose a formidable ethical and intellectual challenge for lawmakers by throwing two essential values—the public's right to safety and the accused's right not to be convicted in the absence of "moral guilt"—into direct conflict. Which value do you feel is more important, and why?

2. Can you suggest an alternative approach to finding all "automaton" accused NCR-MD? How might a trier of law protect the public without unduly limiting the autonomy of the accused?

Sources: *R v Parks* (1992), 75 CCC (3d) 287 (SCC); *R v Luedecke*, 2008 ONCA 716, 2010 ONCJ 59; *R v Stone*, [1999] 2 SCR 290; *Sex Offender Information Registration Act*, SC 2004, c 10.

Intoxication

Intoxication or drunkenness in its extreme form may be used as a defence if it interfered with the ability of the accused to form the required level of intent to commit the offence. There must have been an extremely high level of intoxication for this defence to be accepted. Basically, the accused must have been in such a state that he or she was unaware of the specific criminal act committed.

The common law has held that intoxication is appropriate only as a defence to specific intent offences—offences where the accused must have had a particular intention in mind when committing the *actus reus* (for example, breaking and entering with the intent to commit an indictable offence, as discussed above). The intoxication defence cannot be used for general intent offences such as assault, sexual assault, assault causing bodily harm, manslaughter, and mischief, where the mental element of the offence is simply the intention to commit the *actus reus*. The *mens rea* for assault is simply the intent to strike someone, an intent that can be formed even by an extremely intoxicated person.

Infancy

Under Canadian law (s 13 of the *Criminal Code*), a child under the age of 12 cannot be convicted of a criminal offence. An 11-year-old child who commits any criminal offence in Canada, including murder, cannot be held criminally accountable. The rationale for this law is that a person under the age of 12 does not have the maturity to be accountable for the *mens rea* element of the act.

Young people aged 12 to 17 who commit criminal offences are tried and sentenced according to the *Youth Criminal Justice Act*.[7] If the crime that a youth over age 14 commits is particularly serious, the prosecution may seek to have the youth sentenced as an adult. This is permissible under section 64 of the *Youth Criminal Justice Act*.

Mistake of Fact

Although **mistake of fact** can be interpreted as a defence to a criminal charge, it really amounts to the Crown failing to prove the *mens rea* element of the offence. Mistake of fact can be defined in the following way: the accused did not willingly or knowingly commit

mistake of fact
a defence to a criminal charge that involves the Crown failing to prove the *mens rea* of the offence

the act because he or she believed certain facts to be true. For example, Claire was at a party and took a coat that she believed to be hers from the coat rack. As it turned out, the coat belonged to Maria. Claire had an honest belief that the coat was hers. If Claire is charged with stealing the coat, her defence could be mistake of fact.

Mistake of Law

mistake of law
a situation where someone commits an offence while being mistaken about the legal consequences

Being mistaken about the state of the law or about legal consequences does not provide a defence to a criminal charge. Section 19 of the *Criminal Code* expressly provides that ignorance of the law is not an excuse for commission of an offence. In other words, there is a presumption that everyone knows the law. For example, Ted is a clergy member who officiates a marriage ceremony. He knows that one of the parties is an unwilling participant in the marriage, but Ted performs the ceremony anyway. Even though Ted is unaware that by assisting in the ceremony, he can be charged under section 293.1 of the *Criminal Code* for assisting in a forced marriage, this would not be a defence to the charge.

Entrapment

entrapment
a situation where the police lure, draw, or entice a person into committing a crime

Although included here, **entrapment** is not truly a defence. A successful entrapment argument involves a finding of guilt followed by a decision by the judge to stay the proceedings as a result of the actions of the police.

Entrapment involves a situation where the police lure, draw, or entice a person into committing a crime that he or she may not have committed otherwise. As a society, we do not consider it proper for the police to cause otherwise innocent people to commit offences, and then to arrest and charge them for those offences.

If entrapment is raised by the defence in a case tried before a judge and jury, the jury will first determine whether the accused is guilty or not guilty of the offence. If the accused is found guilty, the judge will then consider the entrapment issue. The accused must prove entrapment on a balance of probabilities. If a court finds that police officers entrapped the accused, the most common remedy is a stay of proceedings, which effectively ends the trial.

Alibi

alibi
a defence based on an allegation that the accused could not have committed the *actus reus* of the crime because he or she was not at the scene of the crime at the time it happened

Alibi differs from most other defences in that, when successfully argued, it contradicts the prosecution's evidence about the *actus reus*, and not necessarily the *mens rea* element of the offence. An accused who presents an alibi defence generally calls witnesses who testify that he could not have committed the offence because he was not at the scene of the crime at the time that it was established to have been committed. One of the most interesting things about an alibi defence is that it creates a rare exception to the general rule that the defence need not disclose its case to the prosecution: where an accused intends to rely on an alibi defence, he must reveal the details of his alibi evidence to the prosecution early enough in the investigative process to permit the prosecution to investigate the alibi prior to trial.

Box 8.1   Offence-Specific Passive Defences

Certain offences are charged so frequently that a pattern begins to emerge with respect to how defence counsel constructs a passive defence. These patterns tend to be dictated by precedent: lawyers who have represented many accused charged with a certain crime come to learn which types of evidence, when presented in court, are most likely to assist in creating a reasonable doubt in the mind of the judge or jury.

These "patterned" defences can be described as offence-specific passive defences, and they tend to remain in use until the case law turns against them—when convictions begin to be achieved in spite of their use.

One example of an offence-specific passive defence that has since fallen out of favour is the "two-beer defence" that was sometimes argued in cases involving federal impaired driving charges under section 253 of the *Criminal Code*. The way the two-beer defence worked was as follows: after the prosecution led evidence of the accused's over-80 Breathalyzer reading, the accused called his friends to the stand. The friends testified that the reading could not possibly have been accurate, because they were with the accused all evening before he got into the car, and he was only seen to have consumed two beers (or a small quantity of some other alcoholic beverage). This testimony, where credible, was sometimes enough to create a reasonable doubt about the accuracy of the Breathalyzer in the mind of the trier of fact.

Then, in July 2008, the federal government introduced new provisions under the *Tackling Violent Crime Act*, including a provision that required Breathalyzer readings to be viewed as conclusive proof of impairment (that is, leaving no room for attempts to create a reasonable doubt). Although the new provisions were challenged under the Charter on the ground that they interfere with the right of the accused to mount a full and fair defence, the provisions were upheld by the courts. The final nail in the coffin of the two-beer defence came in the form of the Supreme Court of Canada decision in *R v Gibson*, in which the court rejected the defence in two separate impaired driving cases, one from Nova Scotia and one from Alberta.

Sources: *Criminal Code*, RSC 1985, c C-46, as amended; *Tackling Violent Crime Act*, SC 2008, c 6; *R v Gibson*, 2008 SCC 16.

CHAPTER SUMMARY

Criminal charges are imposed in one of two ways: by information or by indictment. Charging documents must meet particular standards, and if they are deficient, they can be challenged by the defence. A judge may remedy a deficiency either by ordering that the prosecution give the defence particulars of unclear counts or by amending the charging document. If an information or indictment cannot be remedied, the judge can quash the charging document.

After an accused has been charged and has entered a plea of not guilty, his or her case is set down for trial. At a jury trial, the judge is charged with determining the appropriate legal principles to apply to the facts, and the jury is charged with evaluating the facts and the credibility of the witnesses, and applying the law, as articulated by the judge, to the facts. In a trial by judge alone, the judge acts as both trier of law and trier of fact.

Criminal trials follow a set procedure divided into stages. First, the jury is selected. Pre-trial applications are then heard (often in the absence of the jury). Next, each side makes an opening statement. The Crown and the defence then present their witnesses, in turn; the witnesses are often cross-examined by opposing counsel. Because the standard of proof necessary to support a criminal conviction is the high "beyond a reasonable doubt" criminal standard, the prosecution faces a heavy burden of proof, and must present evidence in support of every element of the offence. The defence, in order to obtain a verdict of not guilty, has a lighter burden of proof: it must successfully create a reasonable doubt, in the mind of the trier of fact, about the accused's guilt.

The defence may create a reasonable doubt simply by undermining the prosecution's evidence, referred to as a passive defence, or it may attempt to prove that circumstances existed that negate the guilt of the accused, referred to as a positive (or affirmative) defence. Positive defences may be divided into four categories: justification (for example, self-defence), excuse (for example, necessity), entrapment, and alibi. In some criminal cases, the defence argues that although the accused committed the *actus reus* of the offence, he or she cannot be convicted because he or she was not criminally responsible for the crime because of a mental disorder. In other cases, the defence presents evidence of an alibi: an alternative explanation for the accused's whereabouts and actions at the time the *actus reus* was allegedly committed.

After the lawyers have made their closing arguments, the judge, in a jury trial, recites a charge to the jury (gives instructions) and the jury deliberates to come to a verdict.

KEY TERMS

alibi, 138
automatism, 134
burden of proof, 128
challenge for cause, 128
charging document, 124
civil standard, 128
consent, 132
count, 124
criminal standard, 128
defence, 122
defences, 129
directed verdict, 129
duplicity, 125
duress, 133

entrapment, 138
evidentiary standard, 128
excuse, 133
indictment, 124
information, 124
instructions, 123
insufficiency, 125
joinder, 126
jury, 122
justification, 130
mistake of fact, 137
mistake of law, 138
particulars, 126
passive defence, 129

peremptory challenge, 127
positive (or affirmative)
   defence, 129
pre-enquete hearing, 124
presumption of innocence, 128
prosecution, 122
quash, 127
self-defence, 130
standard of proof, 128
trier of fact, 122
trier of law, 122
verdict, 123

NOTES

1 *Canadian Charter of Rights and Freedoms*, Part I of the *Constitution Act, 1982*, being Schedule B to the *Canada Act 1982* (UK), 1982, c 11.

2 *Criminal Code*, RSC 1985, c C-46, as amended.

3 *R v Côté*, [1978] 1 SCR 8, (1977), 33 CCC (2d) 353.

4 *R v Jobidon*, [1991] 2 SCR 714, 66 CCC (3d) 454.

5 *R v Rabey* (1977), 79 DLR (3d) 414 (Ont CA), aff'd [1980] 2 SCR 513.

6 *R v Parks* (1992), 75 CCC (3d) 287 (SCC).

7 *Youth Criminal Justice Act*, SC 2002, c 1, as amended.

EXERCISES

Multiple Choice

1. To convict an accused of a crime, the judge or jury must be convinced that
   a. it is more likely that the accused is guilty than not guilty
   b. beyond any doubt the accused is guilty
   c. beyond a reasonable doubt the accused is guilty
   d. the police collected all the relevant evidence

2. For an accused to claim self-defence under section 34(1) of the *Criminal Code*, which of the following conditions must be present?
   a. actual force must have been used against the accused
   b. the actions of the accused must be reasonable
   c. the attack is against the accused only—not others
   d. all of the above

3. The trier of law in a trial is
   a. the prosecution
   b. the judge
   c. the jury
   d. the judge and the jury
   e. the defence

4. During jury selection, the defence and the prosecution
   a. are allowed to exclude a certain number of potential jurors with no explanation
   b. are allowed to challenge each juror
   c. may be granted the opportunity to question each juror for cause
   d. none of the above
   e. a and c

5. Which party bears the burden of proving the elements of the offence and the guilt of the accused?
   a. the defence
   b. the judge
   c. the jury
   d. the prosecution
   e. all of the above

True or False?

_____ 1. The Crown bears the burden of proving that an accused person committed a crime.

_____ 2. Proof beyond a reasonable doubt means the judge or jury cannot convict an accused person if they have any doubt in their minds that the accused committed the crime.

_____ 3. Balance of probabilities means that the trier of fact is more than 50 percent certain of the truth of a fact.

_____ 4. Necessity is an example of the type of defence known as an excuse.

_____ 5. The principle of fundamental justice is guaranteed by the _Criminal Code_.

_____ 6. Two separate charges may be laid out in a single count on the charging document.

_____ 7. For offences that are punishable by more than five years of imprisonment (except in cases that involve first-degree murder or treason), both the Crown and the defence are each entitled to 12 peremptory challenges.

_____ 8. Intoxication is a defence to both general intent and specific intent offences.

_____ 9. Both mistake of law and mistake of fact may be used as a valid defence in criminal law.

_____10. The defence must disclose details of an alibi defence to the prosecution.

Short Answer

1. Explain the concept of reverse onus, and cite an example from the _Criminal Code_ that has not already been provided.

2. Why must a crime be proven beyond a reasonable doubt?

3. a. Why is mental disorder an unpopular defence?

   b. The defence of insanity seems to receive a lot of bad press. Why do you think this is the case?

4. What is the difference between a "passive defence" and an "affirmative defence"?

5. In what circumstances will a directed verdict be entered by the court?

Criminal Offence Sentencing and Appeals

9

LEARNING OUTCOMES

After completing this chapter, you should be able to:

- Describe the objectives of sentencing.

- Explain the different kinds of sentences available to a judge.

- Identify aggravating and mitigating factors that may affect the sentence imposed for an offence.

- Identify the circumstances under which a dangerous offender designation or a long-term offender designation may be imposed on an offender.

- Explain the purpose of the National Sex Offender Registry and understand to which offenders it may apply.

- Understand the grounds available to each party for appealing a trial court decision.

- Identify the powers of the appeal courts to change the decision of a trial court.

- Understand what is meant by a record suspension and summarize the criteria for receiving one.

After the Verdict

The criminal trial ends with the announcement of the verdict: guilty or not guilty. Once the verdict has been announced, the jury is no longer needed and is dismissed by the judge. At that point, certain post-trial issues must be dealt with. The two most important of these are sentencing and appeals.

If the verdict is not guilty, the accused is free to go. In certain circumstances, however, the prosecution (in this case, the attorney general and his or her representatives in the Crown attorney's office) can **appeal** the decision of the court.

appeal
the review or challenge of a legal decision in a court of higher jurisdiction

If the verdict is guilty, the next step is sentencing the accused—deciding what punishment he or she will face. The accused also has certain rights of appeal from a guilty verdict.

Sentencing

sentence
the punishment imposed on a person convicted of an offence

The issue of **sentencing** is dealt with in great detail in part XXIII of the *Criminal Code*.[1] What follows is only an introduction to some of the concepts.

When an accused is convicted of an offence either after a trial or after a guilty plea, the court must impose a sentence. The range of sentences for each offence is described in the *Criminal Code*, often in the section that creates the offence itself.

Rationales for Punishment

The purpose and principles of sentencing are contained in section 718 of the Code (Figure 9.1):

> 718. The fundamental purpose of sentencing is to protect society and to contribute, along with crime prevention initiatives, to respect for the law and the maintenance of a just, peaceful and safe society by imposing just sanctions that have one or more of the following objectives:
>
>   (a) to denounce unlawful conduct and the harm done to victims or to the community that is caused by unlawful conduct;
>   (b) to deter the offender and other persons from committing offences;
>   (c) to separate offenders from society, where necessary;
>   (d) to assist in rehabilitating offenders;
>   (e) to provide reparations for harm done to victims or to the community; and
>   (f) to promote a sense of responsibility in offenders, and acknowledgment of the harm done to victims and to the community.

In general, once a guilty verdict is entered, the judge has the power to decide what sentence to impose, subject to the minimum or maximum sentence (if any) set out in the Code for the offence, the principles of sentencing listed above, and the case law precedents for sentences previously imposed for similar offences and similar offenders.

For example, the offence of assault under section 266 of the Code carries with it, if tried as an indictable offence, a maximum sentence of five years in prison. This means that a judge may not sentence a person convicted of assault to eight years in prison. As well, if every other judge who has dealt with an assault conviction in the past has imposed a sentence of between one and three years, the judge in the present case must impose a similar sentence unless he or she is convinced this case is much more serious.

FIGURE 9.1   Sentencing Objectives

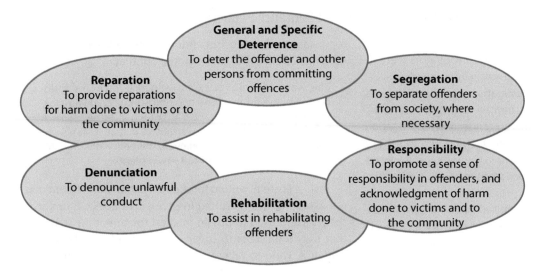

Section 718.1 sets out the fundamental principle of sentencing: "A sentence must be proportionate to the gravity of the offence and the degree of responsibility of the offender." The scope of sentences available under the *Criminal Code* is relatively narrow. Canadian law does not allow capital punishment (the death penalty) or corporal punishment (whipping, beating, or otherwise inflicting physical punishment), in part because of the prohibition against cruel and unusual treatment or punishment in section 12 of the *Canadian Charter of Rights and Freedoms.*[2]

Aggravating and Mitigating Factors

Under section 718.2 of the *Criminal Code*, the court can take into account any aggravating or mitigating factors when imposing a sentence. One or more **aggravating factors** (factors that make the crime more serious) may result in a harsher sentence than the norm; one or more **mitigating factors** (factors that make the crime less serious) may result in a lighter sentence than the norm.

Some examples of aggravating factors that may increase the sentence include the following: the crime was motivated by hatred of an identifiable group (hate crime), the crime was domestic (committed against a family member), the offender breached a position of trust with respect to the victim, or the offence was committed for the benefit of a criminal organization.

Mitigating factors that may lessen the sentence include the following: the accused was provoked by the victim, the accused is a first-time offender, and/or the accused has shown evidence of remorse or rehabilitation. Unfair or improper (though not necessarily illegal) conduct by law enforcement officials or prosecutors may also lead to a reduced sentence. An example is the Crown deliberately delaying the trial.

aggravating factor
in a sentencing context, a circumstance of the offence or the offender that supports a more serious punishment

mitigating factor
in sentencing for crimes, a fact or condition relating to either the offence or the offender that decreases the punishment (for example, an early guilty plea or remorse)

Police Misconduct Affecting Trial Fairness Warrants Stay, Not Sentence Reduction

Beginning in 2002, Mississauga police investigated a series of violent home invasion robberies. Nine conspirators were investigated as suspects and were eventually charged.

During the course of the investigation, one of the suspects, Quang Hoang Tran, surrendered himself to the police for questioning. During the course of that surrender and interrogation, two police officers beat up Mr. Tran, causing him to suffer a broken jaw and what was described in the appeal as a "permanent injury." The officers then took steps to cover up what they had done to Tran.

The police brutality and attempted coverup were uncovered during a *voir dire* (a hearing to assess the admissibility of evidence allegedly illegally collected). Despite the finding that the police beat Tran, the Crown permitted those same officers to continue to participate in the investigation and in the court proceedings until the judge ordered the Crown to ban the officers from any further participation.

The trial judge refused to grant the stay of proceedings that Tran's defence counsel requested as a remedy for the police conduct. Tran's trial proceeded, and he was found not guilty of certain other offences, but guilty of conspiracy to commit robbery. The judge explained that as a remedy for the police brutality he suffered, Tran should receive a sentence that was one-half the sentence that would otherwise be ordered in the case. While certain of his co-conspirators received sentences of approximately three years' imprisonment plus probation, Tran was sentenced to 14 months' custody plus three years' probation.

Tran appealed his conviction, arguing that he should have been granted a stay of proceedings as a remedy for the violation of his Charter rights. He also appealed his sentence, arguing that he should have been given additional "credit" for time served in jail in restrictive conditions.

The Court of Appeal acknowledged that a stay of proceedings is an "extraordinary remedy" and that a sentence reduction has often been considered to be an appropriate remedy

for instances of police misconduct in the course of an investigation. However, the court pointed out that:

> This was not a case of excessive police force in the discharge of their duties. The two officers involved were taking him to the police station after he had turned himself in. No degree of force was warranted. In fact, if Tran's version of the story is to be believed, the police beat him for invoking his Charter right to remain silent.

Justice Epstein, writing for the court, then pointed out that the assault on Tran resulted in permanent bodily harm, that the police refused to obtain medical treatment for Tran, and that they took steps to cover up the assault "by destroying evidence, lying to fellow officers and perjuring themselves before the court during the *voir dire*." The state misconduct did not end there, but continued into the trial, because the officers were allowed to participate in the trial process until banned by the judge. This "cavalier attitude" on the part of the Crown, and the willingness of the Crown to align itself with the police misconduct, Justice Epstein explained, prejudiced the fairness of the trial—an event that threatens to bring the administration of justice into disrepute. This, the judge concluded, is exactly the kind of threat that warrants the granting of a stay of proceedings as a Charter remedy. Quoting defence counsel in the case, Justice Epstein asked: "If this conduct does not warrant a stay of proceedings, what does?"

The Court of Appeal overturned Tran's conviction and entered a stay of proceedings in his case.

Questions for Discussion

1. Do you believe that the remedy of a stay of proceedings is a more effective deterrent to police misconduct than is the remedy of a reduced sentence? Why or why not?

2. Tran was assaulted by police after having surrendered himself voluntarily into custody. Do you think this factor had any influence on the court's decision to grant a stay?

Source: *R v Tran*, 2010 ONCA 471.

In 2015, the government passed certain amendments to the sentencing provisions of the Code. One amendment, which was passed via a bill known as "Quanto's Law," introduced stricter penalties for harming police or military animals.[3] It included a new provision (s 718.03) that provided that "the court shall give primary consideration to the objectives of denunciation and deterrence" when sentencing a person under an amended law enforcement animal harm provision (s 445.01).

Another bill, the *Tougher Penalties for Child Predators Act*,[4] made changes to one of the "Punishment Generally" provisions, section 718.3, by adding a subsection (s 718.3(7)) directing courts to consider consecutive (not concurrent) sentences for offenders convicted of sexual offences against children. This amendment was in force at the time of the June 2016 sentencing of Gordon Stuckless, who pleaded guilty to over 100 separate sexual assaults against 18 children. The announcement that Stuckless was sentenced to a total of 6.5 years' imprisonment for the over 100 offences was met with outrage from his victims and from some members of the public. In her reasons for the sentence, the sentencing judge noted a number of mitigating factors, including that the accused chose to plead guilty, he had taken responsibility for his actions, he had not reoffended since the time of his convictions two years before, and he was voluntarily submitting to chemical castration.

Types of Sentences

The most common sentences imposed include **imprisonment** in a custodial facility (ss 743 to 746), imprisonment to be served conditionally in the community (s 742.1), a **fine** (ss 734 to 737), a **suspended sentence** (s 731(1)(a)), and **probation** (ss 731 to 733.1). It is common, and permissible, to impose a combination of sentences—for example, a fine plus probation. Imprisonment in a state-run custodial facility—a municipal jail, provincial prison, or federal penitentiary—is considered the most serious of the sentences, since it deprives the offender of his or her freedom.

Where an offender has been convicted of multiple offences, he or she may be sentenced separately for each offence. Multiple custodial sentences can be served either concurrently (at the same time) or, in more serious cases, consecutively (one after the other). Certain sentences can be served intermittently—for example, on weekends only. These kinds of arrangements are sometimes made to permit a non-dangerous offender to hold a job and support his or her dependants.

Conditional imprisonment is served in the community. It is a form of house arrest. This type of sentence can only be imposed under certain conditions, including: the length of the sentence is under two years; there is no minimum sentence for the crime and the maximum sentence is 14 years or less; and the offence did not involve bodily harm, terrorism, drugs, or weapons. There is also a list of specific offences for which a conditional sentence is not available.

Fines are often imposed for statutory or quasi-criminal offences, such as minor traffic or environmental offences. The ability of the offender to pay the fine must be considered before a fine is imposed. In some cases, an offender can "work off" all or part of a fine by earning credits for participating in a special government work program (s 736).

imprisonment
incarceration in a prison, the most serious punishment allowable in Canada for persons convicted of offences

fine
a form of punishment, requiring the payment of money, generally used for quasi-criminal or minor criminal offences

suspended sentence
a form of punishment that involves delaying the imposition of the punishment indefinitely if the accused person complies with certain conditions, failing which the punishment is enforced

probation
a type of sentence that does not involve imprisonment but allows the accused to remain free, subject to conditions

Box 9.1   Sentencing and the Victim Surcharge

In 2013, the federal government, via a bill called the *Increasing Offenders' Accountability for Victims Act*,[5] increased the amount of a fee called a victim surcharge that is payable by those who commit offences under drug control legislation. The increase was controversial, and a number of provinces, including Ontario, refused to collect the surcharge. Defence lawyers have successfully argued that the surcharge amounts to cruel and unusual punishment contrary to section 12 of the Charter, because it is frequently levied against individuals of very meagre economic means with no way to pay it.[6] However, by the fall of 2015 more recent Ontario cases have upheld the surcharge, either on the basis that it is not a punishment at all,[7] or on the basis that it is indeed a punishment, but not a cruel and unusual one.[8] Because of these conflicting decisions, it is likely that the issue will eventually be considered by the Ontario Court of Appeal.

probation order
the details of the conditions imposed on a person who has been sentenced to probation, or who has been released on parole

A judge can impose a suspended sentence for offences that do not carry a minimum sentence. A suspended sentence means that the offender is released back into society subject to certain conditions set out in a **probation order**. If the offender breaches the conditions of the probation order before it expires (the maximum length of a probation order is three years), he or she faces being sentenced on the original offence and forced to serve the sentence in custody. Several possible conditions can be included in a probation order, such as a prohibition against carrying firearms, an order not to approach or associate with certain people, or an order to stay away from certain places.

Offenders sentenced to probation must comply with the conditions contained in a probation order. Probation may be ordered on its own or along with a fine or a term of imprisonment, but not both. Thus, a person convicted of assault could be sentenced to one year in prison and two years of probation, subject to the conditions in the probation order. He or she may, instead, be sentenced to a fine of $1,000 plus two years of probation, subject to the conditions in the probation order.

discharge
the release of an accused after a finding of guilt, with or without conditions

In some cases, a person convicted of a less serious offence may be **discharged** either on an absolute basis or on a conditional basis. An absolute discharge (s 730) has no conditions attached to it and takes effect right away. An accused who receives an absolute discharge is not required to serve time or pay a fine, and his conviction does not result in a criminal record. A conditional discharge (s 730) includes a probation order with conditions that can be in effect for up to three years; if the accused does not reoffend during her probation period and complies with all conditions, at the conclusion of her probation period, she will not have a criminal record.

Offenders who are sentenced to a prison term can usually apply for supervised release or parole before they have served the entire sentence.

Credit for Pre-Trial Custody

When ordering a custody sentence for an accused who was held in custody awaiting trial, judges award the accused a "credit" in the form of a deduction from the global sentence for time served before sentencing. How much credit to allow has been a source of controversy in the last decade.

Prior to the fall of 2009, judges had a broad discretion to credit time served according to a ratio of more than 1:1—in other words, an accused often had 1.5 months deducted from his or her sentence for every pre-trial month served. The rationale for this practice was that conditions in the jails in which accused are held pending trial are generally poorer than conditions in prisons. Where an accused was held in a notoriously uncomfortable or crowded jail (Toronto's Don Jail had this reputation), or in a jail that experienced riots or disease outbreaks, the credit ratio could be even higher: up to 3:1 in extreme cases.

In an effort to be seen as getting tougher on crime and to encourage guilty pleas, the Canadian government changed the time-served credit rules in 2009 to strictly limit instances in which credit can be granted at a ratio higher than 1:1, and abolished the granting of credit at any ratio higher than 1.5:1. The 1.5 ratio was designated as available only in exceptional circumstances.

The new limits on credit for pre-trial custody proved unpopular with accused and critics alike, and led to litigation over what was included in "exceptional circumstances." In April 2014, the Supreme Court of Canada released its decision in the case of *R v Summers*,[9] clarifying the issues. In *Summers*, the court held that contrary to some of the cases that had been decided in the previous five years, judges *do* have discretion to award credit at a rate of 1.5:1 even where the accused was denied bail prior to trial, and even where a sentence provided that pre-trial credit was not to be counted when determining the date of parole eligibility. Since the decision in *Summers*, courts have returned to regularly awarding credit at a rate of 1.5:1 in many cases.

Pre-Sentence Report

In deciding the type and harshness of the sentence to be imposed, the judge may hear submissions from both the prosecution and the defence. These take place at a sentencing hearing, without the jury present.

The judge may order a **pre-sentence report** under section 721(1) of the Code. If ordered, the report is prepared by a probation officer before sentencing and filed with the court. The report usually contains information on the background and character of the offender, separate from the offence. The report gives the judge insight into the offender so that the sentence can be effective both in punishing the offender for the offence and in helping his or her rehabilitation.

The court is also permitted to consider another type of report, called a victim impact statement. Provided for by section 722, these reports are prepared by victims to an offence and are intended to describe "the physical or emotional harm, property damage or economic loss suffered by the victim as the result of the commission of the offence and the impact of the offence on the victim." Some victims choose to read their statements aloud in court (with a support person sitting with them, if they desire); others simply file the written report for the court's consideration.

Where the offender is an Aboriginal person, the court is required, under section 718.2(e), to consider "all available sanctions, other than imprisonment, that are reasonable in the circumstances and consistent with the harm done to victims or to the community." While this rule applies to all offenders, the section provides that it should be applied with particular attention to Aboriginal offenders. In 1999, the Supreme Court of Canada set out, in *R v Gladue*,[10] guidelines for the information that ought to be considered to give effect to section 718.2(e). It has since become standard practice, in cases involving Aboriginal offenders, to prepare a special pre-sentence report called a "Gladue report" that addresses these relevant factors, which include the lingering impact of the residential school system and the welfare and adoption systems as they applied to indigenous children, indigenous social history including relocation and the loss of culture, and also exposure to poor living conditions and substandard education.

pre-sentence report
a document prepared by a probation officer at the request of a judge that provides background on the offender for use in deciding on a sentence for the offender

Dangerous and Long-Term Offenders

In certain cases, the Crown takes the position that, on its own, the sentence imposed on a particular offender is insufficient to protect the public from the risks that the offender poses. Prosecutors generally take this position either because the offender seems particularly dangerous or because he or she has demonstrated, through a pattern of reoffending, that he or she is unlikely to be deterred from further offending.

In these cases, the prosecution can apply to have the offender designated as a "long-term offender" or a "dangerous offender." These designations are created by part XXIV of the *Criminal Code*, which sets out the procedure for making the designations, the consequences of being so designated, and the process for appealing a designation.

An offender can be designated as long-term or dangerous only if he or she has been convicted of an offence that falls into certain prescribed categories. In the case of dangerous offender designations, the relevant category is that of "serious personal injury" offences, which are defined in section 752. The category of offences that can lead to a long-term offender designation includes primarily sexual offences, particularly those associated with high recidivism rates (for example, sexual abuse of children). In both cases, the offender must have committed more than one such offence, and the prosecution must be able to demonstrate that the offender poses an ongoing risk to society. To assist in making this determination, the court has the power to remand (place by way of court order) the offender into the custody of a person who can conduct or arrange an assessment of the offender's risk potential (for example, a psychiatrist).

If the prosecution is successful in having the offender designated as a dangerous offender, the court has three options for protecting the public:

1. detention in a penitentiary for an indeterminate period (during which periodic reviews of the offender's risk potential are conducted);

2. imposition of a custodial (prison) sentence of at least two years and a long-term supervision order, upon release, for up to ten years; or

3. imposition of a sentence (just like in the normal course, but often a particularly strict sentence is chosen).

If the prosecution succeeds in its application to have the offender designated as a long-term offender, the court will impose a custodial sentence of at least two years, and, in addition, a period of supervision in the community that is not to exceed ten years.

National Sex Offender Registry

In 2004, the government of Canada proclaimed the *Sex Offender Information Registration Act*[11] (SOIRA) and created the National Sex Offender Registry. The SOIRA created a system for the collection and retention of identifying information about designated sexual offenders for the purpose of protecting the public from these individuals and supporting police efforts to investigate sex crimes.

Where a person has been convicted of a sexual offence included in the definition of "designated offence" in section 490.011(1) of the *Criminal Code*, the Crown can ask the court to issue a sex offender registration order against that offender. In general, the Crown must move quickly to request this order; however, it is possible to have an order issued against certain offenders who were convicted of their offences prior to the coming into force of the legislation in 2004.

In general, the court will grant a prosecutor's request for a registration order. However, section 490.023(2) permits a convicted person to apply, within one year of the imposition of the order, for an order exempting him or her from the order. The court will grant the exemption if it is satisfied that

> the person has established that the impact of the obligation on them, including on their privacy or liberty, would be grossly disproportionate to the public interest in protecting society through the effective prevention or investigation of crimes of a sexual nature.

When a registration order is issued, the offender is required, within 15 days, to attend at a registration centre to provide information and be photographed. The offender must return once a year to update the registration, and must report all absences longer than 15 days from his home address to police (and give details of his whereabouts). If the offender has a change of address, he has 15 days to report it.

CASE IN POINT

Intolerance of Homosexuality in Offender's Culture Doesn't Outweigh Benefits of Registration

A male offender, identified in his registration order appeal as "A.T.," was convicted of sexual assault on two different under-age boys and was sentenced to five years' imprisonment. In 2005, the court ordered the offender to register in the National Sex Offender Registry.

A.T. appealed the order on the grounds set out in section 490—that forcing him to register would have an impact "grossly disproportionate to the public interest in protecting society."

The evidentiary burden for an offender attempting to avoid registration under this provision is extremely high, which means the court will only find that the impact on a person is grossly disproportionate in very exceptional circumstances. In support of his appeal, A.T. presented the following evidence:

- he believed (though he hadn't actually investigated the issue) that being registered as a sex offender would have a negative impact on his career opportunities as a psychologist—the profession for which he was studying;

- he was under stress, had trouble sleeping, had developed nervous tics, and avoided going out in public after someone shouted "pedophile" at him;

- he felt that the prejudice against people who commit homosexual sex crimes was especially strong within his ethnic community (the court decision did not specify his particular ethnicity);

- he feared returning to his country of origin, where his crimes would have attracted the death penalty;

- he was engaged to be married but felt that he could not marry his fiancée because of the risk of people taking a derogatory view of her or her family, or ostracizing her; and

- he was concerned that if he lived in a small town, police might breach the confidentiality protections for registered sex offenders and word of his convictions would get around.

After listening to this evidence, the court dismissed A.T.'s appeal and confirmed the registration order. Judge Godfrey gave the following reasons for ruling that the appellant had not proved that registering would have a disproportionate impact on him:

- the appellant's stress flowed not from the prospect of registration, but from fear that the community would find out about his convictions; however, criminal convictions are a matter of public record anyway;

- with respect to the issue of cultural intolerance, Judge Godfrey wrote: "I am not sure any community is accepting of the criminal offence of anal sex on 12 and 13-year-old boys";

- with respect to the small town issue, Judge Godfrey noted that the offender was free to live wherever he wants, and that allowing all sex offenders who live in small towns to be exempt from registration would defeat the purpose of the legislation;

- there were aggravating factors: the accused "groomed" the victims by befriending them (which shows forethought and planning), he used pornography and alcohol to encourage them, and the boys suffered significant emotional harm; and

- psychological assessments of the offender suggested that he was at low to moderate risk of reoffending violently and/or sexually. However, the offender never made any admission of guilt, and so it was not possible to determine what the triggering factors were in the first place. Therefore, the assessment of his recidivism risk was only an estimate based on incomplete information.

In light of these factors, the court held that the offender had not proved that being required to register would have a grossly disproportionate impact on him.

Questions for Discussion

1. Do you believe that a person convicted of sex crimes against minors has the right to be shielded from potential embarrassment related to the public revelation of those crimes? Why or why not?

2. What about the offender's suggestion that registration in the database would prevent him from returning to his country of origin? Is this likely a valid concern? Why or why not?

Source: *R v AT*, 2007 BCPC 317.

The duration of an offender's registration depends on the nature of the conviction:

- if the offence was prosecuted summarily (via summary conviction procedures, even if it was a hybrid offence) or if the maximum term of imprisonment for the offence is 2 or 5 years, the duration of the registration is 10 years;
- if the offence was prosecuted under indictable procedure and carries a maximum prison sentence of 10 or 14 years, the duration of the registration is 20 years; and
- if the offence was an indictable offence and carries a maximum term of life imprisonment, the registration is for life.

Offenders who have not reoffended can apply for an order terminating their registration early (in general, after half of the applicable term has elapsed). Offenders who fail to comply with the terms of a registration order can be charged under section 490.031 of the *Criminal Code*.

Appeals

The verdict of the judge or jury in a criminal trial is not necessarily the final word. Both the prosecution and the defence have certain rights to appeal verdicts and sentences.

Appeals of decisions about indictable offences are dealt with in part XXI of the *Criminal Code*. Summary conviction offences are dealt with as a whole in part XXVII of the Code. What follows is a very brief introduction to the complex issue of appeals.

Grounds: The Basis for an Appeal

The basis for any appeal must be a party's allegation that some sort of **error** was made at trial by either the trier of fact or the trier of law. The alleged error itself is called the **ground for appeal**. If there is no ground for appeal, no appeal can be made. In most cases, parties who appeal a trial court decision will list several grounds for appeal in their appeal documents.

Grounds for appeal fall into three categories: questions of law, questions of fact, and questions of mixed law and fact. In most cases, the right to appeal is available to either the defence or the prosecution on a question of law; questions of fact or of mixed law and fact can be appealed only by the defence with **leave to appeal** (permission) of the court to which the appeal is to be brought.

When making an appeal on the ground of a **question of law**, the person appealing—the **appellant**—must show that the judge in the trial court misinterpreted or misapplied a legal rule and that the error had a material impact on the verdict. For example, the offence of first-degree murder involves a very specific *mens rea*: the accused must not only have intended to kill the victim, but the killing must also have been planned and deliberate. If, instead, the judge instructs the jury that it can convict the accused of first-degree murder if the jury believes that the accused attacked his or her victim without concern for whether the victim would die, the judge has made an error in law. That error could potentially have led the jury to wrongly convict the accused of first-degree murder even if the required planning and deliberation were not present.

When making an appeal on a **question of fact**, the appellant must show that the trier of fact made an error in deciding, on the basis of the evidence presented at trial, that a certain fact was true or false. The error must be glaring—it cannot simply be a difference of opinion. In general, the decision of the trier of fact must be completely unsupported by the evidence for the appeal court to intervene. For example, if all witnesses to the offence

error
a mistake made by the judge (or, less commonly, the jury) that might lead to an appeal

ground for appeal
a reason—generally an error made by the trier of law or of fact—for a party to be allowed to ask a higher court to reconsider the decision of a lower court

leave to appeal
permission to file an appeal

question of law
a ground for appeal that is available to either the defence or the prosecution that is based on the misinterpretation or misapplication of a legal rule at trial

appellant
the party that decides to appeal a court's decision to a higher court

question of fact
a ground for appeal that is available only to the defence that is based on the validity of a piece of evidence presented at trial

stated clearly that a tiny woman committed the offence and the jury still convicts the accused, a large man, of the offence, it could be argued that the jury has made a finding of fact that is not supported by the evidence.

An appeal on a **question of mixed law and fact** is based on an error that combines elements of the two. This type of appeal tends to arise in cases where the legal rule that was applied is one that turns very closely on particular facts. A case involving sexual assault is a good example. There can be no sexual assault where the contact complained of was consented to by the (adult) victim. From a practical standpoint, participants do not explicitly negotiate every stage in a sexual encounter. This means that where consent is contested, the circumstances must be closely examined on their specific facts. Any errors in this process of examining the evidence may later result in an appeal on a question of mixed law and fact.

question of mixed law and fact
a ground for appeal that is available only to the defence that is based on an error that combines elements of a question of law and a question of fact

Appeal Courts

The decision of a provincial court (for example, Ontario Court of Justice) judge in a summary conviction matter must be appealed to the superior court (for example, the Ontario Superior Court of Justice). The decision of a provincial court judge in an indictable matter is appealed to the provincial court of appeal (for example, the Ontario Court of Appeal). The decision of a superior court judge or judge and jury must be appealed to the provincial court of appeal. In some cases, the decision of the provincial court of appeal may be appealed to the Supreme Court of Canada.

Rights of Appeal of Defence and Prosecution

The defence can appeal a decision of the trial court by right (without leave) on a question of law or, with leave from the court to be appealed to, on a question of fact or a question of mixed law and fact. If leave is granted, the defence can also appeal a sentence.

The prosecution can appeal only on a question of law.

Procedure for Appeals

The appeal is launched when the appellant files (in the appropriate court office) a notice of appeal or, when leave is required, a notice of the application for leave to appeal, which will set out the grounds on which the appeal is based. The notice must be served on the representative of the other party—the **respondent**.

Once an appeal has been launched and, if necessary, leave for the appeal has been granted, the appellant and the respondent must each prepare a detailed document called a **factum** that sets out the position of the party on the grounds for appeal. The factum cites the law (cases, statutes, and regulations), refers to evidence given at the trial and to the trial transcripts, and makes arguments to support the position of the party filing the factum. Once prepared, the factum must be served on the other party and filed with the court of appeal.

Although the court of appeal has the right to hear oral testimony from any witness who appeared at trial (s 683 of the Code), in general the court simply reads the factums of the parties and hears oral argument from the lawyers for the two sides. The judges on the court of appeal are entitled to question the lawyers about legal points or interpretations or to clarify the parties' positions.

At the end of the hearing, the judges of the court of appeal have the power to take any of the actions described in the next section.

respondent
the party that defends the original trial court decision when it is appealed by another party

factum
a document used in an appeal that sets out the grounds for the appeal, the facts of the case, and the legal arguments as to why the appeal should succeed or fail

Powers of the Court of Appeal

Once the appeal hearing is over, the judges of the court of appeal have wide powers to revisit (or leave alone) the trial court decision.

On an appeal by the defence (s 686), the court of appeal for the province can direct an acquittal, direct a new trial, dismiss the appeal, or uphold the conviction and alter the sentence. On an appeal by the prosecution (s 686), the court of appeal can set aside the acquittal and direct a new trial, dismiss the appeal, alter the sentence, or substitute the acquittal with a conviction (if the trial was held with a judge alone). If the trial was held with a judge and jury, the court of appeal cannot substitute a conviction for an acquittal but must order a new trial.

Summary Conviction Appeals

For summary convictions, appeals of provincial court decisions go to superior court. Leave is not required. Further appeals are addressed, only on questions of law and only with leave, by the court of appeal. Further appeals may be launched to the highest court in Canada, the Supreme Court of Canada. The Supreme Court considers only appeals based on questions of law. Leave is always needed to bring an appeal to the Supreme Court of Canada unless one of the judges in the court of appeal dissented on a matter of law or the conviction or acquittal was set aside at the court of appeal level.

Record Suspensions

After a convict has completed his or her sentence, and has lived in the community for a certain number of years without reoffending, he or she may be eligible to apply for a **record suspension** (though colloquially known as a pardon, the terminology was changed to "record suspension" in 2012). The Parole Board of Canada explains that a successful record suspension application results in the convict having his or her "criminal record kept separate and apart from other criminal records."[12] A record suspension does not, therefore, "erase" a criminal record. For practical purposes, however, it does remove some of the barriers to normal life that having a criminal record can create.

When a convict's record is suspended, the information about his or her convictions is removed from the Canadian Police Information Centre (CPIC) database, a computerized information system that provides information on crime and criminals to Canadian law enforcement agencies. Once removed, the information cannot be accessed without permission from the minister of Public Safety Canada.

Removal of a conviction from the CPIC database does not guarantee that the conviction is also removed from provincial and municipal police force records, but according to the Parole Board, these agencies often cooperate by removing the same information.

It is illegal under federal human rights legislation to discriminate against a person because of a record suspension—for example, when that person applies for a job. However, a record suspension will not completely shield a person from being treated differently in all situations:

- other countries may refuse to admit a person into their country, or to issue an entry visa to a person, despite the fact that that person has been "pardoned";
- if the convict committed certain sexual offences, his or her name will be flagged in the CPIC database, and this flag will appear when police checks are performed. This allows certain searchers (for example, employers who serve vulnerable popu-

record suspension
an order allowing a person's criminal record to be kept separate from other criminal records and removed from the CPIC database

lations, such as children or disabled individuals) to be warned that the convict may not be a suitable candidate to work with these populations; and

- a record suspension does not erase a record of prohibition orders—for example, an order prohibiting the convict from possessing firearms.

In 2010, changes to the law were made to alter the application process for record suspensions (then called pardons). These came in the wake of public outrage following two news stories about pardons for sexual offenders. In one case, the media reported that convict Karla Homolka—a woman who assisted an accomplice, Paul Bernardo, in the rape and murder of two teen girl victims—intended to apply for a pardon. In the second case, the media reported that Graham James, the person convicted in the high-profile sexual abuse case involving NHL hockey players Sheldon Kennedy and Theoren Fleury, had already been granted a pardon.

This public outcry led the government to draft and pass amendments to the *Criminal Records Act*,[13] the legislation governing pardons. In 2012, yet another round of changes was made via the *Safe Streets and Communities Act*.[14] This round of amendments replaced the term "pardon" with "record suspension," and introduced stricter eligibility requirements and longer waiting periods for those wanting to apply.

The new waiting periods include:

- for a summary conviction offence other than a sexual offence against a child: five years; and
- for an indictable offence other than a sexual offence, or for a summary sexual offence against a child: ten years.

For those convicted of indictable offences against children, record suspensions are no longer available, except in certain narrow circumstances.

In determining whether an application for a record suspension should be granted, the Parole Board will consider whether, during the waiting period, "the applicant … has been of good conduct" and has not reoffended or been convicted of an offence under an Act of Parliament, and whether granting a record suspension "would provide a measurable benefit to the applicant, would sustain his or her rehabilitation in society as a law-abiding citizen and would not bring the administration of justice into disrepute."[15]

The rationale behind the changes is to introduce greater deliberation and reflection into the record suspension–granting process, which had been criticized as a "rubber-stamp" procedure that allowed the Parole Board little discretion to reject applications.

CHAPTER SUMMARY

If a criminal court finds an accused guilty, the next step is to sentence the accused. A sentence is imposed by a judge, not a jury. In most cases, the accused is not sentenced immediately after the verdict; in some cases, a pre-sentence report is prepared by a probation officer to assist the judge in his or her decision.

The range of sentences available for a crime is defined by the relevant provision of the *Criminal Code*. The Code also includes an entire part (XXIII) that regulates sentencing and that includes provisions explaining the principles of sentencing and the purposes that an appropriate sentence should achieve. These purposes include deterrence, protection of the public, and supporting the rehabilitation of the offender with a view to his or her eventual reintegration into law-abiding society.

In choosing an appropriate sentence from within that range, judges follow the principles of sentencing and take into account legal precedents. They must also consider aggravating factors (those that make the accused's actions more blameworthy) and mitigating factors (those that support a lesser sentence). They may also hear submissions from the prosecution and defence.

Sentences available under Canadian criminal law include custody (prison or penitentiary time), probation, conditional sentences (sometimes called house arrest), fines, conditional discharge, and absolute discharge. Some of these sentences can be combined; for example, an accused can be sentenced to a fine and a term of probation.

In addition to a sentence, certain orders may be imposed on an accused; for example, the accused may be prohibited from possessing firearms. In appropriate cases, the accused may be required to register himself in the National Sex Offender Registry. Finally, certain accused may be made subject, on a judge's order, to a dangerous offender or long-term offender designation. Such a designation affects the liberty of the accused for a longer period than does an ordinary sentence.

In some cases, one of the parties to a criminal trial chooses to appeal the result (defence appeals a conviction, prosecution appeals an acquittal). There are some restrictions on parties' rights of appeal—for example, the prosecution cannot appeal on a question of fact. At the conclusion of an appeal, the court may either confirm the original verdict, change the verdict, or allow the appeal and order a new trial. Offenders can also appeal dangerous or long-term offender designations, or an order to register in the National Sex Offender Registry.

After the offender has lived in the community without reoffending for a certain period of time post-conviction, he or she may become eligible to apply for a record suspension—an order that allows the offender's criminal record to be kept separate from other criminal records.

KEY TERMS

NOTES

1 *Criminal Code*, RSC 1985, c C-46, as amended.

2 *Canadian Charter of Rights and Freedoms*, Part I of the *Constitution Act, 1982*, being Schedule B to the *Canada Act 1982* (UK), 1982, c 11.

3 *Justice for Animals in Service Act (Quanto's Law)*, SC 2015, c 34.

4   *Tougher Penalties for Child Predators Act*, SC 2015, c 23.

5   *Increasing Offenders' Accountability for Victims Act*, SC 2013, c 11.

6   *R v Michael*, 2014 ONCJ 360.

7   *R v Tinker, Judge, Bondoc & Mead*, 2015 ONSC 2284.

8   *R v Larocque*, 2015 ONSC 5407.

9   *R v Summers*, 2014 SCC 26.

10   *R v Gladue*, [1999] 1 SCR 688.

11   *Sex Offender Information Registration Act*, SC 2004, c 10.

12   Parole Board of Canada, "Record Suspensions," online: <https://www.canada.ca/en/parole-board/services/record-suspensions/what-is-a-record-suspension.html>.

13   *Criminal Records Act*, RSC 1985, c C-47.

14   *Safe Streets and Communities Act*, SC 2012, c 1.

15   *Supra* note 13, s 4.1.

EXERCISES

Multiple Choice

1. Which of the following is not a rationale for punishment?

   a. deterrence

   b. mitigation

   c. rehabilitation

   d. protection of society

   e. none of the above

2. Which of the following is not an aggravating factor?

   a. the consumption of alcohol

   b. the defacing of a synagogue

   c. a mob hit

   d. a teacher sexually assaulting a student

   e. none of the above

3. The jury is dismissed from the trial after

   a. the sentencing

   b. the verdict is announced

   c. the Crown presents its case

   d. post-trial issues are dealt with

   e. all of the above

4. Sentences are

   a. decided by the judge based on precedent

   b. decided by the jury based on the relevant *Criminal Code* section

   c. decided by the judge and the jury together

   d. decided by the judge based on the relevant *Criminal Code* section

   e. a and d

5. Which of the following is not a mitigating factor?

   a. the victim taunted the accused

   b. the accused has never committed an offence before

   c. the accused committed the offence on behalf of someone else

   d. the accused seems sorry to have committed the offence

   e. the accused has participated in a rehabilitation program

True or False?

_____ **1.** The court has no discretion in imposing sentences, which are strictly prescribed by the *Criminal Code.*

_____ **2.** The fact that a crime was motivated by hatred of an identifiable group is an example of an aggravating factor.

_____ **3.** An absolute discharge has conditions attached to it.

_____ **4.** Improper or unfair conduct by the police or the Crown may be a factor in reducing a sentence.

_____ **5.** A judge can consider an offender's background and character when deciding on a sentence.

_____ **6.** Sentencing law requires sentences for convictions imposed at the same time to be served concurrently, so the total sentence can only ever be as long as the statutory maximum sentence for the most serious of the offences.

_____ **7.** When sentencing an Aboriginal offender, the court has a special duty to consider all reasonable alternatives to custody.

_____ **8.** A court can sentence an offender to multiple types of sentence (custody, probation, a fine) for a single conviction.

_____ **9.** It is not possible to appeal the validity of a sentence, only the validity of the conviction that led to it.

_____**10.** A record suspension or "pardon" is granted only where the individual has later been found to have been innocent of the crime of which he or she had been convicted.

Short Answer

1. Briefly outline the rationales for punishing convicted persons. Which rationale do you think is the most compelling? Why?

2. Give an example of a ground for appeal on a question of law.

3. Why do you think the prosecution can appeal only on questions of law?

4. There has been considerable controversy, in recent years, over whether accused should be granted credit at a ratio greater than 1:1 for time spent in pre-trial custody. Do you believe that credit at a ratio greater than 1:1 is appropriate? Why or why not?

5. As you learned in this chapter, some offenders are permitted to serve custodial sentences on weekends and/or evenings, so that they can continue to work at their jobs. What do you think was the reasoning behind this kind of custodial sentence? Do you think it's a good idea or not?

PART IV

Introduction to Civil Law Disciplines

Contracts and Torts: The Founding Principles of Civil Law

LEARNING OUTCOMES

After completing this chapter, you should be able to:

- Understand the difference between civil law and criminal law.

- Compare and contrast the way in which legal rights arise under contract law and tort law.

- Describe the basic principles of the relationship between two contract parties.

- Describe the nature of the remedies commonly awarded in a contract dispute.

- List some of the circumstances in which a contract will not be enforced by a court.

- Describe the basic principles of the relationship between a tortfeasor and the victim of a tort.

- Describe the nature of the remedies commonly awarded in a lawsuit based in tort.

- Understand the potential tort liability of a police officer.

Introduction

By this point in your studies, you have come to appreciate that there are differences between policing and other occupations that are based on law. The next three chapters focus on the civil law—that is, the non-criminal side of law. Enforcement of rights and obligations in the civil law takes place in the context of litigation (lawsuits) in the civil courts, not in the context of prosecutions in the criminal courts.

It is important that you, as a student of the Canadian justice system, understand the difference between criminal law and civil law, regardless of your career goal. On a personal level, having the basics of contract law will help you understand what you are agreeing to when signing a lease for an apartment or buying a new car. If you become a law enforcement professional (for example, a police officer, customs officer, or bylaw enforcement officer) and are required to enforce specific laws, it will be critical that you understand the limits of what you can do in any given situation. For example, if you are a police officer responding to a noise complaint in an apartment building, you'll need to keep in mind that if a provision of the *Criminal Code* or a provincial statute has not been violated, there is a limit to what you can do. You will not be able to enforce the obligations in the lease although you may be able to mediate the issue and direct the tenants to other resources for assistance.

You should also be aware that a person may be liable to being charged with a criminal offence for his or her action and also be liable in tort for the resulting damages or losses.

Lastly, you should realize that the law is evolving (changing) such that an officer may be liable in tort for an act committed wrongfully in the course of duty. The case law is expanding to include examples of police officers and bylaw enforcement officers being sued for wrongful arrest or wrongful prosecution.

APPLYING THE LAW

Mustapha v Culligan

The Mustapha family had bought large bottles of water from Culligan of Canada for 15 years. A sales representative for Culligan had convinced Mr. Mustapha to use Culligan bottled water because of Culligan's representations (promises) of its purity and healthy quality, including how much better than tap water it was for pregnant women and children. The Mustaphas drank only Culligan bottled water. Mrs. Mustapha was seven months pregnant at the time. One day, while changing a large bottle of water, Mr. Mustapha noticed a dead fly and part of another dead fly in the new, unopened bottle of water. Mrs. Mustapha was present to wash the neck of the new bottle to make sure that there were not any germs on the outside of the neck before it was placed on the dispenser. Neither drank from the bottle; however, due to the shock of seeing the flies in their drinking water, Mrs. Mustapha was ill immediately, and Mr. Mustapha became ill later.

Both sued Culligan for damages, in tort and in contract, arising out of the dead flies in the bottle of water.

Questions for Discussion

Should the Mustaphas be successful in their lawsuit against Culligan? Why or why not? Do you need more information before you can make a decision? If so, what other facts would you like to know?

As you go through this chapter, you will learn more about the legal concepts involved in this type of lawsuit. You will revisit this case for discussion.

Sources: *Mustapha v Culligan of Canada Ltd*, 2008 SCC 27; *Mustapha v Culligan of Canada Ltd*, 2005 CanLII 11990 (Ont Sup Ct J).

Contracts and Torts: The Distinctions

This chapter introduces contracts and **torts**, the two legal disciplines from which nearly all other civil law principles flow. These two disciplines are hundreds of years old, and it would be impossible to introduce even their most basic principles properly in these few pages. A more realistic goal, adopted here, is to compare and contrast these disciplines in an effort to illustrate how the presence or absence of a contract between two parties influences the way in which legal rights arise and are enforced by the courts in the event of a dispute.

tort
literally, a "wrong"; in law, an injury—whether physical, emotional, economic, or otherwise—suffered by a person for which another person may be held liable

Contracts

Contract law is a very broad legal discipline that encompasses a great number of situations, including commercial transactions, tenancies, family arrangements, employment relationships, personal service arrangements, and many other transactions. All situations that fall within contract law, however, have at their heart one common feature: an agreement (or alleged agreement) between two or more parties. The relationship between the parties is governed by the contract or agreement.

For example, you decide to buy a car. You negotiate the terms of purchase with the dealer, including the make, colour, year, price, and options. The contract will also state when you can pick up the car and when you have to provide payment. Your agreement with the dealer is described in the terms of your contract.

A contract can be oral or in writing. A written contract offers the parties the advantage of proof of the terms, whereas there are potential difficulties in proving an oral contract.

Because of the great differences between the kinds of relationships dealt with by contract, many subdivisions of contract law—such as landlord and tenant law, family law, and employment law—have evolved into specialized disciplines. These subdivisions have their own complexities and are often shaped and supplemented by specialized statutes (such as provincial landlord and tenant acts, family law acts, or employment standards acts), many of which represent the codification of branches of common law.

Nevertheless, a large body of general contract law remains a part of the common law and continues to evolve according to common law principles. This large and ancient body of law continues to govern all contractual relationships that don't fall neatly into a subdiscipline, or that are not adequately addressed by existing statutes. If, for example, a landlord and a tenant enter into a relationship that incorporates rights or responsibilities that extend outside the scope of the applicable landlord and tenant legislation (without violating that legislation) and a dispute arises over those new terms, the court will rely on the common law of contract to resolve the dispute.

In general, all issues that arise under contract law are decided by referring to the underlying agreement between the parties, although in some cases terms that are not explicitly incorporated into that agreement are read into it (added) by the courts. Because of this practice of looking to the agreement to settle the dispute, parties' legal rights in a contract dispute are said to flow from the contract itself.

Torts

"Tort" is a French word that simply means a "wrong." The law of torts deals with wrongs, or injuries (physical, economic, or otherwise), inflicted by one party on another, usually outside the context of a contract. The result of the infliction of the wrong is that the injured party sues the wrongdoer (tortfeasor) for the injury suffered. Thus, although the parties may have known each other prior to the occurrence of the wrong, they are not in this particular relationship by choice. Examples of situations that may result in a tort claim are a car accident and a slip-and-fall accident on a slippery sidewalk.

Tort law is less extensively subdivided and codified than contract law. There are certain distinct branches of tort: intentional torts (such as assault), negligence, and nuisance/trespass. Certain types of tort have become the subject of statutes, such as environmental protection laws, which create offences that may be prosecuted by the government in a criminal or quasi-criminal manner. These statutes are designed to protect the common good by stopping parties from committing torts that will cause damage on a significant scale. As a result, a corporation that pollutes the water source for a community, causing health problems and deaths, can be prosecuted under an environmental protection statute and can also be sued by the individual victims under tort law.

A large number of *Criminal Code*[1] offences (typically, those offences that have an identifiable victim) describe actions that would also qualify as torts under the common law. In theory, most victims of criminal offences have the common law right to sue the perpetrator of a crime in civil court under the law of torts, regardless of whether the offence is prosecuted in the criminal system. In practice, most victims choose not to do this, because the remedies available in a tort dispute (most commonly money damages, discussed later in this chapter) are difficult to enforce against a criminal accused, who may be impecunious (broke) or incarcerated. But parallel criminal and civil tort cases do occur (the Todd Bertuzzi and O.J. Simpson cases are well-known examples), and, partly because of a difference in the criminal and civil standards of proof (criminal standards are discussed in Chapter 8), the finding of culpability and/or liability in the two cases can differ.

In a tort case, in contrast with contract law, no underlying agreement is in place that establishes the rights between the parties. A **tortfeasor** (literally, "wrongdoer") and his or her victim are, in theory, "strangers" brought together by misfortune (although in reality many torts occur as a result of interactions between acquaintances or friends). The absence of an agreed-upon set of rights and responsibilities between the parties places tort liability outside the control of the parties involved: tort rights flow not from the parties' own plans but from the law itself.

tortfeasor
literally, "wrongdoer"; a person who commits a tort

APPLYING THE LAW

Mustapha v Culligan

What kind of case is the Mustapha claim: contract or tort—or both? Organize your answer based on the concepts discussed in the section above.

Basic Principles of Contract Law

breach
the failure of one party to perform a contract or contractual obligation

Strictly speaking, the law of contracts provides a remedy in the event of a **breach** (but will only rarely enforce the specific terms of an agreement) once certain required criteria are proven to exist. A party has breached the contract once there is a failure to do what was promised. The availability of a remedy for breach of a contract depends on the enforceability of that contract; in other words, a court will not provide a remedy unless the contract was created according to the rules of contract law.

Formation of the Contract: Intention to Be Legally Bound

Contracting parties must have the intention to be legally bound by the terms of the contract. The elements of a valid contract are discussed below.

Offer

An **offer** exists at the point in negotiations where the terms of the contract have been set and one party, the offeree, must accept or reject the terms set forth by the offeror. There are four ways in which an offer can come to an end without being accepted:

- **Revocation** As long as the offer has not been accepted, an offeror may revoke (withdraw) or alter the offer at any time. An offeror has no duty to hold an offer open (in the absence of a contractual agreement to do so) because there has not yet been any **consideration** in return for the original offer. The revocation is effective only when it has been communicated to the offeree. This communication need not be direct.
- **Rejection** Once an offer is rejected, it is no longer valid or open for future acceptance.
- **Counteroffer** A counteroffer rejects the original offer by substituting a new or revised offer.
- **Lapse** An offer may lapse (expire) at a stipulated time or on the occurrence of a stipulated event. Alternatively, a lapse date may be implied after a reasonable period of time has passed without the offer being accepted.

Acceptance

In general, a contract is not complete until acceptance is communicated to the offeror. The contract is completed at the time the offeror hears or implicitly knows of the offeree's acceptance. Once a contract is "complete," it is legally binding on the parties—it can be enforced using the courts.

Consideration

In order for a contract to be binding, each party to the contract must receive something—a benefit—under the contract. The benefit flowing to each party is known as "consideration." An entirely one-sided promise is generally not enforceable because it implies no mutuality (something that goes both ways) and therefore no consideration. Moral obligations (for example, wanting to help out a loved one) and present compensation for past performance (for example, wanting to repay a past favour) do not qualify as adequate consideration for a new contract, and courts are not generally entitled or required to consider issues of fairness when determining how much consideration is adequate. In other words, as long as there is some benefit to each party, the consideration does not need to be objectively equal on both sides.

Capacity to Contract

A contract entered into by an individual who is found to be lacking the required **legal capacity** to enter into binding contracts may be unenforceable. Subject to certain exceptions, a party may lack the capacity to contract as a result of mental incapacity, drunkenness, or minimum age requirements.

---

offer
the proposal of a contract or a set of contract terms; an offer is not a contract until it is accepted

revocation
the withdrawal of an offer by its maker

consideration
the benefit(s) flowing to each party under a contract

rejection
the refusal of an offer

counteroffer
a new offer that replaces an original offer, often with revised terms

lapse
the expiry of an offer that has not been accepted by a stipulated acceptance time or on the occurrence of stipulated conditions

legal capacity
the ability to enter into an enforceable contract, based on the absence of factors (for example, cognitive impairment) that might impair capacity

Certainty of Terms

Contract terms must be precise and clear to enable the courts to understand the agreement and to ensure that the contract represents the contracting parties' intention. Previous dealings between the same parties can be consulted by the court to help interpret new contracts. Also, where terms are unclear or missing, they may be interpreted or filled in by the court by referring to an industry standard or norm. For example, Ontario's *Sale of Goods Act*[2] states that, in a contract for the sale of goods, if no agreement is reached as to price but there is an enforceable agreement to sell, the purchaser is held to a reasonable price.

Contract Terms

Written Terms

construction
the process of determining the legal meaning of words or terms in a contract or statute, often by reference to context or external evidence

The interpretation of a contract is subject to established legal rules of **construction**. However, the courts will consider the fact that the meaning of a term may vary depending on local custom or the practices of a specific trade. The **parol evidence rule** provides that, in general, the meaning of the contract is determined without reference to external sources of evidence, such as other documents or oral testimony. This rule is applied less rigidly to standard form contracts, and more rigidly in circumstances involving parties that have individually negotiated the specific terms of their contract.

parol evidence rule
the rule that the meaning of a contract must be determined without reference to external sources of evidence, such as other documents or oral testimony

Implied Terms

The court will generally not imply "missing" terms into a contract; however, in the interests of business efficiency, a necessary term may be "read in." Factors such as past business dealings between the parties or standard business practice may be considered in determining the appropriateness of reading in a particular term. For example, courts have held that it is an implied term of a contract of employment that an employer can reassign an employee to new duties, as long as the new duties are reasonable within the context of the employee's job description.[3]

Terms may also be read in by applying a statute. For example, the *Sale of Goods Act* provides that certain implied terms as to the description, merchantability, and fitness for purpose of goods sold be read into contracts that fall under the application of that legislation.

Exclusion Clauses

exclusion clause
a part of a contract that limits the contractual or statutory liability of a party in the event of a breach of the contract

An **exclusion clause** is a contractual device that limits the liability of a party under the terms of a contract. For example, many home insurance policies cover claims against the owner when a visitor is injured on the property, but exclude coverage for injuries caused by the owner's criminal acts (for example, an assault against a visitor).[4] It is a contract term like any other, negotiated between the parties. The standard rules of construction apply to these clauses no differently from any other term of a contract. However, misrepresentation of the purpose of the exclusion clause, or serious unfairness (unconscionability) in its operation, may render the clause inoperative.

Contractual Defects

A contractual defect is a legal problem with a contract. Serious defects can render a contract invalid; more minor defects can give the party who is adversely affected by them the right to sue the other party for damages, but not the right to repudiate (get out of) the contract.

Misrepresentation

Representations are statements or claims made by contract parties in the course of negotiations. Although they may **induce** a party to make the contract, they are not necessarily incorporated into the document as a contractual term or obligation. As a result, **misrepresentations** do not automatically give rise to an award of **damages** under *contract law* because there has been no breach of the contract. There may, however, be *tort* liability for misrepresentation that is negligent or intentional.

To constitute a **contractual defect** (that is, a factor that affects the enforceability of the contract), a misrepresentation must

- be based on a fact that is asserted to be true,
- have been false when it was acted on, and
- have induced the other party to make the contract.

A representation made on the basis of opinion, and not on fact, may be treated in the same way as a factual misrepresentation if it is provided by a person with special expertise or knowledge of the subject matter. There are three types of misrepresentation:

- *Fraudulent misrepresentation* A statement that is made that is known to be false or is made recklessly, without any regard to its truth, is a fraudulent misrepresentation. Misrepresentations of this type give rise to the tort of **deceit**. Remedies that may be awarded to the innocent party may include an award of damages under tort law and/or the right to **rescind** (to not carry out one's side of) the contract.

- *Negligent misrepresentation* A statement of fact, or a statement of opinion made by a person with special knowledge or expertise, that is untrue or inaccurate and that has been **reasonably relied on** to the detriment of another is a negligent misrepresentation, provided that the person making the statement or the party with special knowledge rendering the opinion did not take reasonable care under the circumstances to ascertain the truth of the claim. The innocent party will be found to have "relied on the misrepresentation to his or her detriment" if he or she has taken action that, because of the misrepresentation, has caused a loss of some sort. Remedies that may be awarded to the innocent party may include damages and the right to rescind the contract. A simple example of a case of negligent misrepresentation would be where the owners of a business provide financial information about the business (without adequately verifying the accuracy of that information) to a potential investor, and it later turns out that the financial information was inaccurate, the business has been overvalued, and the investor loses money (see, for example, *Strand v Strand*[5]).

- *Innocent misrepresentation* A statement of fact that is not true but was made by one who believes it to be true is an innocent misrepresentation. Although this may give rise to a right of the other party to rescind the contract, no damages will be awarded unless the representation can be shown to be either a term of a **collateral contract** (one that is related to but separate from another contract) or an implied term of the main contract.

Mistake

There are three types of mistake under contract law: common or mutual mistake, unilateral mistake, and a situation called *non est factum*. With the exception of common mistakes, once proven, a mistake may render a contract unenforceable.

---

representation
a statement or claim made during contract negotiations that, though not necessarily a term of the contract, may be relied on by a party in deciding whether to enter into the contract

induce
persuade or bring about

misrepresentation
a representation based, either innocently, negligently, or intentionally, on incorrect information

damages
losses suffered as a result of the breach of a contract or the commission of a tort, or compensation awarded for contract or tort losses

contractual defect
a legal problem with a contract that can either invalidate a contract or give rise to damages without invalidating the entire contract

deceit
a tort established where one party makes a factual representation, knowing it is false, and knowing that another party will rely on it and suffer harm or loss as a result

rescind
to opt, generally with good legal reason, not to carry out one's side of a contract, as if the contract had never been made in the first place

reasonable reliance
reasonable actions by one party, generally based on representations or actions by the other party, that may result in losses that a court will compensate

collateral contract
a contract that is related to or depends on, but is separate from, another contract

- *Common or mutual mistake* Such a mistake exists where both parties have made the same error (are mistaken about a fundamental aspect of the contract). If the party requesting the right to rescind the contract on grounds of mistake was at fault in causing the mistake (even if it was accidental), this remedy is not available to him or her.

- *Unilateral mistake* Such a mistake exists where one party, with the full knowledge of the other, is mistaken. This mistake arises both in situations of fraudulent misrepresentation (described above) and in situations involving one party's acceptance of an offer that the offeror knows is a result of a mistake. Obviously, in such cases, only the innocent party is entitled to rescind the contract.

non est factum

Latin for "I didn't sign/ make [this contract]"; a legal doctrine that can be pleaded, based on a narrow set of circumstances, in an attempt to render a contract unenforceable

- **Non est factum** This is a Latin phrase loosely translatable as "I didn't sign that." Modern law has changed the meaning of the phrase to something closer to "I didn't *intend* to sign that" or "This is not my deed or doing." A party may **plead** (base his or her case on) *non est factum* in a situation where he or she has signed the wrong contract or has signed a contract under a complete misunderstanding about its nature. This is an exception to the general rule that, once signed, a document is binding. For a party to successfully plead *non est factum*, the mistaken document must be different in quality or nature, not merely content, from the intended document. Also, the party claiming *non est factum* must not have been careless in signing the document. For example, in *Landry v Tivey*,[6] a man negotiated a mortgage and was told that he needed to obtain his ex-wife's consent to encumber (mortgage) her share of the property. The ex-wife was not involved in the negotiations and was told that she was merely giving consent to the mortgage, not taking on any liability. However, the document she was given to sign provided that she would be liable for a shortfall if the proceeds of a sale of the house were insufficient to cover the mortgage. The court held that *non est factum* applied: Mrs. Tivey thought she was signing a consent form when she was actually signing a mortgage, and the mortgage broker did nothing to alert her to her misunderstanding.

plead

argue or claim

Illegality

The general rule is that illegal contracts are unenforceable. There are two types of illegality:

- *Common law illegality* The common law concerns itself primarily with contracts that are contrary to public policy. For obvious reasons, the court will not enforce a contract to kill someone or to share the proceeds of a robbery. Other examples include contracts to defraud the revenue service, contracts to corrupt public officials, contracts that attempt to deny the jurisdiction of the courts, contracts to commit a tort, or contracts that the court concludes are of an immoral nature.

- *Statutory illegality* This type of illegality arises where a breach of a statute is inherent in the fulfillment of a contractual obligation—one party has promised to do something that is contrary to legislation (such as to divide land in contravention of Ontario's *Planning Act*[7]). In concluding that a contract is void because of statutory illegality, it is often necessary to consider the purpose of the relevant statute.

formalities

procedural or formal requirements, such as writing, a seal, or a signature (typically prescribed by statute), that are necessary to make certain kinds of contracts enforceable

Problems with Formalities

Formal requirements are attached to certain categories of contracts. The absence of these formal requirements, or **formalities**, renders the contract void. The general rule is that an oral contract is enforceable, but this rule is altered by statute in some cases—for example, in the case of contracts falling under the Ontario *Statute of Frauds*,[8] the *Sale of Goods Act*, and the *Consumer Protection Act, 2002*,[9] which all require that certain contracts be in writing. An agreement to sell real estate must be in writing and under seal in order to be enforceable.

Duress

A contract is void for reasons of duress if, in signing the contract, a contracting party was influenced by threats of bodily harm against himself or herself or his or her family.

Undue Influence

A presumption of undue influence may exist in circumstances that involve relationships of a special personal or professional nature: the voluntariness of the contract may be put in question when one of the parties is perceived to be in a position of power over the other. Once raised, the presumption of undue influence must be successfully rebutted (proven incorrect) before the contract is considered valid.

For example, if an elderly woman enters into a contract to sell her house to her lawyer for $50, she, or her heirs, could challenge the contract on the basis of undue influence exerted by the lawyer on the woman. The simple fact that the lawyer is in a position of trust, is feared and respected by the woman, and has some measure of control over her actions is enough to make undue influence an issue. The lawyer is then required to prove to the court that he did not exert undue influence on the woman in convincing her to sign the contract, or the contract will not be enforceable.

Unconscionability

A judge may set aside a contract for gross unfairness by applying the doctrine of **unconscionability**. An unconscionable contract is one in which there is extreme one-sidedness, such that an honest and fair person would not propose it because it is so unfair to the other person. A two-part test must be satisfied to be successful in a claim of unconscionability. It must first be established that a substantial inequality of bargaining power existed between the parties and that the exertion of power by the influential party created the unfair result. Once the inequality of bargaining power is established, the onus shifts to the party in the position of power to establish that, although the power existed, it was not exercised. Because a valid contract need not involve equal consideration (equal benefits on both sides), a "bad" bargain is not in itself sufficient cause for applying this doctrine.

unconscionability
serious unfairness in a contract; unfairness that no reasonable person would accept and no honest person would propose

Performance and Breach

Frustration

A contract may be determined by a court to be **frustrated** in circumstances where false assumptions about future events have substantially altered the contract conditions. In the event that performing the terms of the contract is impossible or increasingly difficult, the doctrine of frustration allows the court to terminate or alter the contract's terms in an attempt to preserve the original "flavour" of the bargain. For example, in *Ens v Pacific Home Products Ltd*, a contract to install a glass sunroom that required ten-foot-deep support pilings was frustrated when the contractor determined that an unusually high water table in the area meant that the holes drilled for pilings continually filled up with wet sand.[10]

The doctrine does not apply in circumstances where a reasonable person could have contemplated the future event and no provision was added to the contract to plan for it.

frustration
a legal doctrine that releases the parties to a contract from their responsibilities under the contract when something (a circumstance or an object, for example) necessary to the performance of the contract no longer exists

The *Frustrated Contracts Act*[11] states that where a contract becomes frustrated, moneys paid are recoverable and sums owing are not enforceable, thus placing parties back, as much as possible, into the financial positions they were in before making the contract. In the *Ens* case, the couple who contracted for the sunroom were given their deposit back, but the costs spent on the project up to the time that it was abandoned were split 35/65 as between the couple and the contractors, since neither party could have foreseen the issue, but the contractor had more experience with barriers to construction (and so could be expected to bear more of the risk of a failure).

Remedies

The party who sues or brings the lawsuit is called the plaintiff; the party who has to defend the lawsuit is called the defendant. Often, when there has been a breach of contract, the innocent party (the party who did not breach the contract) will sue the "breaching party."

A remedy is the order a judge makes to compensate the innocent party for the breach of contract. Contractual remedies offered by the courts are designed either to put the innocent party back into the position he or she would have been in had he or she not entered the contract, or to put the innocent party into the position he or she would have been in had the contract been fulfilled. There are a few situations where the court will order the parties to complete the contract (specific performance), usually only if a monetary payment (damages) will not address the breach of contract appropriately.

Damages may be sought on any one of the following three bases:

restitution
the return of benefits to put contracting parties back into their precontractual position

- *Restitution* The plaintiff may seek reimbursement or return of the benefits conferred on the defaulting defendant. Restitution is most appropriate where the plaintiff, relying on the defendant's promise, has transferred something of value to the defendant. In an attempt to guard against unjustly enriching one party at the expense of another, restitution puts the parties back into their precontractual positions. For example, Joanne agrees to buy Ali's car. Joanne pays Ali a deposit of $500. Ali changes his mind and decides not to sell her the car. Joanne sues Ali. The court orders Ali to return Joanne's deposit of $500, thus putting Joanne in the same position as before they entered into the agreement.

reliance
taking actions based on dependence on a promise or contract, including the expenditure of money in dependence on the contract

- *Reliance* The plaintiff may seek an award of damages that includes expenses reasonably incurred from relying on the contract. Protecting the reliance interest is most often a concern where the plaintiff's position has changed and restitution is not an option. An attempt is made to undo the harm that reliance on the defendant's promise has caused by putting the plaintiff in a position that is similar to the precontractual position.

expectation
anticipation of benefits from a contract being fulfilled

- *Expectation* The plaintiff may seek to recover the value of the benefits he or she reasonably expected to receive upon fulfillment of the contract. This kind of remedy attempts to place the plaintiff in a position similar to what was expected had the contract been performed. Compensation according to expectation is the most common contract law remedy.

specific performance
a court order requiring a party in default to fully perform his or her obligations under a contract

As noted above, a court may also grant an order for **specific performance**, which requires the parties to complete the obligations of the contract. Specific performance is available only where the payment of money damages is inadequate. The sale of real estate is often considered an appropriate situation in which to request specific performance. This is based on the theory that all land is unique and that its loss cannot be compensated with an award of monetary damages.

If specific performance is not ordered, the judge must then determine the appropriate amount of monetary damages to be awarded. In doing so, he or she will consider the following issues: quantification of damages, mitigation of damages, and remoteness.

Quantification of Damages

The burden of establishing with evidence the extent of damages suffered is on the plaintiff as the party requesting the award of damages. Receipts, bank statements, and income tax documents and statements are examples of the kind of evidence that the plaintiff must provide the court in order to support the claim for damages. In situations where damages are impossible to quantify accurately, an estimate based on evidence is sufficient.

Mitigation of Damages

A plaintiff cannot recover damages that he or she could have reasonably avoided. **Mitigation** refers to the avoiding or reducing of the plaintiff's losses, and the plaintiff has a responsibility or **duty to mitigate**. Courts will often reduce an award of damages by the amount that could have been reasonably mitigated. The plaintiff must do that which is expected of a reasonable person to minimize his or her losses resulting from a breach of contract.

For example, if a dentist breaches a contract of employment by firing a dental assistant for no sufficient cause, the dentist is in general liable to pay the employee for her lost income over the life of the contract. The dental assistant is not allowed, however, to just sit at home and collect the money from her former employer; she has an obligation to look for and obtain another suitable job so that her losses (for which the dentist is liable) are reduced. If she does not do so, a judge could reduce the amount of damages awarded to her as a result of her failure to mitigate her damages.

mitigation
minimizing a party's damages from breach of contract or from the commission of a tort

duty to mitigate
a party's responsibility to minimize his or her damages from breach of contract or from the commission of a tort

Remoteness

The **remoteness** test provides that only those losses that flow naturally from the contractual breach are recoverable. Only those damages that can be reasonably foreseen at the time of forming the contract will pass the remoteness test and are therefore recoverable.

For example, if the dental assistant discussed above has been improperly fired by the only dentist in town, she may be able to recover from the dentist her costs of moving to another town to take another job (and, thus, mitigate her damages) because, at the time the contract was entered into, it was reasonably foreseeable that the dental assistant would be forced to move to another town to find work if she were fired. On the other hand, if the dental assistant drives her brand new car into a tree because she is so angry at the dentist that she is not paying attention to her driving, she will not likely be able to force the dentist to pay for the car repairs. It is not reasonable to expect the parties to an employment contract to foresee that improperly firing an employee could lead to a smashed car.

remoteness
the degree to which the consequences of a contract breach or the commission of a tort flow, directly or indirectly, from the breach or the tort

Basic Principles of Tort Law

Tort law applies to a wide range of legal disputes involving injuries to people or property, usually outside the context of contract. Because of the breadth of the doctrine, tort law is divided into subcategories, the most important of which are negligence and intentional torts. The defendant in a tort suit is the tortfeasor, and the remedy sought by a tort victim is almost always monetary damages.

All torts require proof of fault as a basis for imposing liability, although fault is measured differently for different classes of tort. The most important distinction between negligence and intentional tort is the presence or absence of intent. Recklessness lies between negligence and intentional tort in terms of an appreciation of the consequences of one's behaviour. The person who is reckless either does not pay attention to the consequences of his or her behaviour, or else is aware that harm may result but proceeds anyway. Where there is intent, the general principles of intentional tort will apply, but where there is only recklessness, carelessness, or negligence, the principles of negligence will govern. Finally, other torts, such as nuisance, cannot readily be classed in either category.

Negligence

The traditional law of negligence operates independently of both contract and property rights and is based on those rights flowing from interactions between people. The **duty of care** is the central principle of negligence law, without which no liability can flow, no matter how awful the conduct of the alleged tortfeasor.

As its name implies, negligence does *not* depend on intentional wrongful action or recklessness for the imposition of liability. Instead, negligence judges the execution of every duty of care by reference to a corresponding **standard of care**, and imposes tort liability wherever a tortfeasor's behaviour falls below the standard and the damages suffered by the victim are not considered to be too remote.

Duty of Care

One person's duty of care to another person is the foundation on which fault is established in a negligence action. In the absence of a duty of care, there is no liability in negligence because the law is unwilling to place obligations on people without reason or reciprocity.

The successful proof of a duty of care depends on **foreseeability**—that is, the plaintiff must prove, first, that the defendant acted despite a foreseeable risk of injury and, second, that the plaintiff was within the scope of foreseeable victims of that injury. If the defendant, in committing the tort, could foresee that a particular person or class of persons might be injured by his or her actions, then the tortfeasor is said to have had a duty of care to that person or class of persons.

Duties of care often accompany relationships—neighbour to neighbour, host to guest, parent to child—but they can also arise between strangers, as between two drivers on a highway. Foresight need not be actual. A tortfeasor who is thoughtless as to the potential victims of his or her actions will usually be held accountable on the basis that foresight was reasonable in the context. For example, a homeowner owes a duty of care to people using the sidewalk in front of his or her house to make sure that it is as reasonably free and clear of snow and ice as circumstances permit. The law will also impose liability on someone who was not directly involved in the wrongful act but who has responsibility for the tortfeasor in some capacity. The duty of care that is imposed is known as vicarious liability. For example, statute law imposes **vicarious liability** on the owner of a car if the driver is involved in a car accident, even if the owner was not present at the time.

Standard of Care

Once a duty of care has been attributed to the alleged tortfeasor, the court must determine whether that duty has been met. To do that, the behaviour of the tortfeasor is compared with a legal standard of care appropriate to the circumstances. The standard used corresponds with the nature of the duty of care, with some duties, such as those between a parent and child, attracting a higher standard of care than others (such as duties owed to strangers). The basic tort standard of care, applied in the absence of special factors, is that of a reasonable and prudent person in the same circumstances.

---

duty of care
a legal duty owed by one person to another based on a relationship or on the doctrine of foreseeability

standard of care
the standard by which discharge of a duty of care is measured, which depends on the relationship between the parties and the circumstances under which the duty arises

foreseeability
a test to determine whether a reasonable person could expect that a certain result may follow from his or her act; typically, an objective precondition to imposing a duty of care or to imposing liability for a particular class of damages

vicarious liability
imposition of liability on a person for the acts of another, because of the nature of the relationship between the two, even if the person was not present

Causation

Many mishaps involve the convergence of unfortunate circumstances. Multiple tortfeasors acting independently may contribute to one set of injuries, and the victim may even be partially at fault. It is up to the court to allocate fault (and liability) among the different negligent parties according to the rules of causation.

To impose tort liability for an injury, the court must accept the plaintiff's argument that the actions of the defendant were the "cause in fact" of that injury or, in circumstances of multiple causation, that they were a significant and substantial factor in the occurrence of the injury. To establish cause in fact, the plaintiff must prove to the court that the actions of the defendant were a major contributing factor, if not the only contributing factor, to the occurrence of the event that caused the plaintiff's injuries. Where the actions of more than one defendant contribute to the chain of events leading to the plaintiff's injuries, the court must review each individual action in isolation to determine which ones constituted significant and substantial factors. This last inquiry turns on whether there is a substantial connection between the action and the injury. The plaintiff may be found to have contributed to his or her own injury. One of the most familiar examples of this is that of the car accident victim whose injuries are aggravated by failure to wear a seat belt. In such a case, the plaintiff is said to have been **contributorily negligent**.

Once it has been determined that the defendants made significant and substantial contribution to the harm, the court must allocate liability among them. If the individual causes are found to be divisible, each defendant will be responsible for part of the damages. If the causes are indivisible, the defendants will be found jointly and severally liable for the harm. In **joint and several liability**, each defendant and all defendants are accountable for all of the harm, and the plaintiff may pursue any or all of them for payment. For example, car A stops properly for a red light. Car B, following behind, does not stop in time and rear-ends car A. Car C rear-ends car B. The driver of car A is injured and sues the drivers of car B and car C for damages. The judge finds both drivers/defendants responsible (jointly liable) for driver A's injuries. As between the defendants, the judge allocates 60 percent liability to driver B (severally liable) and 40 percent to driver C (severally liable).

In some cases, the multiple causes of an injury do not all occur at the same time. A minor injury may predispose a victim to a future, much more serious, injury, or a later injury may compound an earlier one. In such cases, the court must reconcile the rule that defendants take their victims as they find them (discussed later) with the principle that defendants should be held responsible only for foreseeable damage substantially connected to their own actions. To do this, the court usually tries to determine which part of the injuries proven at trial would have occurred without the defendant's own negligence, and will not hold the defendant liable for that part unless a rule, such as the "**thin skull rule**" (discussed later), dictates otherwise.

Remoteness

One tortious action may trigger a long chain of different kinds of damage. Not every kind of damage in the chain will be a consequence that the tortfeasor might have foreseen, and the severity of damage may also exceed all normal expectations. Common law has limited the scope of tortfeasors' liability in such cases, imposing instead responsibility for a defined scope of damage by reference to foreseeability and remoteness. As in contract law, tort law will not provide compensation for injuries that were not reasonably foreseeable at the time of the improper action.

The foreseeability test in this context is different from the objective measure used in the context of the duty of care. Actual foresight is usually necessary, although a tortfeasor is

contributory negligence
the role that a plaintiff or victim may play in negligently contributing to the cause of or aggravation of his or her own injury

joint and several liability
a rule that allows a plaintiff who suffers damages caused by multiple defendants to recover the full amount of damages from any one of them (and that defendant can sue the others for contribution)

thin skull rule
a rule that provides that a defendant who causes harm through negligence is responsible for the full extent of the harm, even if a vulnerability specific to the plaintiff made the harm more serious than would normally be expected

responsible for all *possible* foreseeable consequences of his or her actions. It is not necessary that a consequence be probable or even likely. Where the variety or the extent of damage far exceeds the defendant's actual foresight, he or she will usually argue that the damage was "too remote" to be foreseeable. As in contract law, the victim cannot claim damages from the defendant for losses that no reasonable person could have foreseen at the time of the action that led to the lawsuit (either the breach of contract or the negligent act).

Before liability will be imposed, it must usually be shown that a reasonable person could have foreseen each type of harm proven to have resulted from the wrongful act. For example, a defendant who hits a poodle with her car may be responsible for the dog's veterinarian bills and even for the tranquilizers required to calm down the distraught owner. However, the defendant will not likely be held responsible for the breakdown of the owner's marriage that arguably occurs as a result of the owner's spouse blaming the owner if the dog ultimately dies from its injuries. Foreseeability of the *extent* of harm, however, is not always necessary. A defendant who is capable of foreseeing one degree of injury will often be held responsible for more serious damage.

Indirect damage or damage aggravated by an intervening act or risk raises issues of causation, discussed above, and a defendant is entitled to argue that he or she is liable for only limited damages or for none at all because of a break in the chain of causation between the wrongful act and the injury. However, not all secondary causes are intervening acts. In some cases, aggravating circumstances may themselves be the subject of foresight (or even of control) by the defendant.

In some personal injury cases, the courts have chosen to modify the normal rules of remoteness. A rule sometimes called the "thin skull rule" applies in circumstances where the tort plaintiff suffers from an unusual physical or mental vulnerability that may not be easily detectable but that predisposes him or her to unusually serious injury. A tortfeasor, in injuring such a plaintiff, "takes the victim as he finds him" and may be liable for damage beyond the damage that would be foreseen by a reasonable and prudent person.

Negligence and Contract Remedies in Business Relations

Because the violation of the terms of an explicit contract is generally easier to prove than the violation of an unwritten duty of care, the choice of contract remedies over tort liability is an important motivation for people to make contracts to govern their relationships. Nevertheless, it is a mistake to view the spheres of tort and contract as completely independent. Business relations, as with social relations, can create duties of care, and a layer of negligence responsibility underlies many contracts. Even virtual strangers, bound only by the simplest terms of bargain and sale, may owe a duty of care to each other. The law of product liability is a good example. Product liability is the name given to a hybrid area of the law that depends on both negligence and contract concepts that allow parties to recover damages incurred through losses or injuries from defective or dangerous consumer goods.

For example, the manufacturer of a sports drink can be found to owe a duty of care to the person who buys it, the customer. A problem with the sports drink that causes the customer to be violently ill gives rise to both a breach of contract (the manufacturer did not provide the customer with the sports drink that was intended to be purchased) and a tort (the manufacturer caused the customer to become ill).

Occupiers' Liability

Occupiers—people who have control over property with or without other ownership rights—have long been considered to have a duty of care to people who are invited onto their property, and even to people who trespass onto the property. In Ontario, this responsibility has been codified in a statute called the *Occupiers' Liability Act*.[12] (Other provinces have similar statutes.) The degree of control required to form the basis of occupiers' liability does not have to be permanent or exclusive—there may be multiple occupiers on one parcel of property, and an occupier can count as an occupier even if he or she is only briefly in control of the property (for example, the operators of an outdoor music festival who have a permit to use a park for a weekend can be liable as "occupiers" for that weekend).

Ontario's *Occupiers' Liability Act* has eliminated the different standards of care owed at common law. Previously, an occupier owed a lesser standard of care to a trespasser than to an invited guest. Now, an occupier of premises has an obligation to take reasonable care that people coming onto the premises are reasonably safe while there. The occupier is held to a standard of what is reasonable under the circumstances.

Although the Act makes it clear that the occupier cannot create a danger for trespassers, the Act also states that a trespasser is deemed (assumed) to have willingly agreed to any and all risks involved in being on the premises.

Consider the situation of someone who snowmobiles across a farm field without permission of the farmer. The Act prohibits the farmer from creating any dangers for the snowmobiler (which the farmer might be tempted to do, to discourage snowmobiling) even though the snowmobiler is deemed to have willingly assumed all risks involved in taking his snowmobile across the farmer's field without permission.

Another application of the duty of care under the *Occupiers' Liability Act* is related to "host liability"—the concept that a host should be responsible for the injuries that a drunken guest suffers while at the host's premises. Injured people (plaintiffs) have argued, with varying degrees of success, that the Act imposes a duty on the host of the party to make sure that guests do not injure themselves or others as a result of being intoxicated while at the party.

As the law with respect to drunk driving and host liability currently stands, commercial hosts (for example, restaurants and bars) can be held liable for injuries to third parties injured by drunk drivers,[13] but social hosts cannot.[14]

Intentional Torts

Intentional torts are different from negligence in that they are committed by a tortfeasor who intends to cause harm, loss, or damage to someone or something. A tort is intentional as long as the tortfeasor foresaw the occurrence of the relevant consequences as substantially certain. An intentional tort is different from the tort of negligence; in negligence, the tortfeasor does not demonstrate the duty of care in doing something that is otherwise permissible.

Trespass to the Person

Assault is an intentional tort that involves a *threat* of contact by a tortfeasor who has the means to carry out the threat. Note the difference here between the tort of assault, which involves only the threat, and the criminal offence of assault, which includes both the threat and the carrying out of unwanted contact with another person. Intentional acts that involve actual direct or indirect physical contact and an intent to threaten, harm, or offend constitute **battery**. Because assault and battery are often present together, there is some blurring of the boundaries between the two; however, each is a separate tort, and assault (threat) by itself can attract liability, although quantifying the damages for an assault alone may be difficult.

assault
under the common law, a threat of injury

battery
under the common law, a usually negligent or intentional act of physical contact

Box 10.1   Emerging Causes of Action

Although case law is based on precedent, the law does change to meet unique situations. One such example is the emerging recognition by the courts that police officers and police services may be sued for the way in which they investigate and prosecute a case. In *Hill v Hamilton-Wentworth Regional Police Services Board*, Mr. Hill was charged with ten counts of robbery but only went to trial on one charge. Ultimately, he was acquitted of that remaining charge. He sued the police services and several officers for damages, alleging, among other things, that police were negligent in the method they used to interview the two bank tellers who identified him as the robber.

The Supreme Court of Canada was split 6–3 on whether there was a tort in Canadian law of negligent investigation. The majority (the six justices) felt that there could be such a tort, based on consideration of the principles of tort. The police owed a duty of care to Hill during the course of the investigation. It is reasonably foreseeable that a suspect will suffer harm if the police are negligent in the course of their investigation. The standard of care is measured against what a reasonable officer would have done in similar circumstances. The majority did not feel that recognizing such a tort would change the reasonable and probable grounds standard required before charging a suspect nor would there be a flood of litigation against police for negligent investigation. Even though the majority recognized the tort of negligent investigation in Canadian law, Hill was not successful in his lawsuit. The evidence did not support a finding of negligent investigation or a finding that the standard of care had not been met.

The minority (the other three judges who disagreed with the majority) believed that the tort of negligent investigation should not be recognized, stating:

> A private duty of care owed by the police to suspects would necessarily conflict with the investigating officer's overarching public duty to investigate crime and apprehend offenders.

Source: *Hill v Hamilton-Wentworth Regional Police Services Board*, 2007 SCC 41.

Intentional torts also include intentionally inflicting mental suffering,[15] false imprisonment[16] (including even momentary detention by any person, not just by the police), and "intrusion upon seclusion," which involves intentionally intruding upon the private affairs or concerns of another person where a reasonable person would find that the intrusion was highly offensive, and caused distress, humiliation, or anguish. In the landmark 2012 decision in *Jones v Tsige*, the Supreme Court of Canada confirmed that the tort of "intrusion upon seclusion" can be argued in certain cases of invasion of privacy.[17] In general, almost any violation of personal integrity can qualify as an intentional tort if the necessary combination of intent and action is found to be present and the tortfeasor cannot prove a defence.

CASE IN POINT

"Public Damages" for Rights Violations

The great majority of claims in tort are made by one private party (a person or corporation) against another private party. However, under certain special circumstances, some private parties have successfully claimed damages against the government for breach of rights (often Charter rights). These damages are somewhat, but not completely, similar to tort damages. Like tort damages, they are designed to compensate the injured party, but they also serve a significant deterrent function: they are intended to discourage the government (often, law enforcement officers or prosecutors) from breaching the rights of citizens (often in the context of a criminal prosecution).

In 2015, the Supreme Court of Canada issued a decision in *Henry v British Columbia (Attorney General)*, in which Henry, who was found to have been wrongfully convicted and wrongfully imprisoned for 27 years, was pursuing public damages against the Attorney General of British Columbia (AGBC) for interfering with his right to defend himself at trial by failing to disclose important evidence.

After he filed his claim, the AGBC applied to have it struck out; the trial court upheld the pleading. The AGBC appealed the trial ruling and won (the Court of Appeal struck out the claim). Henry then appealed to the Supreme Court of Canada.

The Supreme Court identified the issue to be decided as follows:

> Does s. 24(1) of the *Canadian Charter of Rights and Freedoms* authorize a court of competent jurisdiction to award damages against the Crown for prosecutorial misconduct absent proof of malice?

In making his case, Henry alleged that he was unable to mount a full defence in his 1983 trial because the Crown had withheld many pieces of important evidence (for example, witness statements that tended to exonerate Henry). They also withheld information about another sexual assault suspect active in the same neighbourhood, and the fact that even after Henry was in jail, assaults matching the pattern of the ones for which he had been convicted continued to happen. Henry's allegations about the Crown's behaviour were well supported, because they formed the basis of his eventual acquittal on all counts.

In arguing that Henry's claim should be struck out, the AGBC relied on case law about the well-established tort of malicious prosecution, and argued that Henry was not alleging malice on the part of the Crown, and so he had no basis for his damage claim.

The Supreme Court disagreed. In overturning the Court of Appeal decision and finding that Henry's claim could in fact proceed (subject to some amendments), it made the following findings:

- Henry's claim, based on wrongful non-disclosure of evidence, was not analogous to the tort of malicious prosecution.
- The decision to prosecute a suspect is based on the Crown's discretion. In the context of discretion, police and Crown motives (like malice) are important factors. However, once a prosecution has been started, complying with the rules of criminal procedure (like the right to disclosure) is *not* discretionary. The suspect has a right to due process, and so government motives (like malice) are not relevant. Therefore, it is not necessary to prove malice to prove a rights violation.
- However, the threshold for making a damage claim against the government must be set very high because of the public interest in letting police and prosecutors do their job without being "chilled" in their pursuit of justice by the prospect of a flood of lawsuits.
- The standard of conduct that will give rise to public damages is much higher than the normal tort standard of negligence. It is also higher than "gross negligence."

Instead of applying a negligence standard, the court set out a special multi-part test to justify public damages, stating that a claimant would have to convince the fact finder on a balance of probabilities that

1. the prosecutor intentionally withheld information;
2. the prosecutor knew or ought reasonably to have known that the information was material to the defence and that the failure to disclose would likely impinge on his or her ability to make full answer and defence;
3. withholding the information violated his or her Charter rights; and
4. he or she suffered harm as a result.

The court also found that the harm to the claimant had to meet a "but for" standard of causation. In this case, damages would flow if Henry could prove that the court would have to answer "yes" to the following question: But for the AGBC's wrongful withholding of disclosure, would the harm to Henry (wrongful conviction and 27 years of prison) have happened?

As a result of winning his appeal, Henry earned the right to proceed with his claim against the AGBC.

Questions for Discussion

1. Do you agree that individuals have a right to claim damages for police or Crown misconduct when that conduct was not motivated by malice, or should existing remedies (like in this case, releasing the prisoner and entering an acquittal in place of a conviction) be enough?

2. If you agree that individuals have a right to damages for rights breaches, do you think that there should be a special "more serious than even gross negligence" proof threshold that should be applied to these cases, or do you believe negligence is negligence, regardless of whether it's committed by the government or by private citizens? Defend your answer.

Source: *Henry v British Columbia (Attorney General)*, 2015 SCC 24, [2015] 2 SCR 214.

Trespass to Property or Goods

trespass
the wrongful entry onto or damage to the property of another

Because the law accords rights to property owners, establishing a duty of care is unnecessary in **trespass** cases: any intentional entry upon or injury to real property (land) or personal property (possessions) constitutes the tort of trespass. Because property owners have a right to exclusive possession of their property, any invasion of the boundaries of private property is tortious, regardless of whether any damage is done. Trespass to real property is probably the most familiar form, but trespass to personal property (often described as theft or conversion) is also actionable in tort and can attract damages that would be unavailable in a criminal trial for theft.[18]

Intentional Business Torts

The common law also recognizes a number of discrete "business" torts, some with a historical definition. These include deceit (or fraud), conspiracy, interference with contractual relations (including inducing breach of contract), and interference with business relations (a tort that doesn't depend on contract interference). Each of these torts depends for proof on an intent-plus-action analysis, which is done by referring to a historical "formula" of legal requirements. For example, a discount airline sues another airline, alleging that the second airline interfered with the customer relations of the first airline.

Defences

The most important defences to intentional torts are (1) the consent of the victim and (2) the self-defence of the tortfeasor. Other defences include legal licence or authority, and necessity. A defendant seeking to avoid tort liability bears the burden of proof in alleging a defence; and he or she must prove it to the level of the civil standard of proof: that is, he or she must put before the court sufficient evidence to establish, on a balance of probabilities, the validity of the defence.

Nuisance

nuisance
a tort law concept generally used to describe something that interferes with another person's use and enjoyment of his or her property

The doctrine of **nuisance** (in contrast to trespass, discussed above) deals with interference with another person's use and enjoyment of his or her property. To constitute nuisance, an invasion of property need not be intentional or even negligent. As long as the possibility of an impact on the plaintiff's use is foreseeable to the defendant before the action is taken, that action can constitute nuisance. Nuisance need not and often does not involve an entry by the defendant onto the plaintiff's land. It may instead be the result of the defendant's ostensibly legitimate use of his or her own private property, which may have harmful effects on the plaintiff's use. For example, loud noises, bad odours, or shade from a new shed cast over a neighbour's garden may be considered nuisances that attract tort liability. Even a neighbour's noisy air conditioner may give rise to a lawsuit.

In assessing damages, the courts can award a remedy for almost any kind of interference, temporary or permanent, with an owner's "use and enjoyment" of the property in question. Any interference beyond that which would not be tolerated by the "ordinary occupier" in the position of the plaintiff will be compensated with damages.

Strict Liability and the Rule in Rylands v Fletcher

fault
responsibility for an action

Because there is no deterrent value in punishing people for their non-negligent (or non-trespassing) actions, the law of tort requires an element of **fault**, usually described as negligence, before liability will be imposed. However, some circumstances cry out for an exception to this rule, especially where damage from non-negligent actions is serious and prevention may have been possible. Exceptions to the rules of tort law are found most often in legislation. For example, environmental statutes hold present occupiers liable for expensive environmental damage caused by their predecessors.

The common law offers at least one example of such an exception. The *Rylands v Fletcher*[19] doctrine allows for the imposition of **strict liability** (non-negligent liability) in certain cases that involve the escape of water, chemicals, or other dangerous forces from one property onto another. In these cases, the damage to the victim's property does not have to be negligent or intentional—the fact of the damage is sufficient ground for liability in all cases except for those involving an "act of God." The principle behind imposing strict liability is that there is a social benefit in requiring those who make risky or dangerous use of their own land to account for even the non-negligent consequences of that use, because they are presumably the parties most able to control the danger.

strict liability
in the civil law context, liability that depends only on proof of the consequences of an action, even though there is no negligence on the part of the tortfeasor

APPLYING THE LAW

Mustapha v Culligan

At trial, the trial judge was satisfied that Mr. Mustapha had suffered harm from seeing the dead flies and awarded him $80,000 in general damages, $24,174.58 in special damages, and $237,600 in damages for loss of business. (Mustapha owned two salons, had to reduce his work hours as a result of illness resulting from the incident, and lost several clients.) Culligan appealed the trial decision to the Ontario Court of Appeal. The Ontario Court of Appeal overturned the judgment on the basis that the injury was not reasonably foreseeable and hence did not give rise to a cause of action. The case was appealed to the Supreme Court of Canada.

The chief justice, in writing the decision for the unanimous court, stated at paragraph 3:

A successful action in negligence requires that the plaintiff demonstrate (1) that the defendant owed him a duty of care; (2) that the defendant's behaviour breached the standard of care; (3) that the plaintiff sustained damage; and (4) that the damage was caused, in fact and in law, by the defendant's breach. … Mr. Mustapha's claim fails because he has failed to establish that his damage was caused in law by the defendant's negligence. In other words, his damage is too remote to allow recovery.

Questions for Discussion

Consider each of the four points that the chief justice indicated that Mr. Mustapha needed to prove to be successful in his lawsuit, from Mustapha's perspective and from Culligan's perspective. What was the duty of care that Culligan owed (or did not owe) Mustapha? How did Culligan breach (or not breach) that standard? What damage did Mustapha suffer (or not suffer)? How was that damage caused (or not caused) by Culligan?

Source: *Mustapha v Culligan of Canada Ltd*, 2008 SCC 27.

CHAPTER SUMMARY

Contracts and torts are civil law disciplines. A contract is an agreement between two or more parties that governs the relationship between the parties. For a contract to be enforceable, the parties must intend to be legally bound by its terms; there must be an offer, acceptance, and consideration; the parties must have the capacity to contract; and the terms must be clear and precise. Contractual defects, including misrepresentation, mistake, illegality, problems with formalities, duress, undue influence, or unconscionability, may give rise to an award of damages. If there is a breach of a contract, a remedy may be awarded to compensate the innocent party, usually in the form of monetary damages, although a court may instead grant an order for specific performance.

A tort is a wrong committed against a person or property that can result in damages to the person suffering the wrong. The two most important categories of tort are negligence and intentional torts.

The central principle of negligence law is the duty of care. In order for a wronged person to be successful in a negligence lawsuit, the plaintiff must prove that a duty of care was owed by the tortfeasor, what the standard of care was, that there was a breach of the duty of care, and that damages resulted. The court must also determine causation: which party or parties, including the victim, contributed to the event that caused the injury. Before liability is imposed, it must usually be shown that a reasonable person could have foreseen the harm that resulted from the wrongful act. Emerging causes of action include negligent investigation (the right to sue police services and/or the Crown for the way in which they investigate and prosecute a case) and also a tort of wrongful non-disclosure of evidence.

Intentional torts are those committed by a tortfeasor who intends to cause harm, loss, or damage to someone or something. These torts include trespass to the person, trespass to property or goods, and business torts. The main defences to intentional torts are the consent of the victim and self-defence of the tortfeasor.

Another area of tort law is nuisance, which deals with interference with another person's use and enjoyment of his or her property.

Finally, an exception to the tort law rule that fault must be proven before liability is imposed may arise when the damage is serious and might have been prevented. For example, strict liability may be imposed in a case involving environmental damage.

KEY TERMS

assault, 175
battery, 175
breach, 164
collateral contract, 167
consideration, 165
construction, 166
contractual defect, 167
contributory negligence, 173
counteroffer, 165
damages, 167
deceit, 167
duty of care, 172
duty to mitigate, 171
exclusion clause, 166
expectation, 170
fault, 178

foreseeability, 172
formalities, 168
frustration, 169
induce, 167
joint and several liability, 173
lapse, 165
legal capacity, 165
misrepresentation, 167
mitigation, 171
non est factum, 168
nuisance, 178
offer, 165
parol evidence rule, 166
plead, 168
reasonable reliance, 167
rejection, 165

reliance, 170
remoteness, 171
representation, 167
rescind, 167
restitution, 170
revocation, 165
specific performance, 170
standard of care, 172
strict liability, 179
thin skull rule, 173
tort, 163
tortfeasor, 164
trespass, 178
unconscionability, 169
vicarious liability, 172

NOTES

1 *Criminal Code*, RSC 1985, c C-46, as amended.

2 *Sale of Goods Act*, RSO 1990, c S.1, as amended.

3 See e.g. *Bolibruck v Niagara Health System*, 2015 ONSC 1595.

4 For an interesting discussion of what happens when the homeowner, instead, fails to prevent an assault on his or her property, see *Unifund Assurance Company v DE*, 2015 ONCA 423.

5 *Strand v Strand*, 2014 ABQB 754.

6 *Landry v Tivey*, 2014 NSSC 426.

7 *Planning Act*, RSO 1990, c P.13.

8 *Statute of Frauds*, RSO 1990, c S.19.

9 *Consumer Protection Act, 2002*, SO 2002, c 30, Schedule A.

10 *Ens v Pacific Home Products Ltd*, 2008 SKPC 108.

11 *Frustrated Contracts Act*, RSO 1990, c F.34.

12 *Occupiers' Liability Act*, RSO 1990, c O.2.

13 *Stewart v Pettie*, [1995] 1 SCR 131, 1995 CanLII 147.

14 *Childs v Desormeaux*, 2006 SCC 18, [2006] 1 SCR 643.

15 See e.g. *Prinzo v Baycrest Centre for Geriatric Care* (2002), 60 OR (3d) 474, 2002 CanLII 45005 (CA).

16 See *Hill v Hamilton-Wentworth Regional Police Services Board*, 2007 SCC 41, discussed above.

17 *Jones v Tsige*, 2012 ONCA 32.

18 See e.g. *Freitas v Defraga*, 2006 CanLII 17936 (Ont Sup Ct J).

19 *Rylands v Fletcher* (1868), LR 3 HL 330.

EXERCISES

Multiple Choice

1. Which incident(s) can form the basis of both a criminal charge and a tort lawsuit?

   a. a person enters a stranger's house by force and removes valuables

   b. a person enters a stranger's house by force and removes nothing

   c. a person threatens to slash his girlfriend's face with a knife, but doesn't

   d. a and c

   e. all of the above

2. A contract in which one person agrees to transfer a brand new car to another person for $5 is unenforceable

   a. on the basis of insufficient consideration

   b. if it's not in writing

   c. because of the doctrine of *non est factum*

   d. if one of the parties lacks legal capacity to contract

   e. for any or all of the above

3. Could a landowner be liable for a chemical spill that occurred on his or her land (contaminating nearby waterways) before he or she even purchased the land?

   a. no, never

   b. only if he or she knew about it at the time of purchase

   c. only if the possibility of a previous spill was foreseeable at the time of purchase

   d. only if he or she signed a contract guaranteeing that his or her use of the land would be contamination-free

   e. possibly, based on the doctrine of strict liability

4. Adam has his ten-year-old car repainted and tells Barry the car is five years old. Barry buys the car on the basis of its being only five years old. This is a case of

   a. negligent misrepresentation

   b. fraudulent misrepresentation

   c. innocent misrepresentation

   d. mutual mistake

   e. unilateral mistake

5. Adam has his ten-year-old car repainted. Barry buys the car believing it is only five years old, but doesn't tell Adam this. This is a case of

   a. mutual mistake

   b. innocent misrepresentation

   c. unilateral mistake

   d. common mistake

   e. negligent misrepresentation

True or False?

_____ 1. Some aspects/areas of contract and tort law have been codified by statute.

_____ 2. The victim of an assault and battery can sue his or her attacker under tort law, whether or not criminal charges have been laid.

_____ 3. A "not guilty" finding in criminal court means that the victim of the crime will automatically be unable to recover civil damages for the same incident.

_____ 4. A person can be found liable under tort law for the consequences of ostensibly legal activities carried out on his or her own property.

_____ 5. A sales contract is unenforceable if it contains no term setting a price for the goods sold.

_____ 6. A person can be held liable in tort for untrue statements he or she made in the process of negotiating a contract.

_____ 7. A parent cannot enter into an enforceable contract with his or her own child.

_____ 8. A contract designed to allow the enforcement of the bribe of a police officer may be struck down by a court even if the contract conforms with all applicable rules of contract formation.

_____ 9. In the interest of the protection of public safety, police personnel are not held to owe a duty to take reasonable care in investigating crime.

_____10. Citizens can sue the government, in some cases, for damages for the breach of their rights (when they can prove damages).

Short Answer

1. A mother sues a condom manufacturer for the costs of raising her daughter, conceived and born as a result of breakage of a condom during normal sexual intercourse. Based on your knowledge of tort and contract law, do you think her lawsuit will succeed? Should she sue under contract law or under tort law? From an ethical standpoint, do you feel she should succeed or not, and why?

2. Eddie "The Baby" Hertz finds out that his rival Big Dool has a contract out on his head. Fortunately for Eddie, Nubs and Dirt Boy (the goons hired to carry out the deed) have refused to proceed because, based on their knowledge of a recent failed business venture, they don't think Big Dool is good for the money.

   a. Can Big Dool sue for specific performance of the contract? Why or why not?

   b. Can he sue for damages? If so, how might they be calculated?

   c. If you believe that this sort of contract is never enforceable in court, why would parties like Big Dool and the goons enter into a contract in the first place?

3. Two teenage boys are roughhousing in a department store, making loud comments about the other shoppers, and generally being a nuisance. A security guard decides to "teach them a lesson" by detaining them, accusing them of shoplifting, and threatening to call the police. Can the boys—or their parents—sue the guard or the store on the basis of a tort? If so, what tort(s)?

4. Mariam and Shawna meet during a fitness class. Shawna tells Mariam that she works as a security officer with a private security agency. Mariam tells Shawna that she is organizing a neighbourhood street party with live entertainment in her neighbourhood, and that she needs to hire two security guards. She gives Shawna the time and place after Shawna expresses interest in working the event and assures Mariam that she will be able to recruit a second guard to work with her. Shawna gives Mariam the agency's phone number and asks Mariam to call her supervisor with the details.

   The next day, while Shawna is not at work, Mariam calls and speaks to Shawna's supervisor. She explains the details of the work and that she is willing to pay the guards $10 per hour each. The supervisor asserts that this compensation is far below the agency's minimum rate, and that he cannot allow his guards to work for so little pay. Mariam refuses to pay more, and hangs up.

   The supervisor later explains what happened to Shawna, who agrees that he was right not to accept the work at that rate.

   Two weeks later, the agency gets an angry call from Mariam. She says that the security guards who had agreed to work her event never showed up, and two traffic barriers valued at $400 apiece were stolen. She demands compensation for her loss, which she says would not have occurred had the agency abided by the terms of the contract.

   a. Was there in fact a contract between Mariam and Shawna, or between Mariam and the agency? Why or why not?

   b. If there was in fact a contract, and Shawna breached it by not showing up with a second guard, would the agency be liable for the cost of the stolen barriers?

5. Imagine that a young relative of yours has learned that you have taken a law class, and has asked you to "write up a contract" for him to use in his dog-walking business. The business involves him obtaining spare keys from clients so that he can visit their homes during the day when they are away to take their dogs for walks. Make a bullet point list of the terms that you might include in this contract. Be sure to consider potential tort liability issues.

Property, Family Property, and Tenancies: The "Rights To" Disciplines

11

LEARNING OUTCOMES

After completing this chapter, you should be able to:

- Describe the function and status of property rights in Canada.

- Understand the basic principles of property law.

- Describe the basic rights of property owners and the legal mechanisms by which these rights are enforced.

- Explain the impact of familial relationships on property rights.

- List ways in which the criminal law protects property.

- Describe the basic rights and responsibilities of both parties to a landlord–tenant agreement.

The Concept and Function of Property Rights

Perhaps one of the strongest human instincts is to protect property. Because acquiring basic goods (such as food) and territory (such as a place to build a shelter) is essential to survival, human beings have always been motivated to work to acquire these things and to protect them from those who might take them away. Acquiring the necessities of life requires effort. Consequently, community support for a system of rules to protect property has always existed in human societies.

There is enormous diversity in the way in which societies define and administer property rights. Some societies see property as being individual, with items of property belonging to a single owner (even if others are allowed to use the property); others see property as being familial (owned by a family unit); and still others, though less commonly today, see property as belonging to a wider group, even to the community or society as a whole. In many modern societies, all three modes of ownership coexist, depending on the kind of property.

Societies also differ widely in their rules about how property ownership is to be transferred or how property is to be protected. For example, in societies where property and property rights are very highly valued, severe penalties may follow the theft of property of comparatively modest commercial worth. More commonly, however, the goals of property administration are to preserve the peaceful use and enjoyment of the fruits of one's labour, and to allocate those "fruits" among members of the society in an orderly way. Establishing clear rules about who controls what property is simply a way to minimize interpersonal disputes.

The Status of Property Rights in Canada

In Canada, property is protected both under the common law and by statute, and the determination and administration of property rights are dealt with in a wide range of statutes. As a result, we can reasonably conclude that property is a relatively important concept in Canadian society. Nevertheless, Canadian lawmakers and the citizens who elect them have so far declined to take a step that has been taken in some other common law countries—protecting (or entrenching) individual property rights in the Constitution, under the *Canadian Charter of Rights and Freedoms*.[1] Because the Charter, as part of the Constitution, is the highest law of the land, and because it does protect many other types of individual rights, such as the right to "life, liberty and security of the person" (see s 7), our legal system, when considered as a whole, seems to place a lesser value on property rights than on the right to personal security. Because of this hierarchy of values, there are considerable limits on what a person can do to protect his or her property from attack by another person, and the penalties imposed by Canadian law for interfering with property rights are usually less severe than those imposed for physical assaults and other crimes against the person.

Basic Principles of Canadian Property Law

What Is Property?

As a concept, property is subjective—that is, its content and application are subject to the changing values and circumstances of society. There continue to be new disputes about what kinds of things can be the subject of property rights. While tangible resources such as land and objects have been the subject of property protection for centuries, more recent times have seen the granting of property and quasi-property status to **intangibles**.

Individuals or corporations may acquire property rights in, among other things, artwork, music, literary works, trademarks, recipes, and genetically engineered plants or animals. These forms of property are governed by copyright (for example, books, songs, or art), trademark (for example, business logos or slogans), or patent law, and are called **intellectual property**. The technology in your cellphone is protected by patent laws governing intellectual property. Intellectual property can be extremely valuable, as can be demonstrated in the legal disputes between high-tech companies over exclusive ownership of rights to operating systems or the technology behind hardware such as cameras or screens. Around the time that this edition was being prepared, the US Federal Bureau of Investigation and Apple Inc. were embroiled in a legal dispute over a demand, by the agency, that Apple permit investigators to "unlock" the phone of an alleged terrorist. The dispute was eventually rendered moot when a third party developed and shared a method to unlock the phone.

Property status can also be accorded to intangible business assets such as "**goodwill**," a concept that describes a company's ability to retain customers through the benefit of its reputation. The goodwill that has been built up in a company over the years may be very valuable to a new owner.

Finally, the concept of personal property has in some cases been extended to apply to the human body and personality. While tort law deals with resolving disputes that involve physical and emotional injury, property concepts have sometimes been used to protect physical integrity and body parts and substances. For example, some courts have allowed a donor to assert a proprietary interest in semen samples. Some jurisdictions have extended property or quasi-property status to privacy and to "personality" in some circumstances, allowing remedies for the violation of interests in these. For example, in Ontario, the *Freedom of Information and Protection of Privacy Act*[2] regulates access to personal information gathered by public institutions. Protection of personal information on online social networking systems such as Facebook or Twitter has become a concern. The federal privacy commissioner has raised the issue in the media, and the administrators of these networks have been encouraged to implement security controls. Protection of personal information can become a criminal matter with identity theft and fraud. Thus, the outer limits of the property concept continue to be tested as information and innovation become the most valuable commodities of our time, demonstrating that law is responsive to changes in society.

intangibles
things or concepts that may be the subject of a property right without having a physical form

intellectual property
intangible property, including copyrights, trademarks, and patents

goodwill
the economic value of a business's renown and good reputation

CASE IN POINT

Is There Privacy in Facebook?

Sami was in a car accident and was injured. She sued Bali, the driver of the other car, for damages for her injuries. Sami makes the allegation in her Statement of Claim that her life has changed and she no longer can do the activities that she did before the accident, including skateboarding and partying. Bali's lawyer searches the Internet and finds out that, even after the car accident, Sami continues to maintain a very active Facebook page, with many "friends" and references to parties and skateboarding.

Source: *Leduc v Roman*, 2009 CanLII 6838 (Ont Sup Ct J).

Questions for Discussion

1. Has Bali's lawyer violated Sami's privacy by finding her Facebook page and going through it?

2. Should Bali's lawyer be able to use the information from the Facebook page against Sami in the lawsuit?

Real Property and Personal Property

real property
land and affixed
dwellings; real estate

personal property
property without a
land or real estate
component—physical
possessions (chattels)

Canadian law recognizes a distinction between **real property** (generally land) and **personal property** (generally anything other than land). These two broad categories of property are governed by the same basic principles, but these principles are applied differently for each category, notably with respect to transferring and registering rights.

For a summary of the different categories of property, see Table 11.1.

TABLE 11.1   Categories of Property

Tangible	Intangible	Tangible or Intangible
Real property • generally land • we can see it, touch it	*Intellectual property* • property governed by copyright, trademark, or patent law (for example, rights in cellphone technology—you cannot see the ideas inherent in the technology that created your cellphone, even though you can see and touch the phone)	*Personal property* • generally anything other than land • tangible when we can see it and we can touch it • jewellery is tangible • intangible when it cannot be seen and touched • rights you own in a company (for example, shares) are intangible—you can see and touch the paper that is evidence of your rights but you cannot see the rights themselves

Features of the Property Concept

A "Bundle" of Rights

Property may be defined as rules between people in relation to things, and it is useful to understand the property concept as a "bundle" of rights and obligations designed to protect some of the *interests* of property holders. A full complement of rights includes

- the right to possession and use of the property (including the right to alter it),
- the right to exclude others from possession, and
- the right to transfer some of these rights to others.

Not all property holders are entitled to all rights with respect to all of their property. For example, each joint owner of co-owned property lacks rights of exclusion with respect to the others, making proprietorship a matter of degree. Nor are rights absolute. Property owners are obliged to use their property in accordance with common law and statutory rules—for example, a car can only be driven on public roads if it is duly licensed. Finally, a person can have a right to use and possess property (for example, to own and display original artwork), but not to modify it.[3] The more complete the bundle of rights held by one person, the more completely that person's interests will be respected. The flexibility of a property concept based on multiple rights allows for sharing the benefit of property within a society.

Ownership and Title, Possession and Control

One of the most important potential "splits" of the bundle of property rights is that between ownership of property (title) and physical control over property (possession).

Title is a legal concept that guarantees a traditional set of rights, including possessory rights, in property. Title is usually passed through formal means: inheritance, gift, or purchase. It is typically established by **instruments** (documents with legal effect) such as deeds or transfers. Title can include and determine possessory rights.

Possession is a physical fact, and, in the right circumstances, may also be a legal conclusion. A person who can establish physical control over property may acquire rights because of that possession. Possession is normally acquired by action—taking or moving in—combined with the intention to take control. Possession itself is important evidence of title, and in some cases, possession may afford a stronger interest than title. Many legal battles are the result of conflicts over the separation of ownership and possessory rights. For example, a landlord, as owner of an apartment building, may disagree with the way in which a tenant, as the lawful possessor of an apartment, exercises possession.

Real Property (Land-Owning) Concepts

Tenure

The tenurial system—in which all lands are owned by the monarchy—as it existed in England was imported into Canadian common law through colonization, when all Canadian lands became the property of the British Crown. Our Constitution transferred this ownership to the Canadian government. As a result, no Canadian land is ownerless—the Crown is the ultimate owner. This state of affairs has led to problems with respect to the rights of Aboriginal peoples, who have been forced to establish their pre-existing property rights through negotiation with the government. While most ancient tenurial concepts are irrelevant to modern society, the concept of **escheat** still permits the government to reclaim ownership of property when a person dies intestate (without a will and with no legal heirs). Ownership of the land also reverts (goes back) to the government when a corporation ceases to exist while still holding title to the land.[4]

The Physical Scope of Property Rights

In general, a landholder is entitled not only to the surface of the land, but also to the air directly above the land, to the earth below, and to the support provided by the subsurface. The landholder may grant some of these rights to another, such as rights to mineral deposits in the subsurface, or, where property includes the bank of a lake or river, rights of access to and use of the water. Legislation may limit the right of landholders to use water flowing through or under their land, and the law of trespass or nuisance can be used to protect landholders against damage to their own lands from their neighbours' use of water. Finally, the law allocates rights on expanding and reducing land boundaries through the processes of erosion and accretion that occur naturally.

Landholding and Capacity

Both individuals and corporations are entitled to hold Canadian land, but restrictions apply in some cases. Provincial legislation often restricts the rights of minors to dispose of their land with full autonomy and grants disposition rights to the courts or to parents or guardians. Persons ruled mentally incompetent also face restrictions on their rights as owners. Non-citizens may hold Canadian land, but provincial legislatures can restrict ownership rights of non-residents. A corporation's right to hold and dispose of land depends on permission found in the statute or instrument granting corporate status.

title
ownership based on rights acquired or conferred through legal transactions or instruments

instrument
a formal legal document

escheat
a reversion of property to the Crown when there is no will or heir to inherit it or when a corporation that is the legal owner of property is dissolved

Estates in Land

The legal concept of an **estate** describes the extent of an owner's interest in a parcel of land. In a tenurial system like ours, landholders do not own the land itself (since the government is the ultimate owner) but rather an interest in the land. The ownership of an estate in land entitles the holder to possession of the physical land. Our property law is based on the rule that possession must never lapse—all land must always be possessed by someone—and a person in actual possession may exclude others from access to the land.

The following are the three most common kinds of estates in land that a person can hold:

- *Fee simple* A fee simple is the greatest possible estate, with the potential of continuing forever. Ownership of land in fee simple means that the owner has the unfettered right to use and dispose of the land as he or she wishes. Most land in Canada is owned in fee simple, with the owner having absolute right to the property subject only to the underlying right of the government (see the discussion of escheat above).

- *Life estate* The holder of a life estate in land has the right to exclusive possession of the land "for life," after which time the land passes to somebody else. Who that somebody else will be is something over which the life estate holder generally has no control, and he or she cannot sell the land during his or her lifetime. A typical situation that results in a life estate is a gift, by will, of land to a spouse for life and then, on the spouse's death, to a child in fee simple.

- *Leasehold estate* A leasehold estate generally confers rights of possession only to a tenant for a limited time. The landlord and tenant relationship in Canada is now primarily governed by contract and statutory rules, but it has its roots in property law. Most Canadian leaseholds are of short duration, but it is possible for a leasehold estate to last several lifetimes.

Transferring Real Property

Most land is transferred either by deed or transfer document (paper or electronic) or by succession (inheritance). In some jurisdictions, such as Ontario, in both cases the *Statute of Frauds*[5] requires that land transfers be in writing. The written instruments describing transfers are later used to trace title to land, so that an unbroken "chain of title" between the current owner and the Crown constitutes evidence of title. This tracing process depends on the registration of instruments at county registries. Many parts of Canada still rely on this deed registration system. In the remaining jurisdictions, it has been replaced (or is being replaced) by electronic land titles registration systems. These systems provide certified evidence of the *state* of title, rather than the actual instruments, so that title may be guaranteed to a new owner without the necessity of researching the validity of title. Additionally, the availability of title insurance has reduced the scope of title searches.

Government Expropriation of Private Land

In addition to the voluntary transfer of title to land (by gift, sale, inheritance), landholders may lose title when property is **expropriated** or taken over by the government under applicable legislation. Landholders subject to government expropriation can dispute the applicable legislation, the specific mandate of the government body in question, or the amount of compensation offered, but the basic right to expropriate is one of the oldest characteristics of the tenurial system. For example, a government may expropriate land from its owners to build a highway.

Multiple Owners

Individual parcels of land can have multiple owners, and the structure of the co-ownership may be determined by the owners themselves or may be imposed by another, such as in the case of an inherited interest. Co-owners of land can be joint tenants or tenants-in-common, depending on the nature of their rights ("tenants" in this context means owners; the term has nothing to do with leasing or renting).

- *Joint tenants* own a piece of property together. They have identical rights with respect to (1) possession, (2) the type of estate owned, (3) title to the property, and (4) duration of ownership. They obtain title to the property by way of the same instrument, at the same time, and they must transfer title at the same time. Each owner has the right to enjoy the full physical extent of the property, and no tenant can exclude another from any part. Joint tenants enjoy the right of survivorship. When any one of them dies, that person's interest passes entirely to the remaining joint tenants—it cannot be bequeathed to someone else by will. However, it is possible for a joint tenant to sever (cut) the joint tenancy by conveying his or her interest to another person. The joint tenants then become tenants-in-common.

- *Tenants-in-common*, by contrast, can have divergent interests with respect to a single piece of property. They may obtain their interests in the property at different times, under different instruments. They each own a specific share of the property (for example, one tenant may own 10 percent, another 30 percent, and another 60 percent) and may sell, give as a gift, mortgage, or will their share of the land independently of the other tenants.

Rights in the Land of Others

A person can acquire rights in the land of another in several ways. These rights, usually limited and well defined, can arise by contract or by other means (such as use), and they form an exception to the law of trespass.

- **Licences**, as personal agreements, are not property interests but may give rights to use land. Licences are not "attached" to land and generally are valid only between the original parties. They need not be the subject of a contract but may arise through behaviour demonstrating an expectation on the part of one party that is encouraged by another.

- **Easements** are special property interests tied to land. They depend on the existence of both a dominant tenement (the parcel of land that benefits from the easement) and a servient tenement (the parcel of land that bears the easement burden). Dominant and servient tenements must be owned separately, but since the easement is tied to the properties, it binds all successive owners. Common easements in residential areas include power line rights-of-way and mutual driveways. In rural areas they may include access paths to "landlocked" property. Usually, telephone companies and cable companies are able to service individual parcels of land because of easements that not only give these companies access to the land but also allow them to dig, if necessary, to complete the work.

licence
permission to use another's land for a specific purpose; does not give any other rights

easement
a limited property interest (often a right of access) that "attaches" to and is passed on with the land; it can be either a benefit or a burden

Adverse Possession and "Squatting"

Because of the importance in law of possession as an indicator of property rights, it is possible, under special circumstances, for a person in possession (having physical control) of land to exclude the titleholder from possession. This occurs through the doctrine of **adverse possession**. The most notorious adverse possessors are **squatters**, who move onto apparently vacant land and eventually defeat the property rights of the paper title-holder. More common is the adverse possession of much smaller parcels, as in the case of a neighbour who erects a fence beyond the boundaries of his or her own property and through long use acquires rights in the enclosed strip. The modern doctrine of adverse possession is based on the failure of the titleholder to exercise his or her right to exclude trespassers for a period exceeding a provincial statutory limitation. The titleholder loses this right if the adverse possessor can show that he or she took possession with intent to exclude the owner, such that the owner is in fact dispossessed of the land. The true owner cannot be excluded by adverse possession under the land titles system until the land has been in the system for more than ten years.

Personal Property Law

The law relating to personal property is less formal than that relating to land. In general, personal property can be transferred without the need for a written instrument, and it is not necessary to prove ownership through a traceable chain of title. However, systems exist to register and trace the ownership of certain types of property such as cars and firearms. The police need to be able to determine the owner of a car involved in an accident. You, as the potential purchaser of a used car, need to be certain that the seller is indeed the lawful owner of the car. In the case of personal property, possession is generally easy to prove, and in the absence of evidence to the contrary (such as evidence of theft, or bailment, discussed below) the person who has possession of property is presumed to be the owner.

One situation that is an exception to the general "havers keepers" rule of property law is **bailment**, a situation in which one person holds the property of another. In bailment situations, there is generally a responsibility on the part of the holder to protect the property of the owner. Avoiding this presumed responsibility is the reason behind most of the "exclusion of liability" clauses and notices used by parking lots, shipping companies, airlines, and other services that are in the business of temporarily holding the property of others.

How the Criminal Law Protects Property

Because it is impractical to deal with all violations of property rights—especially rights to personal property—through civil lawsuits, the criminal law incorporates a number of property-related offences. The most obvious example is theft, also known as conversion. The theft provisions in the *Criminal Code*[6] protect not only tangible property, but also intangibles. See, for example, section 326, which deals with the theft of telecommunication service.

Although damage to real property (land) is often the subject of civil suits, victims of such damage can also have recourse to the criminal law, which criminalizes activities such as arson or the destruction of documents of title.

Finally, the criminal law protects property in less direct ways as well by making it an offence, among other things, to forge a signature or to possess break-in tools.

Family Property: Balancing Merit and Need

As was mentioned above, although property law has its roots in the common law, in a number of situations the common law rules have been altered by statute. One of these situations is in the context of family relationships.

Marriage and family relations have long been the subject of legislation in the Common-wealth and in Canada. Common law countries have historically viewed women as different from men when it comes to property. For many years, the common law prohibited married women from owning property in their own right, and presumed that women's needs would be met through the financial support of their spouses. Property rights in family law have seen two major shifts: the realignment of property rights for women so that there are no longer any legal restrictions, and the availability of spousal rights and obligations for two people of the same sex.

Notwithstanding these shifts, Canadian family law still concerns itself with the issue of spousal interdependence. There are good reasons for this focus. Many families, often in an effort to care for dependent children and to carry out household chores, arrange their affairs so that, at certain times throughout the course of a marriage, one partner bears a dispropor-tionate share of the burden of income earning, while the other pursues non-earning work. The pattern, of course, is no longer as closely tied to gender as it used to be—although women are still more likely to carry the burden of child care, there are many instances in which a family has a stay-at-home dad. There are also childless families in which one spouse supports both partners for a period of time while the other spouse pursues an education. Although arrangements like these may prove very practical while a marriage lasts, they can lead to in-equalities in property ownership that can operate unfairly if a marriage breaks down.

Equalization Under Provincial Statutes

To reduce the impact of these inequalities, all Canadian provinces have legislation de-signed to "equalize" family property on marriage breakdown. Ontario's equalization provi-sions are found in the *Family Law Act* (FLA).[7] Under the FLA, a spouse (which now includes a same-sex spouse) does not acquire an ownership interest in property owned by the other spouse, but does have a right to an **equalization payment** if the parties separate. The equalization payment equals one-half the difference between the **net family property** of one spouse and that of the other. Net family property is the value of all property owned on a chosen "valuation date" (often the date of separation, but it depends on the circum-stances) after deducting

- debts and liabilities, and
- the value of property owned on the date of marriage.

Certain property is excluded from the calculation of property owned on the valuation date, including gifts and inheritances from third parties after the date of marriage. The **matrimonial home**, however, is never excluded, and the matrimonial home is not de-ducted from the owner's net family property even if it was owned before the marriage.

The Matrimonial Home

A matrimonial home is defined by the FLA as property that the spouses ordinarily occupied as their family residence at the time of separation. The matrimonial home is given special treat-ment in the equalization of net family properties, and the FLA also provides for special rights of possession (occupancy rights) and rights against alienation (rights prohibiting sale) of the matrimonial home. Both spouses have an equal right of possession of a matrimonial home. No spouse may sell or mortgage a matrimonial home without the consent of the other spouse or without a court order. Depending on the needs of the parties, one party may be granted the right to live in the matrimonial home (often after compensation is paid to the other party for giving up his or her own right), or the home may be sold and the proceeds equalized.

equalization payment
a payment ordered from one spouse to another, under family property legislation, that is designed to equalize property holdings on separation

net family property
a statutorily defined value of the property owned by one spouse that may be subject to equalization under family property legislation

matrimonial home
a dwelling that meets criteria making it subject to special treatment under family property law

Bail Conditions and Impact on Family Law Rights

The dissolution of a family relationship often triggers strong emotions, and it is not uncommon for separating partners to seek police involvement when conflicts escalate. However, when calls to police lead to formal charges, those charges can affect family law rights, in some cases, limiting options for successful solutions, and compromising the interests of children. For this reason, law enforcement and justice personnel would be well advised to proceed with the family law context in mind.

For example, there have been cases in Canada in which one partner, by bringing charges against the other, has precipitated a situation in which the other party, by being subject to bail conditions, has become unable to pursue access to the matrimonial home, to see children, or even to contact the ex-spouse to make arrangements for children.

In *Shaw v Shaw*, a husband who had decided to leave his marriage provoked his wife into an argument at a tavern. The wife punched him. He did nothing for a month (except obtain legal advice about how to use charges against her to limit her family law rights). A month later, he reported the punch to the police, who charged the wife with assault, arrested her, and detained her overnight. At her bail hearing, she was released subject to conditions that barred her from returning to the matrimonial home.

The judge, frustrated with what he saw as a disregard, on the part of law enforcement personnel, for the effects of their actions (for example, keeping the accused in custody despite the fact that the assault had occurred a month before), included the following passage in his reasons:

> Spousal assaults are by nature serious and there are very sound policy reasons to lay such charges and have them proceed through the judicial system … . I observe, however, that the damage of which I speak is not from the laying of the charge … . The way that the criminal justice system approaches the commencement of these matters, however, often wreaks family law havoc … . [T]he actions of the system—from the officer who refuses to release the defendant at the station, to the duty counsel who allows the defendant to agree to inappropriate conditions of release out of expediency—affect the lives of the members of the defendant's family. Similarly the Superior Court is tasked with the duty of adjudicating the respective rights of the parties to remain in the matrimonial home pending the resolution of the matrimonial litigation. Routine orders excluding a party from the common home of the parties until the end of the criminal matter without thought to the consequences thereof, and without a remedy short of a bail review, place one party in a position of immediate superiority over the other party for as long as it takes (perhaps a year) for defended criminal charges to be resolved. Such rote treatment of all matters of domestic assault can lead, on the one hand, to concocted or exaggerated claims of criminal behaviour or, on the other hand, to innocent defendants pleading guilty at an early stage out of expediency or a shared desire with the complainant to start to rehabilitate the family unit.

Questions for Discussion

1. Do you agree that law enforcement officers should approach allegations of violence differently when the violence occurs between separating spouses, or is it more fair to simply treat all allegations consistently, without regard to the relationship context?

2. Where a law enforcement officer is aware that an alleged assault has occurred within the context of relationship breakdown, what additional considerations might he or she make when responding to a call?

Sources: *Shaw v Shaw*, 2008 ONCJ 130; see also *Kelly v Kelly*, 2009 CanLII 48506 (Ont Sup Ct J).

Equalization of Property Under Trust Law

While it is easiest and most common for couples to rely on equalization rules under provincial legislation to settle family property disputes, not all separating couples are covered by this legislation. Each family law statute contains a definition of "spouse" that depends on certain conditions (typically the sex of the parties, the duration of cohabitation, and the presence of children). Ontario's *Family Law Act* defines "spouse" as either of two people who have married each other or have entered in good faith into a marriage that may be voidable. As indicated above, the definition no longer refers to just heterosexual spouses. This change occurred as a result of a number of court decisions in the past decade in which the common law definition of marriage (which referred to heterosexual couples) was struck down as being unconstitutional.

Where a couple's relationship falls outside the bounds of family legislation (for example, when an Ontario couple are living together "common law"), a party seeking redress of property-related inequities may assert a claim for property that is legally owned by the other party on the basis of **trust** law. A party who succeeds in bringing such a claim will be granted relief in the form of an order (by the court) that the other party holds an interest in the disputed property "in trust" for the claiming party. The effect of such an order is to prevent the title owner from disposing of or using the property without compensating or taking into account the interest of the other party.

trust
a complex legal doctrine based on the rights of a person in the property of another

Domestic Contracts

Parties may contract out of family law rules by means of a "domestic contract." Part IV of the FLA provides that domestic contracts and agreements to amend domestic contracts must be in writing, signed by the parties, and witnessed. There are three kinds of domestic contracts:

- **Marriage contracts** may be made by people who are married or who intend to marry. These contracts may address the rights and obligations of each party during the marriage or on separation, including ownership or division of property, support obligations, and the right to direct the education of children, but not the right to custody of or access to children. Any provision in a marriage contract that purports to limit a spouse's right to possession of the matrimonial home is unenforceable.

- **Cohabitation agreements** may be made by people who are cohabiting or who intend to cohabit. Cohabitation agreements may address the rights and obligations of each party during cohabitation or on termination of the relationship, including ownership or division of property, support obligations, and the right to direct the education of children, but not the right to custody of or access to children. If the parties to a cohabitation agreement marry, their cohabitation agreement is deemed to be a marriage contract.

- **Separation agreements** may be made by married persons or cohabitants who have separated. A separation agreement may include provisions as to each party's rights and obligations, including ownership or division of property, support obligations, the right to direct the education of children, and the right to child custody and access.

marriage contract
a contract entered into before or during marriage that addresses the rights and obligations of the parties during the marriage or upon separation

cohabitation agreement
a contract entered into before or during cohabitation (the parties are not married) that addresses the rights and obligations of the parties during cohabitation or upon separation

separation agreement
a contract entered into by married persons or cohabitants after separation that addresses the rights and obligations of the parties after separation

Tenancies: Occupancy Rights and the Property of Others

Another key area in which the common law of property has been altered by statute is in the context of residential tenancies. Although most people today view landlord–tenant relationships as being essentially a matter of contract, tenancy relationships have property law roots in the concept of the leasehold estate. Because of the importance that the law accords to the concept of possession, the rights of a tenant, although they may be largely administered by contract, are strengthened by the fact of possession of real property. Another factor contributing to the comparatively strong legal rights of residential tenants is the existence of a public policy motive to promote people's security when it comes to a need as basic as shelter.

All Canadian provinces have passed legislation that imposes certain limits on the terms that landlords and tenants can include in the contracts that they make with each other. The balance between the rights of landlords and tenants has been a "live" political issue in modern times, and landlord–tenant legislation has a history of frequent amendment. Ontario's current landlord–tenant statute is the *Residential Tenancies Act, 2006*.[8] A detailed review of that legislation (and the legislation in place in other provinces) is beyond the scope of this book. However, since law enforcement officers are often called upon to intervene in landlord and tenant disputes, it is useful to have a general knowledge of the kinds of rights typically contained in this type of legislation. A very general discussion of typical provisions follows here. Note, however, that provincial legislation varies; to be certain whether a particular rule applies in a jurisdiction, the legislation itself should be consulted.

A Right to Peaceful and Exclusive Enjoyment

Most landlord–tenant legislation guarantees tenants the right to occupy and "enjoy" (use) the rented premises free from unexpected intrusions by the landlord. In general, a landlord cannot enter the rented premises without being invited (for example, to fix something), or without providing a legislated period of notice to the tenant (usually at least 24 hours). These basic rules may be suspended or altered in cases of emergency, or in cases where the tenant is moving out soon and is required to provide access for the purpose of showing the premises to new or prospective tenants. But, in general, a landlord has no right to perform unannounced "inspections" or to enter rented premises when the tenant is not at home.

Keeping Up the Property

Most landlord–tenant statutes have provisions governing maintenance of the property and the landlord's duty to keep the premises in good repair. Typically, the premises must meet a certain level of livability before they are determined to be "legal" for the purpose of tenancy, and these standards must be kept up for the duration of the tenancy. Tenants, of course, are responsible for day-to-day maintenance such as cleaning, and may be held liable to the landlord for unusual damage to the property (normal "wear and tear" will not give rise to liability).

A Right to Notice of Termination of the Tenancy

Because of the public policy interest in security when it comes to shelter, many provisions of landlord–tenant legislation deal with the issue of termination of the tenancy and the parties' rights to notice of termination. Legislation on this issue varies widely, but all jurisdictions provide for a minimum period of notice on both the landlord's and the tenant's part. Even in the absence of a stated lease term (many tenants rent month to month and not on the basis of a longer lease), it is generally impossible or illegal to exclude a tenant from leased premises without at least a month's notice, even if the tenant is not paying the rent or is otherwise in breach of the tenancy agreement. As a result, a tenant who comes home to find that the locks on the door have been changed and he or she cannot get in is almost always entitled to be let back in (unless the eviction process under the landlord–tenant legislation has been finalized).

Tenants are also required to provide notice of termination, although they often enjoy shorter notice requirements (though rarely less than a month). If tenants leave before the expiry of a term lease (such as a 12-month lease), they may be liable for payment of rent for the months they were supposed to stay, although they may be allowed to sublet the premises to a new tenant, and the landlord has a duty to minimize his or her losses by replacing the tenants as soon as possible. Finally, in some very limited instances, a landlord may have a right to **distrain** (keep and resell) the personal property of an absconding tenant who owes money for non-payment of rent or for damage to the property, but this remedy is usually (in Ontario, always) enforceable only when it is directed by a court order.

distrain
keep and resell the personal property of another; traditionally, a landlord's remedy that allowed the taking of a tenant's property as compensation for a default (typically non-payment of rent or property damage), now either banned or strictly constrained in all Canadian jurisdictions

CASE IN POINT

Unjustified Eviction Renders Police Search Unreasonable Under the Charter

As a protest against their landlord's alleged failure to repair a unit, a tenant couple withheld their rent. The landlord went before the landlord and tenant tribunal and obtained an eviction order.

The tenants sought mediation of the dispute, and in January 2005, the parties entered into an agreement by which the landlord would not proceed with the eviction as long as the tenants complied with a payment schedule. The tenants made the first payment on time, but before the second payment was due, the landlord began the eviction process by contacting the sheriff's office. The landlord later testified that he began the process inadvertently (by accident).

Sheriff's office personnel arrived on February 9, 2005, while the tenants were not home, and the building superintendent let them in. While walking through the apartment, the superintendent and sheriff's office personnel observed two gun cases, and also parts of a Prince Edward Island police uniform (shirt, badge, bulletproof vest). The police were called. When they arrived, the police officers opened the gun cases and found guns. The police then contacted the Major Crime Unit and requested backup, and that a search warrant be arranged. The warrant was issued, but only after the gun cases had already been opened.

The male tenant was eventually convicted of charges related to careless storage of a firearm and ammunition. He appealed his conviction on the basis that the search that led to the discovery of the firearms was unreasonable and a contravention of his rights under section 8 of the Charter.

The Court of Appeal agreed, finding that the police were justified in entering the premises, but did not have reasonable cause to conduct a warrantless search (the opening of the gun cases). The police were called to the premises on public safety grounds (because the gun cases were found). However, once the premises were secured (the locks were changed while they were there), there was no longer a risk to public safety, and so no common law right to search for safety reasons. With no issue of urgency, a properly supported warrant was required to open the gun cases, and the warrantless search was a violation of the suspect's section 8 rights. The search was also not justified on the basis of the landlord's consent, nor on the basis of the existence of an eviction order, because the eviction was carried out in contravention of the agreement signed by the landlord and the tenants after mediation.

The appeal was allowed, and all of the convictions were overturned.

Questions for Discussion

1. One of the arguments made by the Crown in this case was that the gun cases were searchable under the "plain-view" doctrine. Do you think there is any merit to this argument? Why or why not?

2. In finding that the tenants had a legitimate expectation of privacy with respect to the contents of their apartment, the court held that people are entitled to a higher standard of privacy with respect to the contents of their homes than with respect to, for example, the contents of a car on a public highway. Why do you think this is so? Do you agree?

Source: *R v Stevens*, 2011 ONCA 504.

CHAPTER SUMMARY

The law recognizes rights in property of different types—real (generally land), personal (generally anything other than land), and intellectual (property governed by copyright, trademark, and patent law). The law is changing to respond to emerging concerns, such as the protection of personal information.

The property concept may be thought of as a bundle of rights and obligations designed to protect some of the interests of property holders. The bundle of property rights is often split between property owners; an important split is that between ownership of property (title) and physical control over property (possession).

In Canada, the tenurial system of real property ownership is used; landholders do not own the land itself (the government is the ultimate owner) but rather own an interest in the land. Ownership of property may be lost in a variety of ways, including through lack of possession or by purchase by a government.

The law relating to personal property is less formal. Personal property may be transferred without the need for a written instrument, and, generally, ownership need not be proven through a traceable chain of title.

Violations of property rights may be dealt with through civil suits and through the criminal law, and sometimes there is an overlap between a civil remedy and a criminal charge, to protect the same right. Provisions in the *Criminal Code* criminalize activities such as theft (of both tangible and intangible property), arson, and destruction of documents of title.

Family law involves protection of property rights, including protection of rights concerning the matrimonial home and property owned by the spouses. Most couples rely on equalization rules under provincial legislation to resolve property disputes upon marriage breakdown and separation. Remedies include a court order to sell the home and equalize the proceeds. Others may assert a claim on the basis of trust law. Trust law remedies include a court order that one party hold an interest in a disputed property "in trust" for the claiming party. Parties may contract out of family law rules by making a marriage contract, cohabitation agreement, or separation agreement.

Residential tenancy law protects the rights of both landlord and tenant, and sets out obligations for both to adhere to. Most landlord–tenant laws give tenants the right to peaceful and exclusive enjoyment of the rented premises, and obligate the landlord to keep up the property. Both landlords and tenants are required to provide adequate notice of termination of the tenancy, although tenants often enjoy shorter notice periods.

KEY TERMS

NOTES

1   *Canadian Charter of Rights and Freedoms*, Part I of the *Constitution Act, 1982*, being Schedule B to the *Canada Act 1982* (UK), 1982, c 11.

2   *Freedom of Information and Protection of Privacy Act*, RSO 1990, c F.31.

3   Restrictions on the modification of property are common with respect to creative works, like a painting or a song. These restrictions reflect the creator's "moral rights" with respect to the creation; for example, a creator may have a moral right not to have an altered photograph or song associated with him or her, because of potential impacts on reputation.

4 In 2016, new, narrower legislation with respect to both escheat and the forfeiture of corporate property came into effect. Reasons behind the new statutes include a desire to reduce confusion about the status of property, and a desire to limit the government's exposure to costs (for example, the cost of environmental remediation) related to title to forfeited property. See the *Escheats Act, 2015*, SO 2015, c 38, Schedule 4 and the *Forfeited Corporate Property Act, 2015*, SO 2015, c 38, Schedule 7.

5 *Statute of Frauds*, RSO 1990, c S.19.

6 *Criminal Code*, RSC 1985, c C-46, as amended.

7 *Family Law Act*, RSO 1990, c F.3.

8 *Residential Tenancies Act, 2006*, SO 2006, c 17.

EXERCISES

Multiple Choice

1. The *Criminal Code* protects property interests by imposing liability for the following offences:

    a. theft

    b. mischief

    c. unauthorized use of a computer

    d. destroying documents of title

    e. all of the above

2. Canadian law has recognized property or property-like interests in

    a. family pets

    b. Internet domain names

    c. one's spouse's medical school degree

    d. frozen spermatozoa

    e. all of the above

3. Which of the following is not covered under intellectual property law?

    a. a patent for an invention

    b. the copyright for a painting

    c. a trademark for a new laundry detergent

    d. a person's collection of books

    e. the copyright for a book

4. Property rights can apply to

    a. land and buildings

    b. personal possessions

    c. intangible possessions

    d. the human body and personality

    e. all of the above

5. Legal possession of property can result from

    a. legal title

    b. inheritance

    c. physical control of property

    d. long-term use of property

    e. all of the above

True or False?

_____ 1. Under a tenurial system, all land with no private owner automatically belongs to the government.

_____ 2. Under family legislation, part of each spouse's property is deemed to be held in trust for the benefit of the children of the marriage.

_____ 3. A person who owns a life estate in land is not entitled to dispose of that interest by will.

_____ 4. It is possible to have possession of real property (land) without having title to the property.

_____ 5. It is possible to have title to real property without having possession of it.

_____ 6. It is possible to sue a person for theft instead of pursuing a charge under the criminal law.

_____ 7. Upon separation, the spouse with legal title to the family home is entitled to put the house up for sale, as long as he or she provides reasonable move-out notice to the other spouse.

_____ 8. Where a tenant has not paid the rent for three months, the landlord can either give notice of termination of the tenancy or change the locks on the premises doors while the tenant is out.

_____ 9. In Canada, where a person dies with no will and no heirs, his or her property becomes the property of the government.

_____10. The family property equalization rules under the Ontario _Family Law Act_ (and some provincial equivalents) apply to common law partners in the same way they do to married partners.

Short Answer

1. As a law enforcement officer, you answer a call from a homeowner who tells you someone has broken in and is downstairs in his kitchen. When you arrive on the scene, the homeowner greets you at the front door carrying a baseball bat. The invader has fled—luckily, because the homeowner asserts that his home is his castle and that he would have "defended it to the death" had the need arisen.

   a. What if the homeowner had in fact hit the invader with the bat, killing or seriously injuring him or her? What would the legal implications have likely been? Does it make a difference to your answer if the invader had been unarmed and had immediately made it clear that he or she was retreating (albeit carrying a TV)?

   b. Going back to the original scenario (the invader got away), you decide you'd better throw some cold water on the homeowner's plans to defend his home to the death. What reasons do you give him?

2. While executing a search warrant at a personal residence, law enforcement personnel seize a quantity of white powder that proves, on analysis, to consist primarily of diacetylmorphine (heroin). The owner of the white powder is considering suing under property law for return of the material.

   a. Will she succeed? Why or why not?

   b. What if the substance, on analysis, turned out to be bicarbonate of soda (baking soda)?

   c. What if the substance was bicarbonate of soda and there was no warrant for the search?

3. In the last few years of his life, Eduardo became frail and easily confused. Concerned about his father's ability to care for himself, Eduardo's son Michael and Michael's wife Leelah moved out of their rental apartment and moved into Eduardo's house to care for him. Three months ago, Eduardo slipped in the shower, broke his hip, and was transferred to hospital, where he died last month from complications of pneumonia.

Caring for Eduardo put a significant burden on the young couple's marriage. Shortly before Eduardo's death, they decided to separate, but have been living together in the house until they can afford separate residences, and so that they can co-parent their son Jason. Michael runs a web design business from home, and so does much of the hands-on parenting of Jason.

One evening, Leelah came home from work to find the house a huge mess and Jason still in his pyjamas. She and Michael had a major fight in which she accused Michael of being a layabout and a bad parent. In the course of the fight, Michael slapped Leelah hard across the face, and Leelah called 911. Michael was arrested, charged with assault, and held in custody overnight. At his bail hearing the following day, he was released on conditions, which include a prohibition on going within 500 metres of his father's house, and on communicating directly with Leelah. With nowhere else to go, Michael is currently sleeping on his best friend's couch.

a. Michael visits a family law help centre and asks for help in having the police remove Leelah from Eduardo's house, because he needs to get in there to take care of Jason, and also because he is the executor of his father's will and needs to prepare the house for sale. The law student he speaks with tells him the police won't remove Leelah from the house, and even if they did, it wouldn't help. Why do you think this is true?

b. Michael is served with documents that explain that Leelah is going to court to seek exclusive possession of the house. Can she get this, even though Michael's father is the sole owner of the house? Why or why not?

c. What will now need to happen to allow Michael to spend time with his son?

d. What will now need to happen to allow Michael to sell the house so that his father's estate can be administered?

e. What might the police have done differently to prevent these disruptions to the family's life, while adequately protecting Leelah's safety?

f. What might the bail court have done differently?

4. The police get a call from a landlord who expresses a belief that the tenant who is renting the premises is sharing it with two very young women who are being forced to work as prostitutes. The landlord admits that she has no proof of these activities, and no proof that they are taking place at the rental premises themselves—she only knows the girls are living there. The landlord wants the police simply to "put a stop to it"—she doesn't specify whether she means she wants the prostitution stopped, the girls removed from the home, or the tenant evicted.

a. As the responding officer, which statutes would you need to consult to figure out what to do? Assume that the girls are both under age 18. List at least *three* statutes.

b. Which sections of the *Criminal Code* might apply to the circumstances as described?

c. If there is evidence that young women are in fact being forced into prostitution, which agency or agencies might you call for assistance?

d. If the tenant is eventually charged with a crime but is released on bail, can the landlord evict him, even if he has done no damage to the premises and his rent is up to date?

Family and Employment Law: The "Relationship" Disciplines

12

LEARNING OUTCOMES

After completing this chapter, you should be able to:

- Understand the basic principles of the law relating to marriage and divorce in Canada.

- Understand the basic principles of the law relating to child custody, access, and support.

- Explain the basic principles of the law relating to child protection in Canada.

- Describe the role of the police in protecting family members at risk on family breakdown.

- Understand the basic principles of employment law in Canada.

Introduction

The two subject areas mentioned in the title to this chapter—family and employment law—may seem unrelated. However, whereas the previous chapter's topics shared property as a common link, family ties and employment arrangements share a basis in the concept of relationship. Both family and employment relationships are entered into voluntarily, with an expectation of permanence and with obligations flowing from each party to the other. Because of the interdependence created by both family and employment bonds, the breakdown of the relationship, in both cases, presents unique problems that require sophisticated solutions. In Canada, these solutions are prescribed by a mixture of common law and statute law.

Principles of Family Law

Dual Jurisdiction

Canadian family law is characterized by an overlap in legislative jurisdiction. Marriage and divorce are matters of federal responsibility and are governed by the *Divorce Act*.[1] Other aspects of family relationships—notably those that relate to property (discussed in Chapter 11), spousal and child support, and child custody and access—are within provincial jurisdiction by virtue of section 92(13) of the Constitution, which gives the provinces the power to legislate property and civil rights in the province. This generally means that if the disputants in a family law matter are legally married, they can choose to pursue issues of support, custody, or access under either provincial or federal legislation. Remedies for unmarried spouses, where they exist, are found exclusively under provincial law. The content of the provincial statutes varies from province to province. For the purposes of this chapter, we will focus on the Ontario *Family Law Act*[2] (FLA).

Validity of Marriage

annulment
a legal declaration that a marriage was never valid and never legally existed; it permits remarriage without need for a divorce

The requirements for a valid marriage may be an issue where parties seek to obtain a marriage licence, where one party to a marriage seeks an **annulment** (a court order terminating the marriage as if it had never existed), or where the validity of a marriage is relevant to another legal question (for example, rights of inheritance).

Essential Validity

The essential validity of marriage means the capacity of the parties to marry. In Canada, capacity to marry is a matter of exclusive federal legislative jurisdiction. Depending on the defect or deficiency, a marriage could be either void, void but capable of ratification, or voidable.

void
null or of no effect; as if never having taken place

Certain defects or disabilities existing at the time of the marriage render a marriage **void**. A void marriage will be regarded by every court in which the existence of the marriage is an issue as never having taken place and can be treated as such by the parties without the necessity of obtaining an annulment. A marriage will be void if one of the following defects exists at the time of the marriage:

- one or both parties have a prior existing marriage, or
- the parties are too closely related (the federal *Marriage (Prohibited Degrees) Act*[3] sets out what kinds of relationships are too close to permit marriage).

A marriage between two people of the same sex is legal, according to case law and the *Civil Marriage Act*.[4]

A marriage will be **void but capable of ratification**, by continued cohabitation after the defect or disability no longer exists, if at the time of the marriage

- the parties were below the common law marriageable age (14 for boys and 12 for girls),
- one of the parties was mentally ill or mentally defective, or
- one of the parties was intoxicated by drugs or alcohol to the point of lacking capacity.

void but capable of ratification
void but capable of becoming valid by certain actions

Some defects existing at the time of the marriage render a marriage **voidable**. A voidable marriage will be regarded by every court as a valid subsisting marriage unless and until a decree of annulment has been obtained by one of the parties. The validity of a voidable marriage can be questioned only in annulment proceedings brought by one of the parties to the marriage, and can never be questioned by third parties or after the death of one of the parties to the marriage. A marriage will be voidable where

- one of the parties entered the marriage as a result of duress,
- one of the parties was mistaken about the nature of the ceremony or the identity of the other party, or
- one of the parties is physically incapable of fulfilling his or her matrimonial (sexual) obligations.

voidable
valid but capable of being rendered invalid through annulment proceedings by certain actions

Formal Validity

The formal validity of marriage refers to the formalities and evidentiary requirements for marriage (such as the need to obtain a marriage licence and to be of the age of majority). The requirement for formal validity means that even if a marriage meets the essential validity threshold (see above), it may not be recognized in a particular jurisdiction—for example, because the parties are not of the age of majority in that jurisdiction. Formal validity is governed by the law of the place where the marriage was celebrated. In Canada, formal validity is a matter of exclusive provincial legislative jurisdiction. In Ontario, the *Marriage Act*[5] is the relevant legislation.

Divorce

The *Divorce Act* sets out only one ground of divorce: **marriage breakdown**, which may be established on the basis of

- one year's separation,
- adultery, or
- cruelty.

marriage breakdown
the only ground for divorce under Canadian law

Parties may apply for a divorce on the basis of one year's separation at any time after separation, but must wait until the one-year period has elapsed before obtaining the divorce. There must be an intention on the part of the parties to live apart. Living apart without the intention to end the marriage (for example, where one party is required to work abroad for a certain period) is insufficient. It is even possible for parties to satisfy the requirement of one year's separation while living under the same roof if the required intention is accompanied by physical separation.

adultery
voluntary sexual intercourse outside a marriage by one of the partners to the marriage; not a ground for divorce but rather evidence by which marriage breakdown may be proven

cruelty
under divorce law, physical or mental cruelty to a degree that makes continuing a marriage intolerable to one of the parties

Adultery is voluntary sexual intercourse between a married person and a person other than the married person's spouse.

Cruelty must be physical or mental cruelty of such a kind as to render intolerable the continued cohabitation of the spouses.

Various provisions in the *Divorce Act* aim to encourage reconciliation where possible and amicable divorce where reconciliation is not possible. Section 9 requires lawyers to draw these provisions to the attention of clients, to discuss the possibility of reconciliation with clients, to advise clients of the advisability of negotiating issues of support and custody, and to inform clients of mediation facilities that might assist the spouses in negotiating support and custody.

Spousal Support

A party may claim spousal support under the *Divorce Act* if the party is seeking a divorce, or under provincial legislation, which is the *Family Law Act* in Ontario. Under the FLA, spousal support is available to legally married spouses and to people who are not married to each other but who have cohabited continuously for a period of not less than three years, or in a relationship of some permanence, if they are the natural or adoptive parents of a child.

The amount of spousal support that will be awarded depends on many considerations, including

- the need of the dependent spouse,
- the other spouse's ability to pay,
- the economic advantages or disadvantages to the spouses arising from the marriage or its breakdown,
- the financial consequences arising from the care of children, and
- the promotion of self-sufficiency of each spouse where possible.

Where appropriate, spousal support may be time-limited—that is, it may last only for a defined period after the separation.

Child Support

A parent may be ordered to pay child support under either the *Divorce Act*, if the request for child support is part of the divorce proceeding, or the *Family Law Act*, if there is not an ongoing divorce proceeding.

Under the *Divorce Act*, either or both spouses may be ordered to pay support for any child of the marriage. A child of the marriage is a child of the parties who

- is under the age of 16, or
- is 16 or over and under their charge but unable, by reason of illness, disability, or other cause, to withdraw from their charge or to obtain the necessaries of life.

Also included are any non-biological children for whom a party stands in the place of a parent.

Under Ontario's FLA, every parent has an obligation to provide support for his or her unmarried child who is under the age of 18 or is aged 18 or older but is enrolled in a full-time program of education. The obligation to provide child support does not extend to a child who is 16 or older and who has withdrawn from parental control. "Child" includes a person for whom a parent has demonstrated a "settled intention" to treat as a child of his or her family—for example, a stepchild.

The amount of child support payable is determined, in many jurisdictions, by referring to a legislated formula based on the needs of the children and the income of the paying parent.

Custody and Access

In the case of divorce, either spouse may apply for custody of, or access to, a child of the marriage under the *Divorce Act*, and a person who is not one of the spouses may apply for custody or access in the context of divorce proceedings with leave of the court.

Ontario's *Children's Law Reform Act*[6] (CLRA) provides that a parent of a child or any other person may apply for custody or access. Non-parents may apply for custody but, in a contest with a parent, they are rarely successful unless they are the "psychological parents" of the child and have actually raised the child for some period. Parents are rarely denied access, although in cases of violence, possible abduction, or lack of parenting skills, *supervised* access may be ordered. Non-parents are rarely granted access over the objections of parents unless the non-parents have a very significant relationship with the child—for example, grandparents.

Best Interests of the Child

Custody and access are determined according to what is in the "best interests of the child." All circumstances relevant to the interests of the child are considered. The *Divorce Act* states that the court must ensure that a child has as much contact with each parent as is consistent with the best interests of the child, and specifically cites the willingness of a party seeking custody to facilitate contact with the other parent as a factor to consider when determining the best interests of the child. Because the child's interests are determinative, there is no enforceable "right" on either parent's part to have access to the child, regardless of the desire of the parent to have access or the responsibility to pay support for the child.

The CLRA lists many factors to consider in determining what is in the best interests of the child, including the child's emotional ties with each person claiming custody or access, the views and preferences of the child, and the plans proposed for the care and upbringing of the child. A few decades ago, the majority of custodial parents were mothers, but since that time, social norms have shifted. Shared custody is now the most common (and generally, the preferred) custodial arrangement.[7]

Possible Custodial Arrangements

In Canada, the custodial parent has the right and responsibility to make all decisions relating to the upbringing of the child, subject to any agreements or court orders that limit this right. Parents with joint legal custody share decision-making responsibility. Parents with joint legal custody *and* shared residential custody share decision-making responsibility, and each spends substantial amounts of time (40 percent or more each) with the child. Custodial arrangements are diverse, and the ideal is for families to create custody and access arrangements that best serve the interests of the child, modifying the arrangements over time as the family's circumstances and the child's needs and interests change.

Law Enforcement Issues on Family Breakdown

As most law enforcement officers know, not all spousal relationships end in an orderly and civilized way. Spousal or child abuse (whether physical or emotional) can precede a break-up or be precipitated by the departure of a spouse. The FLA contains certain provisions—including provincial offence provisions—that recognize this reality and provide for police involvement in certain situations. These situations and the role of the police are dealt with in greater detail in provincial offences courses. Listed below are some situations that may warrant police involvement:

- Particularly where there has been a history of violence or harassment, police may be called on to enforce an order of exclusive possession of the matrimonial home by one of the spouses.
- The FLA provides for the arrest of an "absconding debtor" (a spouse who is not paying court-ordered support and who is suspected of preparing to leave Ontario) in certain circumstances.
- If a restraining order has been made against a spouse, a former spouse, or someone he or she has cohabited with, and that person violates the order, the police may arrest that person without warrant and charge that person with a criminal offence.

The inclusion of these provisions in the FLA demonstrates a change in focus from civil law to criminal law.

Child Protection

Besides the FLA and the *Divorce Act* and their provisions relating to support, custody, and access, other legislation deals with parental responsibility for the welfare of children.

The *Criminal Code*[8] prescribes several offences with which parents may be charged, including infanticide (murder of children), child abandonment, child abduction (a non-custodial parent can be charged with the abduction of his or her own child), sexual offences against children, and child neglect (failure to provide the necessaries of life).

In many jurisdictions, there is also provincial legislation dealing with child protection issues. For example, the Ontario *Child and Family Services Act*[9] provides for the apprehension of a "child in need of protection"; the definition of a child in need of protection includes children whose parents have subjected them to abuse or neglect, have allowed them to be subject to abuse or neglect by others, or have failed to provide adequate supervision or care.

Employment Law

In essence, employment law is a matter of contract. The employment relationship is based on a contract—express or implied, written or unwritten—between an employer and an employee. In the case of unionized employment, the individual employment contract is replaced in whole or in part by a **collective agreement**—a contract between the union that represents a group of employees and the employer.

collective agreement
an employment contract between a labour union and an employer

However, largely because of the special importance of paid work in employees' lives (employment is, after all, the cornerstone of economic security for a large percentage of Canadians and their dependants), a number of statutes have been passed that influence the employment relationship and limit, to some degree, the freedom of the parties to define the terms of an employment relationship. A discussion of some of the more important employment law issues and the legislation that governs them follows.

Discrimination in Hiring and Employment

All provinces have human rights legislation that prohibits discriminatory hiring. In Ontario, the *Human Rights Code*[10] guarantees equal treatment with respect to employment and provides that that right is violated if an employer advertises a job opening that "directly or indirectly classifies or indicates qualifications by a prohibited ground of discrimination." Each jurisdiction has a slightly different list of prohibited grounds of discrimination, but these typically include

- religious beliefs/creed;
- colour;
- race;
- nationality/national origin/place of origin/ethnic background/citizenship;
- sex/gender (includes pregnancy in some jurisdictions), gender identity, and/or gender expression;
- physical or mental disability;
- marital/family status;
- sexual orientation;
- record of offences;
- political beliefs/opinions; and
- age (although many jurisdictions allow employers to require employees to be between age 18 and 65).

Ontario has changed its definition of "age" in the area of employment from between 18 and 64 to 18 or over. This means that persons 18 or over are now protected against age discrimination. This move also effectively abolished mandatory retirement. Retirement programs can still be created by an employer in Ontario but the retirement program cannot be mandatory.

Some jurisdictions also prohibit discrimination based on a criminal record. However, in Ontario, for example, an employer is permitted, for certain types of employment, to ask for proof of a "clean record" (free of convictions that have not been pardoned) before making an offer of employment. A typical application to a police service in Ontario contains the question whether the applicant has been convicted of any offences for which a pardon has not been granted. Similarly, where a position reasonably requires that an employee be bondable, questions relating to bondability are permissible, or where driving is part of the job, questions about offences under provincial highway traffic legislation may be permitted.

When interviewing job applicants, it is important for an employer to avoid asking any question that might require an employee to disclose information about any of the above-listed grounds of discrimination.

Once an employee is hired, the obligation not to discriminate against him or her continues. Under human rights legislation, discrimination (either direct or indirect) is not acceptable as a factor in decisions related to promotion, continued employment, or termination. In certain narrow circumstances, discrimination based on personal characteristics is permissible if the employer can prove that the employee lacks a quality (such as a specified degree of physical strength) that would allow him or her to meet a bona fide occupational requirement. However, the courts interpret such requirements narrowly, and employers must be able to provide evidence of the reasonableness of their requirements and performance standards.

Employment Standards

All jurisdictions have legislation in place that attempts to regulate the quality of the work environment by imposing minimum standards for the treatment of employees (in Ontario, the relevant legislation is the *Employment Standards Act*[11]).

Wages

Minimum wages are legislated in all jurisdictions. A province's minimum wage is typically prescribed by regulations under its employment standards legislation. The minimum wage varies across the country, and there may be lower minimum wages for certain occupations (typically where employees, such as servers, receive tips), or for employees under the age of 18.

Box 12.1   Protecting Employees' Tips

On June 10, 2016, new *Employment Standards Act* (Ontario) provisions aimed at protecting workers' right to retain tips came into force. The amendments were introduced by Bill 12, the *Protecting Employees' Tips Act, 2015*.[12] While the legislation does permit the pooling and redistribution of tips among employees, it prohibits the employer from confiscating or making deductions from tips in almost all circumstances, and prohibits an "employer or a director or shareholder of an employer," other than a sole proprietor who works alongside the employees performing similar duties, from sharing in pooled tips.

Hours of Work

Many provinces also legislate the maximum hours of work per week and the minimum periods of rest during shifts for most occupations (professional employees are generally excepted, and there are also exceptions for emergency situations and certain kinds of industries). Finally, where an employee works longer than a standard workweek (again, defined differently depending on the jurisdiction), he or she may be entitled to overtime pay, which is usually calculated as a factor (1.5 or 2.0 times) of the regular wage.

Holidays

Employment standards legislation also prescribes a list of public holidays (sometimes called statutory holidays) that employees are entitled to take off with pay if they fall on a regularly scheduled workday. Certain exceptions apply, and employees who are required to be at work on a public holiday are typically entitled to overtime pay (generally time-and-a-half).

Vacations

Once employees have satisfied a minimum qualification period (typically one year), they are entitled, under employment standards legislation, to take an annual paid vacation. The details of vacation entitlements and the amount of vacation pay vary by jurisdiction, but in general, employers are not allowed to substitute pay in lieu of vacation except in very special circumstances.

Leaves of Absence

Finally, all jurisdictions prescribe, under employment standards legislation, that pregnant employees who have met a minimum qualification period may take several weeks or months of pregnancy leave around the time of birth. This leave is unpaid by the employer (though usually covered by employment insurance), but employees taking it are entitled to have their employment benefits continued during the period of leave and to return to their employment at the end of the leave. The federal *Employment Insurance Act*[13] sets out the length of insured absences. Ontario is one province that changed its pregnancy leave provisions to coordinate with the federal provisions. Most provinces also offer parental leave for employees of either sex who have recently become parents, either by birth or by adoption. Many provinces offer other statutory leaves for other purposes, including bereavement, jury duty, voting, and family responsibilities. The law now recognizes the growing demand for job-protected leaves to take care of a seriously ill family member. Ontario, for example, provides a family medical leave, an unpaid, job-protected leave of up to eight weeks. Although the Ontario legislation does not provide for pay during this leave, under the federal *Employment Insurance Act*, six weeks of employment insurance benefits (called "compassionate care benefits") may be paid to eligible employees.

Termination: Statutory and Common Law Rules

The most contentious legal issue in employment law is that of employment termination. The rights of the parties on the termination of employment are governed both by statute (most commonly under employment standards legislation) and by the common law.

Reasonable Notice

Under the common law, an employee who is terminated without **just cause** is entitled to reasonable notice of termination or to pay in lieu of notice. The reasonableness (sufficiency in terms of duration) of common law notice is decided by the court on the basis of the facts of the case. Relevant facts to be considered when determining the adequacy of common law notice include

just cause
cause for terminating a person's employment that meets a standard specified either under the common law or under a statute

- the duration of the employment before the termination,
- the nature of the work performed (more specialized, professional, or senior-level work tends to warrant longer notice),
- the age and re-employability of the terminated employee,
- the conduct of the parties (abuse of the employment relationship by either party can affect the notice granted), and
- any contractual agreements made between the parties with respect to the issue of notice, as long as these are not in conflict with applicable legislation.

Although courts are loath to characterize it as a "rule" (because of the need to weigh all of the facts in any given case), there is a general trend toward granting approximately one month's notice for every year of service, all other factors being equal. Although employers are less likely to sue on the issue of notice, departing employees are considered to be subject to a similar requirement to give reasonable notice to employers on leaving their employment.

Because not all parties are able or are inclined to sue for notice under the common law, statutory provisions (which vary from province to province) exist to guarantee a minimum period of notice of termination (usually between two and eight weeks, depending on an employee's length of service). Employment contract terms that grant less than the applicable minimum notice period are invalid.

Where an employee can successfully prove that he or she has been wrongfully dismissed (without cause or without proper notice), damages over and above any monetary amount granted in lieu of notice may be granted. These damages are similar to tort damages in their nature and basis and are designed to compensate for such issues as serious maltreatment in the termination process or unusual losses related to the termination. For example, if an employer unnecessarily humiliates or embarrasses an employee in the process of firing him or her such that the employee's reputation is damaged, the employer could be found liable for extra damages beyond the usual notice payment.

Just Cause for Termination

Notice of termination or pay in lieu of notice is not normally required if the employer can prove that an employee has been terminated for just cause. The common law and statutory definitions of just cause can be different; be sure to check your provincial legislation. Unless a termination is governed by a particular statute that overrides the applicable common law, courts typically look to the common law for assistance on what is just cause. Some circumstances that can form the basis of termination for just cause include

- dishonesty that is prejudicial to the employer's economic interests or reputation,
- serious insubordination or disobedience,
- chronic lateness or unexcused absenteeism, and
- serious incompetence.

In general, for the conduct to warrant dismissal, the conduct must have occurred more than once, and the employer has to show that progressive discipline (often a series of warnings, or more minor penalties such as suspensions) has preceded the dismissal.

CASE IN POINT

Just Cause or Entitled to Notice?

Boris has worked for the same company for five years operating equipment. Over the five years, he has been disciplined seven times: four times for failing to show up for his shift and three times for accidentally damaging company property. The day after his last absence, the company terminated his employment without notice and without any pay in lieu of notice, claiming that it had just cause.

Questions for Discussion

1. Does Boris's employment record fall within the list of circumstances that would allow the company to terminate his employment for just cause? Why or why not?

2. Is there any other information that you would need before making a decision?

3. What factors would be in Boris's favour if the court decided that he should have had notice? Look at the list of considerations for adequacy of notice under the heading "Reasonable Notice," above.

Source: *Jones v Patriot Forge Co*, 2009 CanLII 2031 (Ont Sup Ct J).

CHAPTER SUMMARY

Family law covers the areas of marriage, divorce, property, spousal support, child support, child custody and access, and child protection.

The legal requirements for becoming married include essential validity (the capacity of the parties to marry) and formal validity (the formalities and evidentiary requirements for marriage). Some deficiencies in validity may be cured while others render the marriage void.

Divorce is governed by the federal *Divorce Act*. A spouse, which the Act defines as one of two people who are married to each other, may seek a divorce on the ground of marriage breakdown. Marriage breakdown is established on the basis of one year's separation, adultery, or cruelty.

Spousal support may be ordered under the *Divorce Act* where a party is seeking a divorce, or under provincial legislation in other situations. Child support may also be ordered under the *Divorce Act* and under provincial legislation. In the event of divorce, either spouse may apply for custody of, or access to, a child. A person who is not one of the spouses may apply for custody or access with leave of the court. Custody and access are determined according to what is in the best interests of the child. Issues of custody and access may veer into criminal law, if there is criminal behaviour involved. Issues of support, property, and custody may be dealt with by the spouses by agreement.

Employment law deals with the relationship between an employer and an employee. The relationship is based either on a contract or, in the case of a unionized workplace, on a collective agreement. A number of statutes also govern the employment relationship. All provinces have human rights laws that prohibit discriminatory hiring and employment standards laws that set minimum standards in the areas of wages, hours of work, holidays, vacations, and leaves of absence.

The rights of employer and employee upon termination of the employment relationship are governed both by statute and by the common law. Under the common law, an employee who is fired without just cause is entitled to reasonable notice or pay in lieu of notice. But because not all parties are able or inclined to sue for notice under the common law, statutory provisions exist to guarantee a minimum period of notice of termination. Notice of termination or pay in lieu of notice is not usually required if the employer can prove that the employee was terminated for just cause.

KEY TERMS

adultery, 206
annulment, 204
collective agreement, 208
cruelty, 206

just cause, 211
marriage breakdown, 205
void, 204
voidable, 205

void but capable of ratification, 205

NOTES

1   *Divorce Act*, RSC 1985, c 3 (2nd Supp).

2   *Family Law Act*, RSO 1990, c F.3.

3   *Marriage (Prohibited Degrees) Act*, SC 1990, c 46.

4   *Civil Marriage Act*, SC 2005, c 33.

5   *Marriage Act*, RSO 1990, c M.3.

6   *Children's Law Reform Act*, RSO 1990, c C.12.

7   However, a private member's bill (Bill C-560) aimed at requiring courts to order shared custody in most cases was defeated in 2014.

8   *Criminal Code*, RSC 1985, c C-46, as amended.

9   *Child and Family Services Act*, RSO 1990, c C.11.

10   *Human Rights Code*, RSO 1990, c H.19.

11   *Employment Standards Act, 2000*, SO 2000, c 41.

12   Bill 12, *Protecting Employees' Tips Act, 2015*, SO 2015, c C.32.

13   *Employment Insurance Act*, SC 1996, c 23.

EXERCISES

Multiple Choice

1. Unmarried spouses can claim support from each other
    a. under the *Divorce Act*
    b. if they have cohabited for three years
    c. on the basis of a prenuptial agreement
    d. if they can prove adultery or cruelty
    e. any or all of the above

2. Twelve-year-old children can
    a. be awarded support from their parents according to their needs
    b. withdraw unilaterally from parental control
    c. be awarded the right to see as much of each of their parents as is consistent with their best interests
    d. determine for themselves who will have custody of them
    e. a and c

3. Employers are normally required to pay their employees at least the provincial minimum wage, although exceptions apply, which may include the following:
    a. employees who work as servers
    b. employees who are not Canadian citizens
    c. employees who are under the age of 21
    d. employees who are on probation
    e. all of the above

4. An employer is required to give a terminated employee the reasonable notice prescribed under the applicable employment standards legislation unless
    a. the employee and the employer have contracted out of the application of the legislation
    b. the employee is over the age of 65
    c. the employee has been terminated for just cause
    d. the employer has made payment in lieu of notice
    e. c or d

5. What constitutes reasonable notice of termination does not depend on
    a. the duration of employment of the terminated employee
    b. the age of the terminated employee
    c. the employer's financial situation
    d. the conduct of the employer
    e. the re-employability of the terminated employee

True or False?

_____ **1.** Whether a parent will be granted access to a child when a marriage breaks down depends on whether that parent has been ordered to contribute to the child's financial support.

_____ **2.** Extreme drunkenness of one party at the time a marriage is performed can render a marriage void.

_____ **3.** Adultery is a ground for divorce in Canada.

_____ **4.** A party to a marriage that has been annulled cannot claim support from the other party.

_____ **5.** Two married people who live in the same house can be "separated" for the purpose of divorce law.

_____ **6.** Provincial employment standards legislation prescribes maximum notice periods in the event an employee is terminated without cause.

_____ **7.** An employee can legally be terminated without cause as long as the employer gives reasonable notice of the termination or makes payment in lieu of notice.

_____ **8.** If an employee is charged with a criminal offence, the employer has just cause to terminate him or her.

_____ **9.** Just as an employer must give notice before terminating an employee, an employee must give notice before quitting.

_____**10.** An employer must not, in a job interview, ask an interviewee whether she intends to have children.

Short Answer

1. It's 10:30 a.m. on a Saturday. You are a police officer called to the scene of a domestic dispute. A woman has asked that her ex-husband be made to leave her front porch, where he has been standing for 45 minutes continuously ringing the doorbell. When you arrive, the woman shows you a court order granting her temporary exclusive possession of the house, which was the matrimonial home during the marriage. There is no restraining order in force against the ex-husband. The ex-husband tells you that he is not interested in entering the house; he simply wants his ex-wife to send out his daughter, Maxine, age three. He shows you his court document, which grants him unsupervised access to Maxine. According to the order, he is supposed to be able to pick up Maxine on Saturday mornings by 9 a.m., returning her to her mother by 7 p.m. When you ask the woman why she won't let Maxine go with her father, she tells you that her ex-husband has not paid his court-ordered child support for the past four months. The woman also tells you that the ex-husband's constant doorbell ringing is harassment and psychological abuse, and that in light of these she is justified in not letting Maxine go with him.

   a. Is the man entitled to take Maxine with him for the day, despite the delinquent support payments?

   b. Do you agree with the woman's actions? Why or why not?

   c. What advice should you give the ex-husband?

   d. What advice should you give the ex-wife?

2. An employer owns an ice-cream store franchise in a busy location. There are between one and three employees working in the store during each of two daily shifts, depending on the expected volume of business. The first shift of the day ends at 5 p.m. The business has nine employees.

   Easter Monday is a beautiful day. Temperatures reach over 15 °C for the first time that spring, and the ice-cream store is very busy. Marcia, a mother of one who has been employed full-time by the store for four years, is working the early shift alone, and is frustrated because business is very heavy. She anxiously awaits the arrival of Stephanie, scheduled to take over for the second shift. By 5:20, Stephanie has not arrived. Marcia calls her employer to say that Stephanie is missing and that she has to leave to be in time to pick up her son from daycare by 6:00. The employer tells Marcia she can't leave until Stephanie arrives. At 5:35, Marcia calls again, and is given the same message.

At 5:45, Marcia, needing to pick up her son, locks the front door of the store, serves the customers still in line, and then closes the store, leaving at 5:50. The next day her employer calls and tells her that she's fired.

a. Was Marcia entitled to close the business early on such a busy day? Could she be held liable to her employer for loss of revenue? Explain.

b. Did the employer have just cause to terminate Marcia for leaving against orders? Why or why not?

c. Does the employer have just cause to terminate Stephanie? Why or why not?

d. If Marcia was dismissed without just cause, how much notice is she entitled to under the Ontario *Employment Standards Act*?

e. How much notice might Marcia be awarded if she sued under the common law? What factors would be taken into account in determining her notice entitlement?

3. You are a family lawyer, and Margaretta is your client. She comes to you to obtain representation in connection with her divorce from Hugh. Hugh and Margaretta have been married for six years and have one child, Dylan, aged 14 months. Margaretta tells you that she still loves Hugh but he has developed a serious alcohol problem and his behaviour has grown increasingly frightening to her. A few months ago, while they were riding in the car, she confronted him about his drinking habits. Although he was sober at the time, he was so angry that he spun the car around recklessly and backed into a fire hydrant. Margaretta sprained a wrist bracing herself against the impact. Then a week ago, in the incident leading up to the separation, he was drunk and flew into a rage in the kitchen, knocking over a skillet full of grease, which spilled onto the gas stove. A fire started and spread to a pair of oven mitts on the counter. Instead of helping Margaretta put out the fire, he stormed out of the house and drove off, this time, drunk. Margaretta assures you, however, that he has never intentionally hurt her or Dylan.

a. Are you required, as her lawyer, to encourage Margaretta to reconcile with her husband instead of divorcing him?

b. Would you actively recommend reconciliation in this case?

c. Do you agree that it is the place of the law and/or government to encourage reconciliation at all, or would this impose a state moral value—that may not be held by all—on private individuals?

4. You are a student in a paralegal program. Your friend Aisha, a Muslim woman who wears the niqab, asks you for advice about a situation she has encountered. She went for a job interview with a medium-sized social media marketing firm. The interview went well, and she got along well with the human resources director and the CEO, who sat in on the interview. She felt she had a very good chance of getting the job. Two days later, she received a phone call from the HR manager, who told her, apologetically, that she was not the successful candidate. Aisha asked what she had done wrong or what qualifications she lacked, and the manager said that she had actually been the best candidate and had interviewed well. However, the CEO had decided that she should not be hired because the vice-president of the department in which Aisha would have been working was an older gentleman, "traditional," and "socially conservative," and the CEO felt that the workplace would not be comfortable for a woman who wears the niqab. Aisha interpreted this conversation to mean that this VP was prejudiced against Muslims and that though the HR manager and CEO liked her, they were concerned that she might face harassment on the job and were ruling her out for her own protection.

    a. Given that the HR manager and CEO were satisfied with Aisha's qualifications, is this discrimination in hiring?

    b. If this is discrimination, what should Aisha do, if she wants to pursue the matter further?

    c. What should the HR manager and CEO have done to avoid this situation?

5. You are the manager in charge of human resources for a small business. One day, an employee with four years' service approaches you and tells you he is transgender and is transitioning to female. He requests to use the women's washroom from now on. You agree, and, with his help, draft an email to the other employees advising of the change. A small group of women employees approaches you to complain that they consider themselves "at risk" because "a man" will be sharing a private space with them. What do you do?

Appendixes

Abbreviations of Case and Statute Reporters

Below is a list of case and statute reporters commonly cited. The full name follows the abbreviation. Some report series have more than one series; the additional series are noted by the number in parentheses after the abbreviation. For example, (4th) means Fourth Series.

AC	Law Reports: Appeal Cases (England)
ACWS	All Canada Weekly Summaries
AR	Alberta Reports
Admin LR	Administrative Law Reports
All ER	All England Law Reports
Alta LR	Alberta Law Reports
Alta LR (2d)	Alberta Law Reports (Second Series)
App Cas	Law Reports: Appeal Cases (England)
BCLR	British Columbia Law Reports
BLR	Business Law Reports
CBR	Canadian Bankruptcy Reports
CBR (NS)	Canadian Bankruptcy Reports (New Series)
CCC	Canadian Criminal Cases
CCC (2d)	Canadian Criminal Cases (Second Series)
CCC (3d)	Canadian Criminal Cases (Third Series)
CCEL	Canadian Cases on Employment Law
CCLI	Canadian Cases on the Law of Insurance
CCLT	Canadian Cases on the Law of Torts
CanLII	Canadian Legal Information Institute
CCSM	Continuing Consolidation of the Statutes of Manitoba
CED (Ont 4th)	Canadian Encyclopedic Digest (Ontario Fourth Edition)
CELR	Canadian Environmental Law Reports
CLR	Construction Law Reports
CPR	Canadian Patent Reporter

CPR (4th)	Canadian Patent Reporter (Fourth Series)
CR	Criminal Reports
CR (3d)	Criminal Reports (Third Series)
CRR	Canadian Rights Reporter
CTC	Canada Tax Cases
CTR	Canada Tax Reports
Can Abr (4th)	Canadian Abridgment (Fourth Edition)
DLR (4th)	Dominion Law Reports (Fourth Series)
ER	English Reports
ETR	Estates and Trusts Reports
FTR	Federal Trial Reports
Imm LR	Immigration Law Reporter
KB	Law Reports: King's Bench Division (England)
LAC (3d)	Labour Arbitration Cases (Third Series)
LR	Law Reports (England)
LR Ch	Law Reports: Chancery Cases (England)
LR Eq	Law Reports: Equity (England)
LR Exch	Law Reports: Exchequer (England)
LRCP	Law Reports: Common Pleas (England)
LRHL	Law Reports: House of Lords (England)
LTR	Law Times Reports (England)
MPLR	Municipal and Planning Law Reports
MVR	Motor Vehicle Reports
Man LR	Manitoba Law Reports
Man R	Manitoba Reports
Man R (2d)	Manitoba Reports (Second Series)
NBR	New Brunswick Reports
NBR (2d)	New Brunswick Reports (Second Series)
NR	National Reporter
NSR	Nova Scotia Reports
NSR (2d)	Nova Scotia Reports (Second Series)
Nfld & PEIR	Newfoundland and Prince Edward Island Reports
OAC	Ontario Appeal Cases
OJ	Ontario Judgments
OMBR	Ontario Municipal Board Reports
ONSC	Ontario Superior Court of Justice
ONCA	Ontario Court of Appeal
ONCJ	Ontario Court of Justice
OR	Ontario Reports
OR (2d)	Ontario Reports (Second Series)

OR (3d)	Ontario Reports (Third Series)
OWN	Ontario Weekly Notes
RFL	Reports of Family Law
RFL (2d)	Reports of Family Law (Second Series)
RSA	Revised Statutes of Alberta
RSBC	Revised Statutes of British Columbia
RSC	Revised Statutes of Canada
RSM	Revised Statutes of Manitoba
RSN	Revised Statutes of Newfoundland
RSNB	Revised Statutes of New Brunswick
RSNWT	Revised Statutes of Northwest Territories
RSO	Revised Statutes of Ontario
RSPEI	Revised Statutes of Prince Edward Island
RSQ	Revised Statutes of Quebec
RSS	Revised Statutes of Saskatchewan
RSYT	Revised Statutes of Yukon Territory
SA	Statutes of Alberta
SBC	Statutes of British Columbia
SC	Statutes of Canada
SCC	Supreme Court of Canada
SCR	Supreme Court Reports
SM	Statutes of Manitoba
SN	Statutes of Newfoundland
SNB	Statutes of New Brunswick
SNWT	Statutes of Northwest Territories
SO	Statutes of Ontario
SPEI	Statutes of Prince Edward Island
SQ	Statutes of Quebec
SS	Statutes of Saskatchewan
SYT	Statutes of Yukon Territory
Sask LR	Saskatchewan Law Reports
TLR	Times Law Reports (England)
UCCP	Upper Canada Common Pleas Reports
UCQB	Upper Canada Queen's Bench Reports
WCB	Weekly Criminal Bulletin
WDCP	Weekly Digest of Civil Procedure
WLR	Weekly Law Reports (England)
WWR	Western Weekly Reports
WWR (NS)	Western Weekly Reports (New Series)

Case Brief

B

CASE BRIEF

R v SCHWAB
2015 ABPC 180

<http://www.canlii.org/en/ab/abpc/doc/2015/2015abpc180/2015abpc180.html>

Procedural History

This is a first-instance decision after the hearing of a *voir dire* in the Alberta Provincial Court of Justice by the Honourable Judge B.D. Rosborough. (In Canada, a *voir dire* is a mini trial-within-a-trial used to decide whether evidence proposed to be used in the main trial should be excluded, in this case, because of an alleged infringement of a Charter right.) According to a procedure in use in Alberta, this *voir dire* was held before the trial itself began.

Facts

In the pre-dawn hours of March 15, 2015, Constable Wright of the Camrose, Alberta police force observed a driver apparently committing a (minor) highway traffic offence while driving through an industrial area of Camrose. Cst. Wright pulled the driver, Michael Schwab, over. The driver's documents (insurance, licence, registration) were in order, and the driver complied readily with the officer's instructions. The officer observed, however, that Mr. Schwab's face was flushed, his eyes were bloodshot, and there was an odour of alcohol coming from the car, so he requested that Mr. Schwab submit to a roadside approved screening device (ASD) test.

Cst. Wright had been taught, during his training, to conduct these tests in the back of the cruiser, and to perform a pat-down "safety search" of the driver first. He did so, conducting a "top to bottom, front to back" pat-down that included putting fingers into the accused's front pants pockets and checking his jacket pockets. The accused submitted to the pat-down search and to the ASD test without resistance. On the basis of the results of the test, he was charged with operating a vehicle while impaired by alcohol (*Criminal Code* s 253(1)(b)).

At trial (actually, before the trial—at the *voir dire*), the accused argued that the pat-down search violated his right to be free from unreasonable search as protected under section 8 of the Charter.

Issues

Was the pat-down search of Michael Schwab an unreasonable search prohibited by section 8 of the Charter, and if so, did Cst. Wright's violation of Mr. Schwab's section 8 right require the exclusion from admission at trial of the ASD evidence on grounds that admitting that evidence would bring the administration of justice into disrepute (Charter s 24(2))?

Related issues in this decision included:

1. Does a "routine" pat-down search, in the absence of a perceived threat to the officer's safety in the specific circumstances, fall within the "safety search" exception to the rule against unreasonable searches?

2. Was the ASD evidence related to the search (such that it could be excluded if there was a Charter violation)?

3. If the answer to #1 in this list is "no" and the answer to #2 is "yes," could the admission of this ASD result bring the administration of justice into disrepute?

Decision

Warrantless searches are presumptively unreasonable under Canadian law, but "safety searches" of suspects for the protection of law enforcement officers are a well-established exception to the rule against warrantless searches. Courts must recognize the need for law enforcement officers to make safety decisions in high-pressure situations and the need for the law to provide for officer safety. However, these interests must be balanced against the privacy and security rights of accused people. For this reason, the use of safety searches must be reserved for situations in which the officer perceives a threat to his or her safety that is specific to the circumstances of the particular traffic stop, and the officer in this case admitted that he did not feel unsafe around Mr. Schwab but only performed the stop as a part of the routine he had been taught during police training. That routine is contrary to the state of Canadian law with respect to safety searches, and had been contrary to the law for 11 years (since the 2004 decision in *R v Mann*, 2004 SCC 52). The routine pat-down search violated Mr. Schwab's section 8 right to be free from unreasonable search.

The case law has established that in order to lead to the exclusion of evidence, there need *not* be a causal connection between violation of a constitutionally protected right and the acquisition of evidence. Instead, the rights violation and the acquisition of evidence need only to be part of the same general transaction or course of conduct. In this case, the obtaining of the ASD result and the pat-down search were part of the same general transaction, and so, the evidence could be excluded if it had the potential to bring the administration of justice into disrepute as per section 24(2) of the Charter.

There are three things to consider when deciding whether the admission of evidence gathered in violation of a Charter right can bring the administration of justice into disrepute:

1. whether the admission may send the message that the justice system condones serious state misconduct;

2. whether the admission may send the message that individual rights count for little; and

3. society's interest in the adjudication of the case on its merits (that is, to not have charges dropped because of Charter violations).

In this case, the court found that to condone the Camrose police force's procedure of having officers conduct routine pat-down searches in the absence of a specific threat to officer safety could send the message that the justice system condones serious state misconduct, especially since the law with respect to routine pat-downs had been settled for 11 years before this traffic stop happened. Also, the court found that there are other ways to conduct an ASD test safely (and without unnecessary embarrassment to the suspect) without doing a pat-down—for example, conducting the test outside the vehicle at the roadside, or through the driver's window. The inappropriate police procedure had the potential to bring the administration of justice into disrepute; therefore, the evidence was excluded under section 24(2) of the Charter.

Ratio

Where a safety search is conducted merely as a measure of routine police procedure, rather than in response to an officer's reasonable perception of a threat to his or her safety under the specific circumstances, that threat violates the suspect's section 8 Charter right to be free from unreasonable search. The entrenchment of routine safety searches in the normal procedures of a police force has the potential to bring the administration of justice into disrepute and justifies the exclusion of evidence so collected under section 24(2) of the Charter.

Glossary

abet: intentionally encourage the commission of a crime

absolute liability offence: an offence that permits a conviction on proof of the physical elements of the offence (*actus reus*), with no proof of intention to commit the offence (*mens rea*) required

abuse of process: a course of action on the part of the police or the prosecution that misuses court process or ignores the spirit of that process and interferes with the accused's ability to make full answer and defence, threatening to bring the administration of justice into disrepute

accessory after the fact: a person who, knowing that another person has committed an offence, helps that person to commit a related offence (for example, converting stolen goods) or to escape prosecution

accused: a person against whom a criminal or quasi-criminal charge has been laid, but who has not yet been convicted

acquit: find an accused not guilty of an offence

act: something done or committed

actus reus: Latin for "criminal act"; the objective element of an offence, which may be an act, an omission, or a state of being

adjournment: postponement of a trial

adultery: voluntary sexual intercourse outside a marriage by one of the partners to the marriage; not a ground for divorce but rather evidence by which marriage breakdown may be proven

adverse possession: a legal doctrine by which rights in land are acquired or are sought to be acquired through possession unaccompanied by title

aid: knowingly assist the commission of a crime

alibi: a defence based on an allegation that the accused could not have committed the *actus reus* of the crime because he or she was not at the scene of the crime at the time it happened

aggravating factor: in a sentencing context, a circumstance of the offence or the offender that supports a more serious punishment

amend: change a law or rule

analogous: sharing similar qualities or characteristics in some aspects, yet being different in other aspects

annotate: supplement published statutes by giving references to cases that have considered the application of statutory provisions

annulment: a legal declaration that a marriage was never valid and never legally existed; it permits remarriage without need for a divorce

appeal: a review or challenge of a legal decision in a court of higher jurisdiction

appearance notice: a formal document, given to a person charged with a minor offence, that sets out the requirement to attend court for trial at a certain date and time

appellant: the party that decides to appeal a court's decision to a higher court

arrest: the act of taking a suspect into police custody

assault: under the common law, a threat of injury

authority: a previously decided case that supports a particular position or conclusion about a question of law

authorized by law: conducted under the authority of a statute or with judicial authorization

automatism: involuntary or unconscious behaviour

autrefois acquit: French for "previously acquitted"; a special plea by which the accused alleges that he or she has already been charged, tried, and acquitted of the offence that is currently being charged

autrefois convict: French for "previously convicted"; a special plea by which the accused states that he or she has already been charged, tried, and convicted of the offence that is currently being charged

bail: the release of a person accused of a crime before trial, with or without conditions

bailment: a delivery of physical possession of goods, without transferring ownership, from one person to another

battery: under the common law, a usually negligent or intentional act of physical contact

binding: in common law, the determinative quality of a legal decision on future decisions (assuming similar facts) if it was decided in a court of superior jurisdiction

breach: the failure of one party to perform a contract or contractual obligation

burden of proof: the requirement that a certain party prove a particular fact at trial

bylaws: laws made by a municipality that govern such issues as parking, noise control, licensing, and property standards; can include offences and penalties

Canadian Charter of Rights and Freedoms: the constitutional document that sets out the rights and freedoms affecting people in Canada; the people entitled to the specific rights and freedoms vary by the particular right or freedom

carelessness: a level of intent (*mens rea*) where a person fails to appreciate a risk that a reasonable person would have foreseen

case brief: a summary of a legal judgment prepared for research purposes

case law: reported decisions of judges from trials or appeals that are used to interpret the law

causation: the element of an offence that involves whether an act or omission of one party resulted directly in the injury to the other party

caution: a statement made by a peace officer to a person who is detained, advising that person of his or her right to remain silent and to hire a lawyer

challenge for cause: the right of either party in a criminal jury trial to require that prospective jurors be questioned about certain aspects of the offence or the accused that may result in bias on the part of the jurors

charge screening device: *see* preliminary inquiry

charge screening form: a form filled in by Crown counsel that sets out the charge(s) the Crown will be proceeding on and the penalty the Crown will be seeking upon a guilty plea or upon conviction after trial

charging document: a written document, either an information or an indictment, that sets out the charges against a person accused of an offence

citation: an expression, in standard form, of the bibliographical information for locating a case or legislative document

cite: describe or refer to, orally or in writing, a legislative provision or legal decision

civil standard: the level of proof that a party must achieve in a civil trial to be successful—proof on a balance of probabilities

codify: formalize a law or rule by incorporating it (usually in print form) into an existing or new code

cohabitation agreement: a contract entered into before or during cohabitation (the parties are not married) that addresses the rights and obligations of the parties during cohabitation or upon separation

collateral contract: a contract that is related to or depends on, but is separate from, another contract

collective agreement: an employment contract between a labour union and an employer

commit: declare an accused ready to stand trial after the preliminary inquiry, if any, has been completed, and the accused's not-guilty plea has been accepted by the court and entered into the trial record; this act is known as the "committal"

common law: a legal rule or a body of legal principles, established through judicial decisions, that deals with particular legal issues or subject areas

community justice worker: person who attends court on a regular basis, receives referrals from the Crown for diversion, and assists the accused in registering for and fulfilling the conditions

condition: a requirement that limits the freedom of an accused who has been released on bail or on parole

consent: a defence that arises when the accused has an honest yet mistaken belief in the complainant's consent to an action

consent: the informed, voluntary approval by one party of the actions of another

consideration: the benefit(s) flowing to each party under a contract

considered: applied or interpreted in a court case; refers to statutory provisions

construction: the process of determining the legal meaning of words or terms in a contract or statute, often by reference to context or external evidence

constructive possession: a person can be found to be in possession of something, under the criminal law, when she acquiesces to another person's (unlawful) actual possession of the thing while they are together

contractual defect: a legal problem with a contract that can either invalidate a contract or give rise to damages without invalidating the entire contract

contributory negligence: the role that a plaintiff or victim may play in negligently contributing to the cause of or aggravation of his or her own injury

conviction: a guilty verdict, where an accused is found, beyond a reasonable doubt, to have committed an offence

counsel: advise another person to be a party to an offence

count: a single charge on a charging document

counteroffer: a new offer that replaces an original offer, often with revised terms

criminal negligence: actions that are defined as criminal under the *Criminal Code* even though they incorporate a level of *mens rea* falling below conscious intent—for example, indifference

criminal standard: the level of proof that the prosecution must provide in a criminal trial to obtain a conviction—proof beyond a reasonable doubt

cruelty: under divorce law, physical or mental cruelty to a degree that makes continuing a marriage intolerable to one of the parties

culpability: guilt or responsibility

culpable intervention: an unexpected action, often by a third party, that contributes to or causes a chain of events

damages: losses suffered as a result of the breach of a contract or the commission of a tort, or compensation awarded for contract or tort losses

deceit: a tort established where one party makes a factual representation, knowing it is false, and knowing that another party will rely on it and suffer harm or loss as a result

defence: the person accused of an offence in a criminal trial and his or her lawyer(s)

defences: the arguments that the defence uses to contradict the prosecution's evidence against the accused

deposit: partial payment of a surety

direct intent: a level of intent (*mens rea*) where the accused has a clear intent to commit the offence or to cause certain results

directed verdict: an early verdict of acquittal based on the prosecution's failure to meet its standard of proof

discharge: the release of an accused after a finding of guilt, with or without conditions

disclosure: the requirement that the prosecution provide to the defence any and all evidence relevant to the charges against an accused

distrain: keep and resell the personal property of another; traditionally, a landlord's remedy that allowed the taking of a

tenant's property as compensation for a default (typically non-payment of rent or property damage), now either banned or strictly constrained in all Canadian jurisdictions

diversion program: an alternative to a criminal proceeding; typically available to an accused person who does not have a criminal record and who is charged with a very minor offence

duplicity: a flaw in a charging document where a single count contains two or more alternative offences so that the accused does not know against which offence to defend

duress: a defence that allows the accused to be acquitted if he or she committed the offence under threat of immediate death or bodily harm

duty of care: a legal duty owed by one person to another based on a relationship or on the doctrine of foreseeability

duty to mitigate: a party's responsibility to minimize his or her damages from breach of contract or from the commission of a tort

easement: a limited property interest (often a right of access) that "attaches" to and is passed on with the land; it can be either a benefit or a burden

election: choice

element: a part of an offence that must be proven

entrapment: a situation where the police lure, draw, or entice a person into committing a crime

equalization payment: a payment ordered from one spouse to another, under family property legislation, that is designed to equalize property holdings on separation

error: a mistake made by the judge (or, less commonly, the jury) that might lead to an appeal

escheat: a reversion of property to the Crown when there is no will or heir to inherit it or when a corporation that is the legal owner of property is dissolved

estate: an interest in land

evidence: oral or physical proof of the truth of an allegation

evidentiary standard: a basic level of proof; an alleged fact meets the evidentiary standard when there is at least some evidence that the allegation might be true

excluded: barred by a judge's order from being used as evidence at trial, often as a result of a breach of a Charter right in producing the evidence

exclusion clause: a part of a contract that limits the contractual or statutory liability of a party in the event of a breach of the contract

exculpatory: proving innocence; of evidence, tending to show that a person did not commit an offence

excuse: a defence that concedes that the accused's actions were wrong but claims that external or internal forces influenced the accused

expectation: anticipation of benefits from a contract being fulfilled

expropriation: the reclaiming of private land by the government

factual causation: the situation where a certain result would not exist if a specific action or event had not occurred

factual mistake: an error made about the truth of a fact or the existence of a condition

factum: a document used in an appeal that sets out the grounds for the appeal, the facts of the case, and the legal arguments as to why the appeal should succeed or fail

fault: responsibility for an action

fine: a form of punishment, requiring the payment of money, generally used for quasi-criminal or minor criminal offences

first instance: the first time a dispute appears before the court (at the original trial level, not the appeal level)

fitness to stand trial: the accused's mental competence, at the time of trial, to understand the trial and what is at stake and to communicate with counsel

foreseeability: a test to determine whether a reasonable person could expect that a certain result may follow from his or her act

formal equality: a measure of equality based on equality or inequality of opportunity

formalities: procedural or formal requirements, such as writing, a seal, or a signature (typically prescribed by statute), that are necessary to make certain kinds of contracts enforceable

frustration: a legal doctrine that releases the parties to a contract from their responsibilities under the contract when something (a circumstance or an object, for example) necessary to the performance of the contract no longer exists

full answer and defence: a principle of fundamental justice whereby the accused person must be provided with the information and the means to have the opportunity to defend against the charges

fundamental justice: the basic tenet of the Canadian system of rights and freedoms that requires that all persons investigated for and accused of a crime receive procedural protections to ensure that they are treated fairly throughout the process

general intent: a level of *mens rea* where the accused need not have intended to commit the offence or cause certain results but must have intended to act in a way that resulted in the offence occurring

goodwill: the economic value of a business's renown and good reputation

ground for appeal: a reason—generally an error made by the trier of law or of fact—for a party to be allowed to ask a higher court to reconsider the decision of a lower court

headnote: an unofficial summary of reasons for decision that may precede the full text of a published case in a commercial case reporter or an online legal database

hearsay evidence: information that comes from a source that does not have direct knowledge of the truth of the information

"housekeeping" provisions: provisions found at the end of some statutes that deal with such administrative issues as the timing of coming into force of individual provisions

hybrid offence: a crime that allows the prosecution to elect to proceed by way of summary conviction or by way of indictment

imprisonment: incarceration in a prison, the most serious punishment allowable in Canada for persons convicted of offences

inadmissible: refers to evidence that was obtained in a manner that breached a Charter right and is disallowed by a trial judge so that the prosecution cannot use it as part of its case against the accused

inchoate crime: a crime that is incomplete or attempted

included offence: a less serious offence that might be proven even when the more serious offence charged is not

inculpatory: proving guilt; of evidence, tending to show that a person committed an offence

indictable offence: a serious crime that attracts more serious penalties and that is prosecuted using the more formal of two possible sets of criminal procedures

indictment: a form of charging document used for serious (indictable) offences

induce: persuade or bring about

informant: (for a document) the person, usually a police officer, who swears the facts in an application for a search warrant or on a charging document

information: a form of charging document used for less serious offences

information to obtain a search warrant: a sworn affidavit that serves as an application for a search warrant

instructions: directions given to the jury by the judge at the end of a trial advising it on how to apply the law to the facts of the case

instrument: a formal legal document

insufficiency: a flaw in a charging document that causes it to fail to contain the required information to sustain the charge

intangibles: things or concepts that may be the subject of a property right without having a physical form

intellectual property: intangible property, including copyrights, trademarks, and patents

joinder: where two or more charges or two or more accused persons are tried together in the same trial

joint and several liability: a rule that allows a plaintiff who suffers damages caused by multiple defendants to recover the full amount of damages from any one of them (and that defendant can sue the others for contribution)

judicial interim release: bail; also known as pre-trial release

jurisdiction: authority to make law, either by governments or by courts

jury: a group of 12 citizens who are chosen to act as the trier of fact in a criminal trial

just cause: cause for terminating a person's employment that meets a standard specified either under the common law or under a statute

justification: a rare defence that negates the objective wrongfulness of an act and exempts the accused from the application of the *Criminal Code*

lapse: the expiry of an offer that has not been accepted by a stipulated acceptance time or on the occurrence of stipulated conditions

leave to appeal: permission to file an appeal

legal capacity: the ability to enter into an enforceable contract, based on the absence of factors (for example, cognitive impairment) that might impair capacity

legal causation: the situation where one or more actions could have caused a certain result and, for the purposes of a legal decision, the action that was most responsible for the result must be determined

licence: permission to use another's land for a specific purpose; does not give any other rights

marriage breakdown: the only ground for divorce under Canadian law

marriage contract: a contract entered into before or during marriage that addresses the rights and obligations of the parties during the marriage or upon separation

matrimonial home: a dwelling that meets criteria making it subject to special treatment under family property law

mens rea: Latin for "guilty mind"; the subjective element of an offence that describes the state of mind or required intention necessary of the accused

mental disorder: a disease or condition of the mind under section 16 of the *Criminal Code* that results in the accused lacking the mental ability to intend to commit a crime

misrepresentation: a representation based, either innocently, negligently, or intentionally, on incorrect information

mistake of fact: a defence to a criminal charge that involves the Crown failing to prove the *mens rea* of the offence

mistake of law: a situation where someone commits an offence while being mistaken about the legal consequences

mistrial: a declaration by a judge that the trial of an accused cannot be allowed to continue because of unfairness to the accused, and that a new trial must be conducted

mitigating factor: in sentencing for crimes, a fact or condition relating to either the offence or the offender that decreases the punishment (for example, an early guilty plea or remorse)

mitigation: minimizing a party's damages from breach of contract or from the commission of a tort

motive: the reason a person committed an offence

negligence: the failure of a person to respect or carry out a duty of care owed to another

net family property: a statutorily defined value of the property owned by one spouse that may be subject to equalization under family property legislation

neutral citation: a form of citation for a case that is not tied to a particular report series or database, but includes the year of the decision, the court or tribunal that made the decision, and a number indicating the place in sequence of the decision

non est factum: Latin for "I didn't sign/make [this contract]"; a legal doctrine that can be pleaded, based on a narrow set of circumstances, in an attempt to render a contract unenforceable

non−section 469 offence: a less serious *Criminal Code* offence for which, at a bail hearing, the onus is on the prosecution to show cause why the accused should not be released pending trial

offence: an act or omission that breaches a law and leads to a penalty; a crime codified in a statute such as the Criminal Code

offence grid: a feature of some annotated versions of the *Criminal Code* that provides, in chart form, a summary of the elements, punishment, and other aspects of different offences

offer: the proposal of a contract or a set of contract terms; an offer is not a contract until it is accepted

official source: a version of a statute or regulation that meets the courts' standards for legitimacy, accuracy, and currency

omission: a failure to do something that is required by statute or by common law

onus: burden of proof; the necessity for a certain party to prove a certain fact

oral testimony: evidence provided verbally by witnesses

overruled: rejected or contradicted in a decision of a court of higher jurisdiction

parol evidence rule: the rule that the meaning of a contract must be determined without reference to external sources of evidence, such as other documents or oral testimony

particulars: details of a count

party: a person who has involvement in the commission of an offence, whether direct or indirect

passive defence: a defence by which the accused and his or her lawyers simply assert (through cross-examination or in closing arguments by counsel) that the prosecution has failed to prove the accused's guilt beyond a reasonable doubt

penalty part (of an offence): the part of a section of the *Criminal Code* that sets out the maximum or minimum punishment, or both, for the particular offence

peremptory challenge: the right of either party to a criminal jury trial to reject a prospective juror without giving a reason

person of interest: a person the police wish to speak to in order to obtain further information

personal property: property without a land or real estate component—physical possessions (chattels)

persuasive: the quality of a legal decision or precedent that influences later decisions on the same or similar legal issues

physical evidence: proof of the truth of an allegation in the form of actual objects (for example, a gun, bloody clothes, photographs)

plea: a statement of a legal position (guilty or not guilty); a legal argument or basis for a claim

plea bargain: an agreement between the defence and the prosecution as to how the accused will plead and what punishment the prosecution will seek

plead: argue or claim

positive (or affirmative) defence: a trial defence where the accused and his or her lawyers actively attempt to refute the evidence of the prosecution and perhaps introduce evidence of their own to clear the accused

possession: ownership based on rights acquired or conferred through physical occupancy or control

preamble: an introduction, made up of one or more provisions, that sets out the objectives and guiding philosophy of a statute

precedent: a court decision that influences or binds future decisions on the same issue or similar facts

pre-enquete hearing: a hearing that is not open to the public

preliminary inquiry: a judicial hearing where the prosecution must demonstrate that it has enough evidence to prove, if uncontested and accepted by the trier of fact, that the accused is guilty of the charges against him or her

pre-sentence report: a document prepared by a probation officer at the request of a judge that provides background on the offender for use in deciding on a sentence for the offender

presumption of innocence: the basis of criminal legal procedure and rules of evidence—that an accused person is considered innocent until proven guilty

principal: a person who is directly involved in committing an offence

probation: a type of sentence that does not involve imprisonment but allows the accused to remain free, subject to conditions

probation order: the details of the conditions imposed on a person who has been sentenced to probation, or who has been released on parole

procedural law: law that establishes the process by which substantive issues will be addressed

procedural part (of an offence): the part of a section of the *Criminal Code* that identifies the type of offence created by indicating the procedure by which an offender will be tried—indictment, summary conviction, or hybrid

proof beyond a reasonable doubt: the level of proof that the prosecution must provide in a criminal trial to obtain a conviction

proof on a balance of probabilities: a level (standard) of proof determined on the basis of whether something is more likely to be true than not; the standard that someone accused of a section 469 offence must provide at a bail hearing in order to be released pending trial

prosecution: the Crown attorney or attorneys who are given the task of proving an accused guilty of an offence

quash: overthrow or void

question of fact: a ground for appeal that is available only to the defence that is based on the validity of a piece of evidence presented at trial

question of law: a ground for appeal that is available to either the defence or the prosecution that is based on the misinterpretation or misapplication of a legal rule at trial

question of mixed law and fact: a ground for appeal that is available only to the defence that is based on an error that combines elements of a question of law and a question of fact

ratio decidendi: Latin for "reasons for decision," but often used to describe the few words or phrases that form the most essential part of a legal decision for precedent purposes

read into: process of interpretation that allows the reader to insert or to include a meaning in a passage that is not specifically there

real property: land and affixed dwellings; real estate

reasonable: a subjective standard, used in the Charter or common law rules, of what is acceptable to society under the circumstances

reasonable person: a hypothetical person on which a standard of behaviour is based for comparison with someone's actual behaviour

reasonable reliance: reasonable actions by one party, generally based on representations or actions by the other party, that may result in losses that a court will compensate

reasons for decision: the written expression of a legal decision; some decisions include reasons from more than one judge or justice

recklessness: a level of intent (*mens rea*) where the accused knows the potential consequences of his or her action and takes an unjustifiable risk despite that knowledge

recognizance: a promise; in the context of a bail hearing, a promise to return for trial

record suspension: an order allowing a person's criminal record to be kept separate from other criminal records and removed from the CPIC database

rejection: the refusal of an offer

reliance: taking actions based on dependence on a promise or contract, including the expenditure of money in dependence on the contract

remedy: an award or order provided by the court to compensate a victim for the commission of a legal wrong, such as a tort or a breach of contract

remoteness: the degree to which the consequences of a contract breach or the commission of a tort flow, directly or indirectly, from the breach or the tort

repeal: terminate the application of a statute or statutory provision

representation: a statement or claim made during contract negotiations that, though not necessarily a term of the contract, may be relied on by a party in deciding whether to enter into the contract

res judicata: Latin for "already decided"; a special plea with which the accused argues that the charges against him or her have already been dealt with in a court of law

rescind: to opt, generally with good legal reason, not to carry out one's side of a contract, as if the contract had never been made in the first place

respondent: the party that defends the original trial court decision when it is appealed by another party

restitution: the return of benefits to put contracting parties back into their precontractual position

reverse onus: a situation where, instead of the prosecution being required to prove all aspects of an offence (which is the norm), the accused bears the burden of proving a fact or allegation

revocation: the withdrawal of an offer by its maker

search and seizure: part of investigating offences, where the police inspect people or places and take into custody any physical evidence of crime that is found

search warrant: a written authorization to conduct a search

secular: non-religious

self-defence: a defence that can be used against assault if the force used was no more than was necessary to protect against the assault

sentence: the punishment imposed on a person convicted of an offence

separation agreement: a contract entered into by married persons or cohabitants after separation that addresses the rights and obligations of the parties after separation

show cause: another name for a bail hearing, where the prosecution is required to show cause as to why the accused should not be released before trial

special plea: a statement, other than guilty or not guilty, made by an accused when he or she is required to enter a plea to the charges

specific intent: a level of *mens rea* that requires the prosecution to prove that the accused meant to commit the offence or to cause the harm that resulted

specific performance: a court order requiring a party in default to fully perform his or her obligations under a contract

squatter: a person who occupies or controls property to which he or she does not have formal legal title

standard of care: the standard by which discharge of a duty of care is measured, which depends on the relationship between the parties and the circumstances under which the duty arises

standard of proof: the level to which a party must convince the trier of fact of a given allegation

statute law: legal provisions, in codified form, that are developed and adopted by the parliamentary and legislative process

stay of proceedings: a decision by a judge to drop the charges against an accused; usually the result of improper actions on the part of the police or the prosecution

strict liability: in the civil law context, liability that depends only on proof of the consequences of an action, even though there is no negligence on the part of the tortfeasor

strict liability offence: an offence that depends for conviction only on proof of the physical element of the offence; a court will assume that the accused was negligent unless he or she can prove otherwise

struck down: made null or void; applies to laws that are found to infringe on individual rights and freedoms

substantive equality: a measure of equality based on equality or inequality of outcomes, regardless of opportunity

substantive law: law that addresses the substance or factual content of a legal issue

substantive part (of an offence): the part of a section of the *Criminal Code* that identifies the actual elements of the offence created

summary conviction offence: a less serious crime that carries a light penalty; the accused is tried before a judge in a provincial court (for example, the Ontario Court of Justice) without the benefit of a jury or a preliminary hearing

summons: a document that may be delivered to a person accused of a crime requiring that person to be in court at a certain date and time to answer the charges

sureties: monetary guarantees that a person will appear at court to answer the charges against him or her; this money is forfeited if the accused does not appear as required

suspect: a person the police are actively investigating with regard to an offence but who has not yet been charged

suspended sentence: a form of punishment that involves delaying the imposition of the punishment indefinitely if the accused person complies with certain conditions, failing which the punishment is enforced

telewarrant: a search warrant that is issued by telephone or other telecommunication method, such as fax

thin skull rule: a rule that provides that a defendant who causes harm through negligence is responsible for the full extent of the harm, even if a vulnerability specific to the plaintiff made the harm more serious than would normally be expected

title: ownership based on rights acquired or conferred through legal transactions or instruments

tort: literally, a "wrong"; in law, an injury—whether physical, emotional, economic, or otherwise—suffered by a person for which another person may be held liable

tortfeasor: literally, "wrongdoer"; a person who commits a tort

trespass: the wrongful entry onto or damage to the property of another

tribunal: a formal body established, often under a statute, for the purpose of adjudicating disputes within the ambit of the statute

trier of fact: the person or people who must decide what facts have been proven at a criminal trial (either the judge or the jury)

trier of law: the judge who interprets the law and applies it to the facts as found by the trier of fact at a criminal trial

trust: a complex legal doctrine based on the rights of a person in the property of another

unconscionability: serious unfairness in a contract; unfairness that no reasonable person would accept and no honest person would propose

undertaking: a promise or monetary payment made as security for a recognizance

verdict: the decision as to the guilt or innocence of the accused

vicarious liability: imposition of liability on a person for the acts of another, because of the nature of the relationship between the two, even if the person was not present

void: null or of no effect; as if never having taken place

voidable: valid but capable of being rendered invalid through annulment proceedings by certain actions

void but capable of ratification: void but capable of becoming valid by certain actions

waive: give up a legal right

wilful blindness: a person is wilfully blind to something when he deliberately fails to turn his mind to that thing despite the fact that he could be expected to know about it

Index